PREFACE

This book presents material drawn from the public record of General John W. Vessey's service—22 June 1982 through 30 September 1985—as the Tenth Chairman of the Joint Chiefs of Staff. Arranged in chronological order, the material is drawn from his speeches, Congressional testimony, published articles, selected correspondence and interviews. It reflects General Vessey's work to rebuild and upgrade the armed forces of the United States. Of particular interest are his efforts to improve the quality of the Joint Staff and his emphasis upon the importance of the unified and specified commands which foreshadowed important provisions of the Goldwater-Nichols Department of Defense Reorganization Act of 1986.

Selection of the volume's contents was the responsibility of the Joint History Office and Major General Julian Burns, USA (Ret.), who had served on General Vessey's staff. Special thanks to Ms. Jacqueline Burns for typing portions of the text and to Lieutenant Colonel Jerry Brooks and Ms. Penny Norman of the Joint History Office for preparing this manuscript for publication. This volume is an official publication of the Office of the Chairman of the Joint Chiefs of Staff but, inasmuch as the text has not been considered by the Joint Chiefs of Staff, its contents do not represent the official position of the current Chairman or of the Joint Chiefs of Staff.

BIOGRAPHY

John William Vessey, Jr., was born in Minneapolis, Minnesota, on June 29, 1922. In May 1939, thirteen months before graduating from Roosevelt High School, he enlisted in the Minnesota National Guard as a motorcycle rider.

During World War II, General Vessey served with the 34th Infantry Division as First Sergeant of a field artillery battery in the North African and early Italian campaigns. He was commissioned a second lieutenant of field artillery at the Anzio beachhead and continued with the 34th Division until the end of the war in Italy.

After the war, most of Vessey's service continued to be in field artillery assignments. In the 1950s he served with the 4th Infantry Division in Germany and the Eighth US Army in the Republic of Korea. During this period he also attended the Command and General Staff College at Fort Leavenworth, Kansas.

General Vessey received a Bachelor of Science degree and Master of Science from George Washington University while he commanded the 2nd Battalion, 73rd Field Artillery in the 3rd Armored Division; then he spent a year as a student at the Industrial College of the Armed Forces.

In Vietnam, General Vessey served as Executive Officer of the 25th Infantry Division Artillery. In March 1967, while acting as Commander of the 2nd Battalion, 77th Artillery, he received the Distinguished Service Cross and the Battalion received the Presidential Unit Citation for actions during Operation JUNCTION CITY.

From Vietnam, he went to Germany, to serve as Commander of the 3rd Armored Division Artillery from October 1967 until March 1969 and then as Division Chief of Staff for a year. He went back to Southeast Asia in December 1970 to head the US Army Support Command, Thailand. In January 1972 he went into Laos to coordinate all US military operations in support of the war in Laos.

Upon his return to the United States, General Vessey became Director of Operations in the Office of the Deputy Chief of Staff for Operations and Plans. In August 1974 he assumed command of the 4th Infantry Division (Mechanized) at Fort Carson, Colorado. He became the Army's Deputy Chief of Staff for Operations and Plans in September 1975.

From 1976 to 1979 General Vessey served as Commanding General of the Eighth US Army; Commander of US Forces, Korea; and Commander-in-Chief of the United Nations Command. In 1978 he became the first Commander-in-Chief of the Republic of Korea-United States Combined Forces Command.

From July 1979 until June 1982 General Vessey served as Vice Chief of Staff of the Army.

On 18 June 1982 he became the tenth Chairman of the Joint Chiefs of Staff and the last World War II combat veteran to serve in the position. During his tenure there was increased emphasis on decentralization. Secretary of Defense Caspar Weinberger authorized General Vessey to direct military operations on the Secretary's behalf. He oversaw execution of the operation that rescued US citizens and brought a pro-US government into power.

There was also an increased emphasis on space as a theater of operations. In early 1983 the Joint Chiefs mentioned to President Reagan that defense against nuclear missiles might be technically feasible in the next century and on 23 March 1983 he announced his vision of the Strategic Defense Initiative (SDI). Realizing the enormous military advantages to be gained from operations in space and to support SDI, the JCS recommended the establishment of a unified command for space. US Space Command was activated on 23 September 1985.

General Vessey retired on 30 September 1985 at the age of 63, several months before the expiration of his second term as Chairman. He was the last four-star World War II combat veteran on active duty and, with 46 years of service, had served the longest of anyone then in the Army. General Vessey was the only Chairman who had been neither a Service Chief nor commander of a unified or specified command.

PROMOTIONS	DATES	
	Temporary	*Permanent*
2LT	06 May 44	
1LT	01 Apr 46	13 Jun 51
CPT	04 Jan 51	29 Oct 54
MAJ	14 May 58	26 Jan 62
LTC	07 Jan 63	02 Jan 69
COL	28 Nov 67	12 Mar 73
BG	01 Apr 71	23 Dec 74
MG	01 Aug 74	23 Aug 76
LTG	01 Sep 75	
GEN	01 Nov 76	

ASSIGNMENTS

	DATES	
	From	*To*
National Guard enlisted service	1939	1944
34th Division Artillery, Camp Claiborne, LA, Northern Ireland, North Africa, and Italy as S/Sgt, 1st Sgt, and then battlefield commission to 2Lt (Communications Officer/Forward Observer/ Air Observer)	1941	1945
US Army Field Artillery School, Fort Sill, OK	1945	1949
Student, Field Artillery Officers Advanced Course, Field Artillery School, Fort Sill, OK	1949	1950
Battery Officer; then Battery Commander, 18th Field Artillery, Fort Sill, OK	1950	1951
Assistant S-3 and Liaison Officer; then Headquarters Battery Commander; then Assistant S-3 and Liaison Officer, 4th Infantry Division Artillery, US Army Europe	1951	1954
Student, Artillery Officer Advanced Course, Artillery and Guided Missile School, Fort Sill, OK	1954	1955
Battery Commander, Artillery and Guided Missile School Officer Candidate School	1955	1956
Gunnery Instructor, Artillery and Guided Missile School, Fort Sill, OK	1956	1957
Student, US Army Command and General Staff College, Fort Leavenworth, KS	1957	1958
Artillery Section 8th US Army with duty station CINCPAC Coordination Center, Philippines	1958	1958
Chief, Operations Branch, Artillery Section, 8th US Army, Korea	1958	1959
Assignment Officer, then Executive Officer, Artillery Officers Division, Office of Deputy Chief of Staff for Personnel, Washington, DC	1959	1963
Student, Armed Forces Staff College, Norfolk, VA	1963	1963

Commander, 2nd Battalion, 73rd Artillery, 3rd Armored Division, US Army Europe	1963	1965
Student, Industrial College of the Armed Forces, Washington, DC	1965	1966
Executive Officer, 25th Infantry Division Artillery, Vietnam	1966	1967
Commander, 3rd Armored Division Artillery, US Army Europe	1967	1969
Chief of Staff, 3rd Armored Division, US Army Europe	1969	1970
Student, US Army Primary Helicopter School, Fort Wolters, TX; later US Army Aviation School, Fort Rucker, AL	1970	1970
Commanding General, US Army Support Command, Thailand	1970	1971
Deputy Chief, JUSMAGTHAI (Chief MAAG, Laos)	1972	1973
Director of Operations, Office Deputy Chief of Staff for Operations and Plans, Washington, DC	1973	1974
Commanding General, 4th Infantry Division (Mechanized), Fort Carson, CO	1974	1975
Deputy Chief of Staff for Operations and Plans, US Army, Washington, DC	1975	1976
Commanding General, 8th US Army; and Commander in Chief, US Forces, Korea; and Commander in Chief, United Nations Command; and (1978) Commander in Chief, Republic of Korea-United States Combined Forces Command, Korea	1976	1979
Vice Chief of Staff, US Army, Washington, DC	1979	1982
Chairman, Joint Chiefs of Staff, Washington, DC	1982	1985

PRINCIPAL US MILITARY DECORATIONS

Distinguished Service Cross
Defense Distinguished Service Medal (with oak leaf cluster)
Army Distinguished Service Medal (with 2 oak leaf clusters)
Navy Distinguished Service Medal
Air Force Distinguished Service Medal
Legion of Merit (with oak leaf cluster)
Bronze Star (with oak leaf cluster)
Air Medal (with 4 oak leaf clusters)
Joint Service Commendation Medal
Army Commendation Medal (with "V" device)
Purple Heart

TABLE OF CONTENTS

24 Feb 83	Address—The Economic Club of Chicago, Chicago, IL
25 Feb 83	Remarks—Naval Recruit Graduation Review, Recruit Training Command, Naval Training Center, Great Lakes, IL
19 Mar 83	Remarks—General Mark Clark Volunteers 42nd Annual Banquet, Charleston, SC
28 Mar 83	Interview in *US News and World Report*
21 Apr 83	Statement—House Armed Services Committee on Strategic Nuclear Force Modernization
9 May 83	Address—Prayer Breakfast, St Paul, MN
9 May 83	Address—Minnesota Meeting, St Paul, MN
13 May 83	Remarks—New Orleans Chamber of Commerce, New Orleans, LA
25 May 83	Remarks—U.S. Southern Command Change of Command Ceremony, Howard Air Force Base, Panama
May 83	Portion of Interview for *Armed Forces Journal*
10 Jun 83	Address—National Defense University Foundation, Fort McNair, Washington, DC
14 Jun 83	Statement—House Armed Services Committee, Subcommittee on Investigations, on JCS Organization
24 Jun 83	Remarks at the Graduation Ceremony for the Empire State Military Academy, Camp Smith, Peekskill, NY
30 Jun 83	Address—25th Division Officers and Men Breakfast, Schofield Barracks, HI
5 Aug 83	Remarks—Opening Ceremonies for the 22nd Class of the U.S. Army Command Sergeants Major Academy, Fort Bliss, TX

1982

Selected Works

Confirmation Hearing before the
SENATE ARMED SERVICES COMMITTEE
On Appointment of General John W. Vessey, Jr.
As Tenth Chairman, Joint Chiefs of Staff
11 May 1982

Mr. Chairman and members of the Committee. I am honored to be here today, but I must tell you that I am also humbled and quite surprised to have been chosen for this job.

As Senator Durenberger said, I have been in the military service quite a long time—over 41 years of active service. I have risen to a rank that is far higher than any I ever expected or hoped to achieve.

I realize that the promotions I have had are due to the fact that I have had some of the best people in the world working for me and due to the fact that I have had the honor to work for and with some of the finest military officers in the world.

When I look at the job of Chairman and the giants who have held the job in the past—including my friend, Dave Jones—I frankly asked myself the question: "Why in the world am I here?" Nevertheless, the President did ask me to take this job and I accept the duties without reservation. I think that I understand fairly well the duties and the grave responsibilities involved.

I pledge to you that, if confirmed by the Senate, I will carry out those duties as well and as faithfully as my abilities permit.

I also understand the grave responsibilities of this Committee to help provide defense for the United States, and I pledge to you that I will work openly and honestly with you to help you inform the Congress and, through the Congress, the American people about the very important defense issues that this country faces.

Address at PENTAGON HONORS CEREMONY
For General John W. Vessey, Jr.
As Tenth Chairman, Joint Chiefs of Staff
Washington, DC
22 June 1982

Mr. Secretary, my colleagues on the Joint Chiefs of Staff, distinguished guests, and soldiers, sailors, airmen, Marines, and Coast Guardsmen.

At the turn of the century when Elihu Root was instituting his reforms, something he said gave the Army War College its motto. He said, "We study war not to promote war but to preserve the peace."

These fine men and women out here today represent two million men and women in the Active forces and over 900,000 men and women in the National Guard and Reserve forces—soldiers, sailors, Marines, airmen, Coast Guardsmen—who study war not because they want to but because they realize that their dedication, their training, their discipline, and their willingness to do what the citizens of this country want them to do—risk their lives to defend our values—comprise an important instrument for the President of the United States, the people of the United States, and you, Mr. Secretary, to preserve the peace. And, I can tell you they will work very hard at it. Thank you.

Address to the
DWIGHT EISENHOWER SOCIETY
Gettysburg, Pennsylvania
14 October 1982

It is an honor to join in paying tribute to one of this nation's greatest soldier-statesmen, Dwight Eisenhower. His place of honor in our military history is inscribed forever as the Supreme Commander of the victorious allied forces in Europe. As time goes on, however, it is important to recall the totality of his contribution to the Nation. The breadth of skills and depth of dedication that he brought to his WW II task should serve to inspire us all to meet our own obligations as citizens of this great nation.

Called to Washington shortly after Pearl Harbor and put in charge of the Army's War Plans Division, General Eisenhower had the vision and courage to champion the setting of strategic priorities while others wanted to fight everywhere at once. His capacity for leadership was awesome as Commander in Chief during the Allied invasions of North Africa, Sicily, and Italy, as well as the Normandy landing and the final push into Germany. Not only did he plan and coordinate the most massive military operations the world had ever known, he did so by harmonizing the efforts of a set of brilliant but strong-willed commanders. At the same time, he was instrumental in convincing Allied governments with sometimes divergent goals to pull together in executing a forceful and coherent strategy. General Eisenhower was indeed the consummate multinational military commander. And having performed in similar roles, I have a great appreciation for what he was able to do.

President Eisenhower, who knew well the horrors of war, was a man of peace. But he also knew from experience that in a less than perfect world peace could only be maintained through the military strength necessary to deter would-be aggressors, and that free nations would have to pull together to provide that strength. His strategy of peace through strength, our own in the United States as well as alliance strength and solidarity, included a strong nuclear deterrent, an alliance structure—particularly NATO—to deter or meet conventional aggression, and a willingness to negotiate arms reductions, provided compliance could be verified.

Those principles remain the cornerstone of our national security policy today. But the world today is perhaps even more complex and more dangerous than that of the 1950s. There are many more nation-states than there were in the 50s and the pressures from political, religious, and ethnic factions within and among them seem to be greater. Economic changes and technological developments have led to far greater interdependence among all nations. The result is that a dispute which erupts in what once was a relatively isolated spot on the globe has the potential of threatening the interests of many far-flung nations.

Add to this the relentless buildup of Soviet military power, both nuclear and conventional, and an increasing willingness to use that power as demonstrated over the past three years in Afghanistan, and we have a dangerous world indeed. If we as a nation are going to continue to steer a safe course through these troubled waters, we must show that we can and we will meet threats of military aggression with force—not to invite a confrontation but to preserve the peace.

In the simplest and most direct terms I know how to use, I must say we do not want a war. We especially do not want a nuclear war. The United States needs to pursue sensible policies to reduce the probability of nuclear war—or any war—while at the same time preserving and improving the security of our nation and its allies and the liberty of the people. Reducing the probability of war and maintaining the security of the Nation must be treated together; they are inseparable. We don't want war, but we don't want to be paralyzed by the fear of war as we go about our business in this world of nation-states.

Our goal is to preserve peace through strength and resolve. Our hope is that, as we persevere, the Soviets may finally conclude that their interests would be best served by joining us in meaningful and verifiable arms reduction agreements that will lead to a safer world. In President Eisenhower's Farewell Address, he warned us against being reduced by emotionally appealing, miraculous solutions to the problems of peace and security. Were he with us today, I'm convinced he'd warn us again to be wary of some of the emotionally attractive but strategically dangerous suggestions we hear today—such as nuclear freezes and no-first-use pledges. If we are to succeed, we will have to muster those same qualities that Eisenhower brought to his efforts to preserve our security:

—Strategic vision—the ability to see the forests for the trees and to focus on what must be done for the common good.

—Moral courage and strength of character to stay the course against pressures for expediency and short-sighted solutions. I would like to read to you from his Farewell Address to the Nation on January 17, 1961:

"Progress toward these noble goals is persistently threatened by the conflict now engulfing the world. It commands our whole attention, absorbs our very beings. We face a hostile ideology—global in scope, atheistic in character, ruthless in purpose, and insidious in method. Unhappily, the danger it poses promises to be of indefinite duration. To meet it successfully, there is called for not so much the emotional and transitory sacrifices of crisis, but rather those which enable us to carry forward steadily, surely, and without complaint the burdens of a prolonged and complex struggle—with liberty the stake."

—The leadership capacity to help others see their responsibility for the greater good.

—And, above all, dedication and service to the Nation.

The concept of service is what has made this country great. It is based on the recognition that life has little meaning if we as individuals are not part of something greater than ourselves. This nation was founded on a mutual commitment of its citizens to the highest ideals of human dignity for ourselves and all mankind. There is nothing in which we as citizens should take greater pride as a people. But, with that pride also comes a responsibility to guard and nurture the values upon which this nation was founded.

One thing that has concerned me of late is that our use of pronouns often tends to undermine the spirit of unity and mutual responsibility that our citizenship demands. It seems to me that as we learn more and more about the wants and imperfections and human frailties that plague this great and beautiful nation of ours, our tendency is to associate responsibility with "they." Whether it be pollution in the air, defenses too weak, taxes too high, poor education for children, rebellious youth, rising prices, not enough jobs, or failure to provide help for the needy, the ubiquitous "they" seem to be the objects of our blame—"They did it!"

I want to suggest to you that the *Great American Pronoun* ought to be "we." When our forefathers set this country on the course that has brought us here today, "we" was the pronoun of choice. In the Declaration of Independence, they pronounced:

> "*We* hold these truths to be self-evident, that all Men are created equal, that they are endowed by their Creator with certain unalienable rights, that among these are Life, Liberty, and the Pursuit of Happiness."

And the Great American Pronoun is the first word in our Constitution:

> "*We* the People of the United States, in Order to form a more perfect Union, establish justice, insure domestic Tranquility, provide for the common defense, promote the general Welfare, and secure the Blessings of Liberty to ourselves and our Posterity, do ordain and establish this Constitution for the United States of America."

We the people established those noble goals. We the people adopted a constitutional system that has survived all others. We the people are responsible for whatever we are or are not as a nation and what we will be in the future. We the people of today have an equal responsibility to secure the blessings of liberty for *our* posterity.

I want to skip back to the Declaration of Independence for another "we" that I find particularly meaningful in the life of the man we honor today. This quote comes from the last lines of that great document:

> "And for the support of this declaration, with a firm reliance on the protection of Divine Providence, *we* mutually pledge to each other *our Lives, our Fortunes*, and *our sacred Honor*."

Those words embody the very essence of service to our country. Many men and women from that day to the present have sacrificed their lives and their fortunes and kept sacred their honor in meeting their commitment to this nation. If we ever lose that spirit of service, then we will have lost what is America.

I am delighted to see so many young people here today to help pay tribute to a man who dedicated his entire adult life in service to his country. Your interest in our heritage and those who have given so much to preserve it is heartwarming because you are our future. Soon you will be choosing what to do with your lives. Some will continue to study and some will join the work force. Because this nation is what it is—a free society dedicated to the worth of the individual—you will be expected to work hard and you can expect to be rewarded for your efforts. And, if you make no effort, then you won't be rewarded.

As you ponder your choices, allow me to presume what I think Ike would have said if you had asked him what his greatest reward in life was. I think he would have said. "Service to your country is its own reward." There is nothing more satisfying in life than knowing that you have contributed to the betterment of society.

There are many ways to serve your country. In peacetime, particularly, civic service is as important as military service. I think military service, though, has given me something that I might have missed in other pursuits. There is a special feeling of belonging, a special cohesion, that comes from being a part of a team effort. That is what service in the Army, Navy, Air Force or Marines means—being part of a team with an important responsibility. I hope many of you choose the opportunity to experience the kind of satisfaction that comes from being a member of such a team dedicated to preserving world peace, to protecting our security, and to serving fellow human beings.

In closing, I pray that we in the military and you as citizens maintain our resolve and our dedication to the ideals that Dwight David Eisenhower stood for. Our willingness to sacrifice for the good of our country and for mankind will preserve the peace. The cost of vigilance is sometimes high, but never as high as the price of wars that come from a lack of vigilance. That price is not paid simply in dollars but in the blood of our citizens. If we the people stand ready to shoulder the responsibilities passed on by those who have preceded us with honor, then we the people will preserve the blessings of liberty for ourselves and *our* posterity.

**From a Letter to an American
Citizen in Massachusetts
16 October 1982**

You can't spend as many years as I have in uniform without making some difficult decisions; but one thing seems clear. My most difficult decisions all revolved around ordering people to do something in combat when I was not completely confident about the prospects for success. There are a number of examples, but let me offer one such instance by way of illustration.

As a commander of a relatively small counterattack force in Vietnam, we were attacked by a far larger enemy unit. I was ordered to commit my men in response. There was small chance for success, but we did what we had to do. We sustained heavy casualties, but succeeded in taking the pressure off our main defenses until they could respond with even greater strength.

What conclusions can be drawn? Namely, a military leader should not commit the forces under his charge lightly, but when faced with military necessity, he may be required to sacrifice for greater good. This concept is inherent in our understanding of service to the citizens of our great country.

**Speech before the Greater Tampa
Chamber of Commerce
Tampa Bay, FL
22 October 1982**

A nuclear freeze would also almost surely end any hopes of a nuclear arms reduction agreement. If we know anything about the Soviets, we know that they are tough negotiators; that they prefer to negotiate from strength, and always seek agreements that they see as clearly advantageous to them. What gives us hope that we can achieve significant, equitable and verifiable reductions both in START and in the INF negotiations is that the Soviets fear that we can offset their advantages through our modernization programs, and therefore see reductions as the lesser of evils. The best way to bring them to that point is to show firm resolve in our plans to deploy Pershing II and Ground-Launched Cruise Missiles in Europe to offset the already-deployed Soviet SS-20s as well as to modernize our strategic nuclear force. A nuclear freeze would stop those programs dead in their tracks and the Soviets would have no need—no incentive—to negotiate seriously.

**Address to the NAVY LEAGUE
New York City, New York
3 November 1982**

Thanks very much. Thanks for inviting me to be here with you tonight for this wonderful 78th Anniversary Dinner to help you honor officers and sailors of the United States Navy—the best navy in the world. When asked some months ago to participate in tonight's activities, I went to my friend, Admiral Jim Watkins and said, "What will be expected of me?" He told me that I would have to come here and say some nice things about the Navy. I told him I could do that both easily and honestly. Then I got a little skittish and I went back and asked him to tell me very frankly if I would have to get up here and embarrass myself tonight by saying, "Beat Army."

The reason that I am a little apprehensive about letting this very important policy meeting of the Navy League Council slip into athletic rivalry has to do with last year's Army-Navy game. Somehow, Admiral Bill Small's aide and my aide had convinced the two of us to make a wager on the game. And we were betting our pride, actually, because the agreement was that we would exchange game balls with the score inscribed and display the balls in our offices for the next year. Well, those of you who have followed Army football at all for the last 10 years will recognize that my agreeing to the wager was a stoic recognition that life has some self-inflicted wounds rather than any calculation of the odds. But after that miraculous 3-to-3 tie, I did get a game ball. I put the score on it and delivered it to Bill Small's office. My gracious act was answered by weeks, nay months of silence from the Office of the Vice Chief of Naval Operations. In February, I finally got a ball box; but it was a big box and I opened it up and it had a basketball in it, not a football, and it was inscribed, "Navy 62 – Army 59."

You've asked me here tonight, I guess, because I'm the Chairman of the Joint Chiefs and I believe that perhaps you want me to tell you a little about what I see from the foxhole that I now occupy.

One of the sights I see regularly is a group of four people that work with me, the other members of the Joint Chiefs of Staff. And I want to tell you that I am very pleased with what I see. The Nation is blessed with four top-notch Service Chiefs to head its Armed Services: General Bob Barrow, the Commandant of the Marine Corps, an outstanding Marine and soldier; General "Shy" Meyer, Chief of Staff of the Army, the same; General Charlie Gabriel, the Chief of Staff of the Air Force, top-notch fighter pilot, great leader; and topped by Admiral Jim Watkins, my friend sitting here beside me on the dais tonight.

These officers are all respected, battle-proved veterans, true experts in their own Services. And I want to tell you that they're working diligently to improve those Services. But I can also tell you that they're men of broad strategic vision who understand that the defenses of this nation are only as good as the ability of those four Services—and the Coast Guard, in time of war—to work closely together. They understand that President Eisenhower was right in 1958 when he told the Congress that wars in the future could only be won if the four Services are working closely together under unified command.

I can tell you also that those four Service Chiefs are addressing in a business-like, professional manner the duties that you the people of the United States have spelled out for them in the law as members of the Joint Chiefs of Staff.

Now, according to some of the stories that I read in the newspapers and hear on the radio and television, I'm supposed to see quite a lot of inter-Service bickering in that crowd. In fact, according to some of the stories, I'm supposed to partake in that bickering myself. Let's be very clear. Those Chiefs don't always agree; and I don't think you expect them to agree or necessarily want them to agree. When they occasionally disagree, the points on which they disagree are very clear. Since by law I'm charged with explaining their disagreements to the Secretary of Defense and the President, I'm happy to have the disagreements be clear.

Another view that one gets from that foxhole of mine is a good view of the very dangerous world we live in. We see a greater independence of the economies of the Free World and the consequences for our own economy—the economy and our economic well-being are inextricably tied to raw material providers and finished goods suppliers from all around the world. At the same time we see a Soviet Union willing to spend 14 to 15 percent of its Gross National Product for defense. "Defense"—that's a euphemism. In fact, it's an inaccuracy. It should be "offense" because neither by character or size can the Soviet arms build up of the last 20 years be justified by legitimate defense needs. We see that same Soviet Union willing to dabble in all parts of the Free World, attempting to upset the freedom of peoples who are friends and allies of ours.

Mr. Brezhnev's truculent remarks a week ago need to be answered quite clearly by the American people. The message to Mr. Brezhnev should be, "We don't want war. We don't want a nuclear war. We don't want a conventional war or any kind of war in between. But we have no intention of being paralyzed by the fear of war as we pursue our life in this world on nation-states. We plan to do all we can to prevent war by remaining very strong while trying to convince you, Mr. Brezhnev, to negotiate seriously towards arms control agreements that will genuinely reduce the danger of war."

Another view I get from my foxhole is of the men and women in the Services, and I want to tell you that their pronoun is "*we*." Wherever I go, it's *we* can do it; *we* are ready; and *we* will do what needs to be done.

In the short four and a half months that I have been the Chairman, I've visited all the Services and I have had some good looks at the Navy and Marine Corps. I have visited a variety of Marine Corps activities. I've seen the Navy on aircraft carriers, in submarines and hydrofoil patrol craft, in aviation operational units and training units, in those wonderful SEAL units, and at the Naval War College.

Now, I am neither a naval officer nor naval expert. And I understand that there are some naval officers who aren't naval experts and there are an awful lot of people who think they're naval experts who aren't naval officers. But I do want to tell you that I'm an experienced naval watcher, having started taking an interested and concerned look at the Navy during an exciting convoy trip to Britain in 1942 and I have continued those observations through the last forty years. During many of those years, my own safety and the well-being of my command have depended on the United States Navy doing its job correctly. At no time in my 43 years of service has that been more important than it is right now.

From the perspective of a naval watcher, I can't tell you whether or not those sailors I saw were doing their jobs correctly (I can check the Marines a little better); but, I can tell you a few things about the sailors that I did see. First, "*we*" was their pronoun—*we* can do it. *We* will do it. Secondly, there was unbounded enthusiasm. There was a clear spirit of teamwork and willingness to take on difficult tasks, and to see them through. There was an extraordinary base of knowledge about a lot of complex, interrelated equipment and a firm knowledge of tactics. They knew how they were going to fight and were confident in their ability to fight well. But most important of all, there was a solid foundation of military discipline. You can be proud of our Navy.

How did it get that way? How do we keep it that way? Well, one answer, of course, is good leadership at the top and the support of the American people and the Congress. But that's not enough. It also depends on the patriotism, dedication and loyalty of those Blue Jackets. How do you get that? Edmund

Burke best described the source of those commodities. He was at the time, of course, talking about the British forces, but I submit to you that the same thought applies to our own forces today. Burke said, "It is the love of the people. It is their attachment to their government from the sense of the deep stake they have in such a glorious institution which gives you your Army, your Navy and infuses into both that liberal obedience without which your Army would be a rabble and your Navy nothing but rotten timber."

As long as the people of this great country of ours recognize that they are *our* Armed Forces—*our* Army, *our* Air Force, *our* Marine Corps, *our* Navy, our Coast Guard—and that we need them to protect our liberty, then those extraordinary young Americans will be out there in strange lands or on, over and under the seas doing extraordinary things to keep this country free.

And the work of this Navy League, in many ways—all the ways from the support you provide for a strong national defense to projects like the INTREPID here, and your other educational projects—are outstanding examples of the love that the American people have for our great institutions, including your Armed Forces. And I thank you for that work and I salute you. Thank you very much.

**From a Letter to the President
Of the Vietnam Veterans Memorial Fund
10 November 1982**

The dedication of the Vietnam Veterans Memorial culminates the labors of many Americans to recognize the service and sacrifice of the Nation's men and women in uniform during the war in Vietnam.

These blocks of granite bear eloquent witness to their noble efforts.

Putting aside personal consideration, they accepted a call to duty. These names are our comrades, friends, parents, sons, and daughters. They served as we wanted them to serve, by obeying an oath. It is the strength of that commitment that enables every American to share the precious gift of freedom we have in our great land.

We owe our Vietnam veterans dignified thanks and recognition for their loyalty and courage. I salute you.

**Statement before the
SENATE ARMED SERVICES COMMITTEE
On the PEACEKEEPER ICBM Program
8 December 1982**

Mr. Chairman and members of the Committee. Thank you for inviting me to testify about the very important matter you are addressing.

You have heard Secretary Weinberger's description of the PEACEKEEPER missile and his explanation of the basing mode and the reasons for choosing it. The Secretary also discussed the missile's relationship to deterrence and to the U.S. arms control policies. I will try to avoid repeating what the Secretary has told you and will amplify the military aspects of the new land-based ICBM. Nevertheless, because a key aspect of our strategy is deterrence and because arms control negotiations are an important part of our security policy, some of my points will overlap with those of Secretary Weinberger.

In his acceptance speech on being elevated to the top Communist party position last month, Mr. Andropov said, "We well know that peace cannot be achieved by begging from the imperialists. It can be defended only by relying on the invincible might of the Soviet Armed Forces." It is not Mr. Andropov's words that need be our primary concern; it is the fact that his country has built a massive military machine which to us seems to be far greater than required for any legitimate defense needs. That military machine, with over 180 army divisions supported by about 7,000 combat aircraft and backed by thousands of theater nuclear warheads and thousands more for strategic nuclear weapons, threatens our allies and us. Hence, the need for us to maintain forces to deter the use of those Soviet forces, if we want peace. Certainly, all of our strengths—moral, social, political, economic, and military—contribute to our deterrent strength. Today we are addressing military strength and its contribution to deterring war.

From the military point of view, deterrence results from a great deal of uncertainty in the minds of the Soviets that their war aims can be achieved. The entire range of U.S. and allied forces contribute to this deterrence. In today's world, strategic nuclear forces alone will not provide deterrence, but the strategic nuclear forces are an important part of our deterrent force. For all who may read the record of these hearings, I want to say as clearly as I can that that United States does not want a war, any kind of war, and especially a nuclear war. We want to prevent war. Paradoxically, the success of our deterrent posture results from a clear perception on the part of the Soviets that the U.S. is capable—however unwilling—of engaging in the nuclear conflict we seek to deter. It is an understanding of the war-fighting capability of the forces that will help lead us to the right mix of forces to prevent a war.

During the Brezhnev years, the Soviets went to great efforts to modernize their strategic and theater nuclear forces. They have fielded and continue to field new, accurate ballistic missile systems with multiple, independently

11

targetable reentry vehicles, the so-called MIRVs. The United States did not undertake a comparable modernization program.

In order to judge what is necessary to deny the Soviets their war aims and hence effect deterrence, it is useful to consider what those aims might be. We know a good deal about the Soviet war aims. They are:

—To ensure continuity of the Communist party of the Soviet Union control of the Soviet government, military, police, and internal security organs and the population.

—To provide continuity of functioning of the Soviet politico-military economic system to prosecute the war to a victorious conclusion, to repair immediate damage and to organize recovery.

—To defeat NATO forces, to occupy NATO countries as intact as possible and to use Europe's economic assets to assist Soviet recovery.

—To neutralize the United States and the People's Republic of China (P.R.C.) by destroying their military forces and preventing the reconstitution of U.S. and P.R.C. military forces.

—To minimize losses to Soviet leadership, scientific-technical elites and other essential personnel, to the unessential population, and to the economy.

—To dominate the post-war world in which "socialism" (read "Soviet-style communism") will have replaced "imperialism" (read Western democracy) as the basic politico-economic system in all nations.

The Soviets have built the forces, both conventional and nuclear, to pursue their war aims. I find it hard to believe that the Soviets or anyone can want a nuclear war; certainly, we do not. Yet, the Soviets have, in fact, allocated vast resources to build the forces and harden the command structures to attain their war aims in a nuclear war. Therefore, the United States and its allies need to have the forces and capabilities to prevent the Soviets from achieving those war aims. When it is clear that we do, deterrence exists and the probability of war is greatly reduced.

Today, we are concentrating on strategic nuclear forces. As the members of this committee know well, the United States has for years relied on the so-called TRIAD of strategic nuclear forces, bombers, submarine-launched ballistic missiles, and land-based intercontinental ballistic missiles. Each leg of the TRIAD has its own strengths and weaknesses, unique capabilities, and vulnerabilities. Our strategic analyses through the years have continued to confirm that maintenance of modern, effective forces in each leg of the TRIAD complicates greatly the Soviet chances for achieving war aims through a nuclear strike on our forces, gives us the flexible sort of forces we would need to respond to any attack and thus contributes greatly to deterrence of war. As the committee knows, we have programs to modernize all three legs of the TRIAD. Our B-52 bombers are 25 years old, on the average. Modern technology permits us to build far more effective bombers with capability to penetrate Soviet air defenses well into the late 1990s in the case of the B-1 and well beyond the year 2000 in the case of the Advanced Technology Bomber

(ATB). The first of the new TRIDENT submarines has just become operational. The TRIDENT itself is a much-improved submarine with additional missile capacity. A very important future addition to the TRIDENT is the D-5 missile now under development. The D-5 will have the accuracy to give the submarine missile forces the ability to attack hard targets. At the same time we are moving to modernize our strategic forces; we are undertaking important modernization of our strategic command, control and communications systems. The modernization will enable us to provide better attack detection and ensure the National Command Authorities have necessary communication with the forces.

A critical element of the modernization program is the new ICBM—the MX or PEACEKEEPER. The accuracy improvements and its ability to carry ten warheads give us the ability to attack hard targets quickly, the so-called time-urgent, hard-target-kill capability.

The Soviets also maintain a triad of forces, but theirs is considerably different from ours. Where we have only about one-third of our missile warheads in ICBMs, the Soviets have about two-thirds of theirs in ICBMs. As I said earlier, in recent years the Soviets have modernized their ICBM force. The over 300 SS-18 missiles with up to 10 accurate warheads each and 300 SS-19s with six accurate warheads, all in super-hard silos, are the heart of that modernization effort. The Soviet ICBM force can attack the fixed targets of the United States, with assurance of high levels of damage on those targets, and can at the same time maintain a large reserve of weapons for follow-on attacks.

At this time, it is worth saying a little about the targets we and the Soviets present to each other. If I put myself in the shoes of the Soviet planner attacking the fixed military targets of the United States, I see a target base that is less than half the size in numbers and only about half as hard in terms of protection as the target base the Soviets present to us. The Soviet planner also sees a lot of targets that are not fixed, our alerted bomber force and our deployed submarines; and, of course, we see a somewhat different mix and a larger set of non-fixed targets in the USSR. Simply said from the war planner's point of view, the United States is an easier target than the USSR.

The hardened fixed targets in the Soviet target base, the missile silos with reserve missiles and the hardened command and control facilities which would play a key role in follow-on attacks, are the targets we want to be able to attack quickly—the time-urgent, hard targets. The accuracy and warhead combination of our present MINUTEMAN missile force does not give us high confidence of destroying those targets rapidly. The vulnerability of the MINUTEMAN force to a first strike adds to our operational problems. Therein lies the need for the PEACEKEEPER with its improved accuracy and increased warhead-carrying capacity. It will give us the capability of attacking those hard targets promptly with high confidence of inflicting damage sufficient to contribute to greater uncertainty in the minds of the Soviets that their war aims can be achieved.

The planned Closely Spaced Basing (CSB) for the PEACEKEEPER adds greatly to the survivability of the missile. It complicates the Soviet attack problem and further creates more uncertainty that war aims can be achieved and thus makes a further substantial contribution to extended deterrence.

The current Soviet systems are not designed to attack CSB. While the Soviets could seek to make CSB vulnerable in the future, it would require them to redirect their current efforts at great cost in both time and resources. We are confident we would detect such efforts on their part and, if needed, make necessary improvements in survivability. The net result will be a continuing high degree of uncertainty on the part of the Soviets that they can successfully attack the system.

In the context of current strategic arms control negotiations, the modernization of the ICBM leg of the TRIAD in CSB will provide an important incentive for serious negotiation. We do not enhance prospects for arms control by failing to correct existing vulnerabilities or failing to modernize our strategic forces. As we seek significant reductions in strategic armaments, modernization will be an essential element in preserving our deterrent at reduced force levels.

The Joint Chiefs of Staff firmly support the President's arms control initiative for substantial reductions in strategic nuclear arms. The JCS support for the reductions recognized that, with both sides at lower levels of forces, any disparity in the quality and capabilities of the forces would be even more pronounced than at today's levels. Therefore, their support for the reductions was with the understanding that all three legs of the TRIAD would be modernized.

The JCS were unanimous in their recognition of the need and in their support for fielding the MX or PEACEKEEPER missile system. There were differing views on the basing scheme for the missile and these differing views were all presented to the Secretary of Defense and the President before the decision was made. The JCS support the President in the implementation of the decision he has made.

1983

Selected Works

Remarks at the
U.S. CENTRAL COMMAND ACTIVATION CEREMONY
MacDill Air Force Base, FL
5 January 1983

By law, the Joint Chiefs of Staff have the mission to establish unified and specified commands in strategic areas.

On 1 January 1983, by order of the President, the Joint Chiefs of Staff established the United States Central Command—USCENTCOM—and Lieutenant General Robert C. Kingston was designated as Commander. Forces were assigned and are represented here today. CENTCOM now joins eight other unified and specified commands worldwide helping the U.S. in maintaining the peace.

CENTCOM's area of responsibility is large geographically. It extends from Egypt east to Pakistan and from Jordan south to Kenya. It includes vast land areas on two continents.

The region has great historical significance. It is the birthplace of Western civilization and the genesis of three of the world's great religions; it has been the historic land-bridge for trade between Europe and the East. It has been the scene of battles, conquests, and empires whose numbers alone stagger the imagination.

Most important for us here today, the region has great contemporary importance. It is comprised of diverse, proud peoples who love freedom and share a common hope for peace. It continues to encompass important trade routes. The area contains mineral wealth that is absolutely vital to the world's economic well-being. It contains nineteen independent nations with a variety of governmental forms and political leanings.

Unfortunately, at this moment the region is not totally at peace; there are wars and rumors of war. That's not unusual; that's part of the world. For the United States the region is truly a strategic area. It is indeed fitting that this command be established.

It is important for the world to know why it has been established. The Command is established to represent the United States militarily in the region. The Command will be the U.S. vehicle for military cooperation with friendly governments in the region when the governments concerned, our own, and those of our friends, agree that military cooperation is necessary. The Command will administer the U.S. security assistance program in the region. It will control U.S. military forces that may be in the region for exercises or peacetime operations. It will plan for other peacetime functions that our unified commands perform, such as noncombatant evacuation and emergency disaster assistance to nations in the region.

The Command will make its contribution to that fundamental element of United States strategy, the prevention of war, and do it in the same way that the other unified and specified commands do. The Command will be ready to carry out its directed wartime missions in the region as circumstances should require.

There are several things the Command will not become. It is not a force built to meddle in the affairs of countries in the region. It is not a force built to acquire territory for the United States.

The Command is a signal to everyone concerned, friends and possible foes, that the United States has great interests in the region, that we stand ready to defend those interests and to help promote peace and stability in cooperation with our friends in the region. The Command will be a force for peace by being ready for war.

I have known and worked with General Kingston for some years. He is an officer with great talent as a planner and trainer, but it is his reputation for audacity and success on the battlefield for which he is most widely known. You soldiers, sailors, Marines, and airmen who will work for him need to know that you have a top-notch commander in whom the President, the Secretary of Defense and the JCS have great confidence.

I bring you special greetings from Secretary Weinberger, who regrets his absence. On behalf of the Secretary and all members of the Joint Chiefs of Staff, I wish you Godspeed as you take on your important duties.

Address at the
WINTER COMMENCEMENT EXERCISES
University of Maryland, University College
College Park, MD
8 January 1983

Thank you very much. It is indeed an honor and privilege for me to be here today.

In preparing for this address, I asked a member of my staff to think about some possible topics and prepare a draft. Instead, he sent back a short outline and a note that read, "Graduation speeches are a bore. Give them two jokes, one thought to take with them, and stop!" Now, if you'll count my two stories as the jokes...you'll see that we're two-thirds of the way through this exercise.

Well, I know you've got a lot of things on your mind and that most graduation speeches fall by the wayside at about the same time the caps and gowns come off. But let me give you that "one thought" to take with you— perhaps two connected thoughts.

The last time I spoke in this building I spoke to a group of educators. For my theme I used an essay, in fact a speech, by Nicholas Murray Butler entitled, "Five Evidences of an Education." The speech was given in 1901, but I assure you that I first read it a number of years later. I have never forgotten that essay, and I'd like to draw on Butler's thoughts again today.

Butler said the first of the five evidences of an education was correctness and precision in the use of the mother tongue. From my own experience I can tell you more has been misdirected on the battlefield and misunderstood in the Pentagon because of a lack of understanding of the English language than any other single factor.

Butler said that the second evidence was refined and gentle manners. Now you might ask how that applies in this hustle-bustle world of today. I would use Butler's own words to describe the applicability. He said, "Manners don't make the man, but manners reveal the man. It is by the amount of respect, deference and courtesy shown to human personality that we judge whether one is on dress parade or whether he is so well-trained, well-educated, and so habitually ethical in thought and action that he realizes his proper relation to his fellows."

The habit of reflection was Butler's third evidence of an education. Eighty-two years ago he found it necessary to raise the allegation that the busy lives of Americans might cause us to lose the habit of reflection. He went on to say that "the educated man has the standards of truth, of human experience and of wisdom by which the new proposals are judged and those standards can only be gained through reflection." When we're dealing with things such as nuclear weapons, the MX missile system, war and peace, world hunger, our social infrastructure, alternative sources of energy, or the Social Security system, we need the habit of reflection in order to understand where all that fits in the scheme of human things.

Butler's fourth evidence was the power to grow. He said that if the impulse to continuous study and self-education, the conditions for permanent, intellectual growth are wanting, education has failed in one of its primary purposes.

His last evidence was the power to do, or efficiency. Butler alleged that knowledge and information for their own sake are at best questionable—but that the established and habitual relationship between intellect and will was the means by which the possessors of knowledge turn knowledge into action. From my own personal experience, it is not useful for someone to know how to do something if he is unwilling to do it when the time comes for that job to be done.

I want to expand a bit on Butler's last evidence of education. This willingness to turn knowledge into action can also be called "service." The concept of service is what has made this country great. It is based on the recognition that life has little meaning if we as individuals are not part of something greater than ourselves. This nation was founded on a mutual commitment of its citizens to the highest ideals of human dignity for ourselves and all mankind. As a people, there is nothing in which we should take greater pride. But, with that pride also comes a responsibility to guard and nurture the values for which this nation stands.

One thing that has concerned me of late is that our use of pronouns often tends to undermine the spirit of unity and mutual responsibility that our citizenship demands. It seems to me that as we learn more and more about the imperfections and human frailties that plague this great and beautiful nation of ours, our tendency is to associate responsibility with "they." Whether it be pollution in the air, defenses too weak or too expensive, taxes too high, poor education for children, rebellious youth, rising prices, not enough jobs, or failure to provide help for the needy, the ubiquitous "they" seem to be the objects of our blame—"They did it."

I want to suggest to you that the *Great American Pronoun* ought to be "we." When our forefathers set this country on the course that has brought us here today, "we" was the pronoun of choice. In the Declaration of Independence, they pronounced:

> "*We* hold these truths to be self-evident, that all Men are
> created equal, that they are endowed by their Creator with certain
> unalienable rights, That among these are Life, Liberty, and the
> Pursuit of Happiness."

And the Great American Pronoun is the first word in our Constitution:

> "*We* the People of the United States, in Order to form a more
> perfect Union, establish justice, insure domestic Tranquility,
> provide for the common defense, promote the general Welfare, and

secure the Blessings of Liberty to ourselves and our Posterity, do ordain and establish this Constitution for the United States of America."

We the people established those noble goals. We the people adopted a constitutional system that has survived all others. We the people of today have an equal responsibility to secure the blessings of liberty for ourselves *and* our posterity.

We need to take a lesson from our Forefathers when they committed themselves to the Declaration of Independence by saying:

> "...with a firm Reliance on the Protection of Divine Providence, we mutually pledge to each other our Lives, our Fortunes, and our sacred Honor."

What is my thought for you to take away? Well, to paraphrase slightly the comic strip character Pogo, "*You is now 'they'*." If we are going to overcome the opprobrium attached to being "they," we must all work together, because whatever we as a Nation are or are not, whatever we do or fail to do—we will be responsible. What ever you do, don't give up that participation. Take stock of your education occasionally, and you might find Butler's five evidences a useful starting point.

Thank you.

Interview in *National Guard* Magazine
January 1983

Question: If you had to tell the average company or battalion commander one thing, what—in terms of advice for next year's annual National Guard training—would you advise?

Answer: Concentrate on training for the most important command task that your unit has to perform. When I was Vice Chief of Staff of the Army, I worked with members of the Army Reserve Force's Policy Committee and the Army Staff to find a way to reduce the administrative burden on the commanders of our Guard and Reserve units. That just can't be done here at the Pentagon. It has to be done all the way down through the chain—so that those officers and soldiers, the men and women out there in the operating units, get to spend those 39 or so days a year on the most important tasks and aren't overburdened with day-to-day administrative chores and things of that nature. And that's one of the reasons that the Army has moved toward a greater mixture of full-timers with the Guard and Reserve units to help take up the slack so that the part-time soldier can get on into the training for the main part of his combat task.

Statement before SENATE ARMED SERVICES COMMITTEE
Subcommittee on Defense
On the FY 84 DOD Authorization
1 February 1983

Mr. Chairman, members of the Committee. I appreciate the opportunity to share with you my views on the defense needs of the Nation.

The capabilities of United States forces are improving to face the growing threat. Clearly, they are stronger now than at any time in the recent past; and many needed programs have been set in motion. We can have considerable confidence in the forces we have, in their readiness and in their ability to undertake assigned tasks. My confidence has been bolstered by what I've seen of our troops at home and abroad. But military strength is relative. The capability to deter threats against our interests cannot be viewed in isolation. Our posture must be judged against the capabilities of potential adversaries today, and the likely threats of the years ahead. Our national security is far from assured. We need to work together to reduce the risks to our security now and in the future.

The Soviet Threat

Peace in the world and our own security are challenged by the sustained growth of Soviet military power and compounded by instabilities in many areas of the world—instabilities which are all too often exploited by the Soviets and those who assist them.

Soviet military power is a reality with which we must deal. Soviet military forces are large—about 5 million active in contrast to our 2 million active. Their forces are also well-organized, well-trained, and well-equipped for a full range of military operations.

Soviet forces are designed for offensive operations while at the same time protecting the homeland from attack.

Soviet weapons are good, and the extraordinary Soviet effort in research and development, over 50 percent greater than ours, should guarantee that their weapons will also be good in the years ahead.

The Soviets continue to modernize their forces across the board and at a rapid pace.

Soviet training demonstrates the ability to use the forces effectively.

Strategic Modernization

We and our allies need military forces which, combined with our other strengths, will deter the Soviets from using their forces to threaten our interests. We need to continue the recent momentum in improving the manning, modernization, and readiness of our forces.

Few programs have received the attention now focused on our strategic nuclear force modernization. While we have been debating the need to modernize, the Soviets have been fielding modern systems and developing and testing the next generation of improvements for their strategic forces. In the past two years, the Soviets have fielded many hundreds of new ICBM warheads with greater accuracy and improved hard-target-kill capability while we've fielded none. Another measure of Soviet activities in strategic forces can be seen in the test and training launches of strategic ballistic missiles. Last year the Soviets launched about 150 missiles compared to less than one-third that number for the U.S.

The Soviet nuclear threat makes clear the need to give our strategic forces the highest priority in modernization. We delayed modernization and now we are faced with the need to modernize all legs of our TRIAD at the same time. To maintain our strategic deterrent, we need to go ahead with the prompt deployment of the PEACEKEEPER missile, TRIDENT submarine, B-1 bomber and cruise missile.

Theater Nuclear Weapons

This committee is well aware of the details associated with our planned deployment of ground-launched cruise missiles and the PERSHING II missile under NATO's dual-track decision of 1979. SS-20s continue to threaten the nations of NATO Europe and the forces of the Alliance. Since last February, the Soviets have deployed over 50 additional SS-20 intermediate-range missiles pointed at our Western allies; we have yet to deploy anything comparable. Our commitment to the elimination of the most destabilizing longer-range systems in Europe was reemphasized by the President just last month. There should be no question about the determination of the United States to strive for an arms control agreement which addresses legitimate security issues of the NATO Alliance. But, barring a satisfactory agreement, it is essential that we move forward with plans to deploy the PERSHING II and ground-launched cruise missiles.

Arms Control

We should continue to pursue nuclear arms reduction earnestly. Comprehensive, equitable, and verifiable arms reduction agreements could lessen the danger of nuclear war. But we must be guided by Soviet actions, not just their words. It is clear to me that our nuclear weapons modernization programs are needed not only to spur serious arms reduction negotiations and meaningful restraint, but to provide our security after the negotiations are over.

Alliances

The defense of the United States will continue to depend upon a strong system of alliances and other security coalitions. Our firm commitment to NATO and other allies is consistent with the global defense requirements of this country. Our friends and allies contribute weapons, trained manpower, and facilities which support us and help defend shared interests.

There is an important interdependency among us. We should continue to refine with our allies the division of labor in our mutual security effort and encourage improvements in readiness and sustainability of combined forces. U.S. and allied forces must continue to strive for a high degree of interoperability. The Joint Chiefs of Staff and major commanders will continue to stress combined training and operations.

Allied host nation support for our forces can assist in implementing the agreed Alliance strategy at reduced costs and it should be supported.

The forward deployment of U.S. air, land, and naval forces remains a key ingredient of our strategy. Such forces demonstrate the strength of the U.S. commitment to collective defense and help provide a forward shield to permit reinforcing our allies when needed. The planned levels of those forces will allow necessary modernization to proceed and preserve their deterrent value.

Strategic Mobility

Our strategy will continue to depend heavily on strategic mobility. Mobility forces work hand-in-glove with forward-deployed units to demonstrate our strength and bolster our deterrent capabilities. Today, our strategic mobility is improving, but it is not yet adequate to move and support our forces for the tasks that may be assigned. The airlift and sealift improvements in the budget need to be pursued.

Technology

Sensible use of high technology multiplies the effectiveness of our forces. The size of the Soviet forces dictates that we use technology to overcome part of the disadvantage. We need to field high quality weapons and equipment efficiently and quickly. We must press on with programs which allow our forces to maintain a technological edge and we need to get modern equipment into the hands of the troops so we can begin getting the benefits from it. We should lay to rest the notion that U.S. soldiers, sailor, airmen, and Marines can't operate modern equipment. At the same time, we need to recognize that modern defense forces require good people. Our manpower programs must continue to be aimed at recruiting and retaining people with the aptitudes and motivations to operate modern weapons.

People

People will remain the cornerstone of our forces. The support of the Congress has been a key factor in the programs that have so greatly improved our total posture over the past two years—programs which reversed downward trends in recruiting and retention. Well-trained, highly motivated Service members will continue to be the heart of our combat readiness.

Pay and allowances, living and working facilities, the level and quality of the training, confidence in equipment, and the quality of leadership all have a great influence on the retention of good people in military service. This year the President found it necessary for military personnel, as well as all our other recipients of governmental payments, to forego pay raises. The Joint Chiefs of Staff understand the President's decision and, with the Secretary of Defense, hope the action will not cause recruiting and retention to suffer. We cannot afford to commit the same mistakes we made in the 70s if we are to maintain the modern, ready forces this nation needs to deter war.

As you deal with the budget and programs for the years ahead, I urge you to do so in the light of the very real security threats the Nation faces today and those it will surely face in the future. Much as we might like to do so, we cannot roll back the calendar to days when we could rest safely behind our two ocean frontiers, mobilize our forces to go off and fight our wars in distant lands, and do it in our own time. Our safety and security are inextricably tied to peace in the rest of the world. Military force alone will not guarantee our security, but the lack of sufficient modern, ready military forces of the kind needed to deter attack may well guarantee that we could lose our security.

Remarks at the NATIONAL PRAYER BREAKFAST
Washington, DC
3 February 1983

Mr. President, Mrs. Reagan, friends and—to borrow from Archbishop Sheen's greeting of a few years ago—Fellow Sinners. What a great occasion this is: 3,500 people, 120 countries represented, the entire range of our political spectrum present, people with widely divergent views on what to do about the Federal budget, defense spending, social programs, nuclear weapons and almost any other issue of the day. We are here together acknowledging our own human frailty, our lack of omniscience, and our dependence on God. Even more important, this diverse group is here together to ask God's help, not just for ourselves, but for each other and our fellow humans everywhere, as we wrestle in the days ahead with the world's problems, the Nation's problems, and our own personal problems. The power of God is truly here; it will touch us all and we will surely be helped.

Many of you are probably wondering why in the world a soldier is standing here behind the podium and I want you to know that I have pondered the same question. We have had a few soldiers, even some generals, who have been great orators. In fact, General MacArthur's words in your program are an indication of that fact. But most of us are awful at it. I, myself, have three basic speeches. One is on tank maintenance; one is on helicopter maintenance; and the third is on reenlistment.

Last weekend the seriousness of the task I had accepted for today began to weigh heavily on me. My thoughts kept turning to some of the truly great speakers I had heard at these breakfasts—Archbishop Sheen, Senator Hughes, Congressman Guy Vander Jagt, to mention a few. I thought that the best solution might be to go back and get a record of Mr. Vander Jagt's speech of a few years ago and play it here today.

But on Sunday, the Old Testament lesson was from Jeremiah, and Jeremiah was writing about a problem somewhat similar to mine. Jeremiah had written:

"Now the word of the Lord came to me saying ... 'I appointed you a prophet to the nations.'

"Then I said, 'Ah, Lord God! Behold, I do not know how to speak, for I am only a youth'"—that part's not similar—'but the Lord said to me, 'Do not say, I am only a youth; for to all to whom I send you you shall go, and whatever I command you you shall speak. Be not afraid of them, for I am with you to deliver you," said the Lord.

"Then the Lord put forth His hand and touched my mouth; and the Lord said to me, 'Behold, I have put My words in your mouth'."

I reread the passage from Jeremiah a couple of times Sunday after the Redskins' game and then the message seemed quite clear to me and the message was, "Give them the reenlistment speech." I want to talk reenlistment—reenlistment in the Army of the Lord. I know this talk goes to our forces overseas and to our ships at sea. All those members of the Armed Forces know that the fellow in my job represents all the Armed Services; so, if it suits you, please substitute Navy, Marine Corps, Air Force, or Coast Guard for Army.

Does God have an Army? Sure he does. The Biblical references to God's Army or the Host of the Lord are so frequent that we needn't spend much time on the point. Joshua was accosted by a captain in the Lord's Host. The writer of the Chronicles judges David's army by the standard of the Army of the Lord. Luke speaks of the multitude of the Heavenly Host. The psalmist in today's Old Testament lesson tells us that the King of Glory is the Lord Almighty in battle—the Lord of the Army. Paul told Timothy to be a loyal soldier in Christ's Army.

How does a person join the Lord's Army? What sort of mental and physical examinations must we take? How do we sign up?

The qualifications are simple. We can look in the Bible at the enlistment of Levi and we can understand how the process works. Jesus saw Levi sitting at his desk in the tax office and said to Levi, "Follow me," and the Gospel of Mark tells us that "Levi got up and followed Him." The enlistment qualifications become clear when Jesus said, "I did not come to invite the righteous, but to invite the sinners."

Those of you who have been in national service in the military of your own countries know that there is a great difference between military life and civilian life. You don't work for the Army, the Navy, the Air Force, the Marine Corps; you serve in them. Once you're in, you are in for all of it. The same is true in God's Army—you're in for all of it and the action starts immediately! The point is best illustrated by Jesus' conversation with some potential recruits on the road to Jerusalem. Jesus said to a man, "Follow me." And the man replied, "Let me go bury my father first." But Jesus told him, "Leave the dead to bury their own dead. You must come away and preach the Kingdom of God."

Another man said to him, "I am going to follow you, Lord, but first let me bid farewell to my people at home." But Jesus told him, "Anyone who puts his hand to the plow and then looks behind him is useless for the Kingdom of God." So, I tell you when you're in God's Army, you've got to be ready for action—and be ready right now!

What about the pay? It doesn't seem reasonable to ask men and women to sign up in anybody's forces these days without some display of the pay system. The pay table for God's Army is prominently displayed and easy to read. Saint Paul lays it out by saying, "Now that you are employed by God, you owe no duty to sin, and you reap the fruit of being righteous, while at the end of the road there is life evermore. Sin pays its servants; the wage is death, but God *gives* to those who serve Him; His free gift is eternal life through Jesus Christ our Lord." Simple, isn't it? Same pay for everybody—privates, captains, generals—even Cabinet officers, Congressmen, and Presidents. No budgetary problems either, Mr. President. It never varies; it's not tied to the Consumer Price Index, and even if it were, the entire cost of the annuity has already been paid by the Lord Himself.

The Secretary of Defense and I have spent the last two days on Capitol Hill introducing the 1984 Defense Budget to the Senate and House Armed Services Committees. About 94 billion dollars of that budget will go to buy equipment and supplies to be used by the men and women of America's Armed Forces to defend the Nation. The equipment includes the entire range of military hardware, all the way from what we formerly called steel helmets (which are no longer steel) to nuclear-powered submarines. Needless to say, many of the questions about the Defense Budget concern equipment procurement. Are we buying good equipment for our people? Is it simple enough to operate easily and, at the same time, can it do the intended job? Does it cost too much? Have we tested it adequately? Do we know it will work as intended? Good questions because much of the spirit and morale and effectiveness of armed forces is tied to confidence in the equipment.

What about God's Army? What sort of equipment is issued to the soldiers? Again, we go to the Bible for the answer. Incidentally, God's Army isn't strangled with paper work. Only one field manual! The Bible has the administrative instructions, the training instructions, and the operations orders. The equipment table is in Saint Paul's Letter to the Ephesians and it tells us, "We are up against the unseen power that controls this dark world, and spiritual; agents from the very headquarters of evil. Therefore, you must wear the whole armor of God that you may be able to resist evil in its day of power and that even when you have fought to a standstill, you may still stand your ground. Take your stand then with truth as your breastplate, the gospel of peace firmly on your feet, salvation as your helmet and in your hand the sword of the spirit, the Word of God. Above all be sure to take faith as your shield, for it can quench anything and every burning missile the enemy hurls at you." That equipment has withstood a 2,000-year operational and reliability test that would dazzle even the General Accounting Office or the House Armed Services Procurement Subcommittee.

What are the standards of service in God's Army? Is there some sort of code to guide new recruits? Yes, there is; and, of course, it's in the basic field manual, too—it's in II Peter, and it says, "You must do your utmost from your side, and see that your faith carries with it real goodness of life. Your goodness must be accompanied by knowledge, your knowledge by self-control, your self-control by the ability to endure. Your endurance too must always be accompanied by a real trust in God; that in turn must have in it the quality of brotherliness, and your brotherliness must lead to Christian love."

On the face of it, that seems like a good guide to action for a new recruit, but will it and the equipment we've been issued stand up on the battlefields of this century? We could look at a lot of examples, I think, in this century, but I'd like to go back exactly 40 years because today is 3 February—in fact, 40 years and about 8 hours ago.

The troopship *SS Dorchester* was nearing Greenland with 900 souls aboard, including 600 U.S. servicemen, mostly soldiers, when she was hit by a torpedo from German submarine U-456. She began to sink rapidly. There were four U.S. Army chaplains aboard: Alex Goode, a Jewish rabbi; Clark Poling, a Dutch Reformed pastor; George Fox, a Methodist minister; and John Washington, a Catholic priest. The four had bunked together during the trip. When the torpedo hit, they went to the deck together and worked together. They prayed together with the men. They helped rig rafts and passed out life vests from the storage box. When the vests were exhausted, they gave up their own. The ship sank in 20 minutes. A lot of the 229 survivors remembered seeing the chaplains standing on the heaving, squall-tossed deck as the ship sank. Their arms were linked and they were praying.

Today, the Chapel of the Four Chaplains stands in Philadelphia. Its first chaplain, Clark Poling's father, gave it its theme "Unity Without Uniformity." A theme which fits this breakfast group and this great country of ours—and it certainly fits God's Army, "Unity Without Uniformity."

The *Dorchester* sank 40 years ago. Maybe the equipment and the code fit that situation, but a lot has changed since then. Man has been to the moon; we have supersonic jet airplanes; we have intercontinental ballistic missiles and nuclear weapons. If we use that old equipment I outlined, how will the battle come out? Will it work today?

Again, the field manual gives us the promise of victory, and I would use just one of the sets of words that gives us those promises. I'd like to read from Paul's letter to the Romans:

"In the face of all this, what is there left to say? If God is for us, who can be against us? He who did not shield His own Son but gave Him up for us all—can we not trust such a God to give us, with Him, everything else that we can need?"

"Who would dare to accuse us, whom God has chosen? The Judge Himself has declared us free from sin. Who is in a position to condemn? Only Christ, and Christ died for us, Christ rose for us, Christ reigns in power for us, Christ prays for us!"

"Can anything separate us from the love of Christ? Can trouble, pain or persecution? Can lack of clothes and food, danger to life and limb, the threat of force of arms? Indeed, some of us know the truth of that ancient text:

'For thy sake we are killed all the day long; We were accounted as sheep for the slaughter.'

"No, in all these things we win an overwhelming victory through Him who has proved His love for us."

"I have become absolutely convinced that neither death nor life, neither messenger of Heaven nor monarch of Earth, neither what happens today nor what may happen tomorrow, neither a power from on high nor a power from below, nor anything else in God's whole world has any power to separate us from the love of God in Jesus Christ our Lord!"

The U.S. Army has a catchy recruiting slogan that says, "Be all that you can be—in the Army." That slogan fits God's Army better than the U.S. Army, and I say to you, "Be all that you can be—in God's Army." Enlist or reenlist today.

Thank you.

Address to the
ECONOMIC CLUB OF CHICAGO
Chicago, IL
24 February 1983

Around 500 B.C., Heraclitus put forth the theory that the "one-stuff," the basic substance, the constant of the universe, was flux or change. I believe that if Heraclitus could have shown his colleagues in Miletus the changes that I have seen in 43 years in uniform, they'd probably not have disputed his theory. As many in this room know so well, we live in an age of fundamental change that affects our country and the world community on a vast, virtually unprecedented scale.

We live in a complicated world of nation-states whose variegated politics seem almost inexplicable and whose economies are inextricably intertwined. Economic interdependence has grown astoundingly. In the year I joined the Army, the United States was a net exporter of about twenty thousand barrels of oil a day. In 1979, some 40 years after I enlisted, we imported six million barrels of oil a day. In the year that I took the oath of enlistment, we imported one million tons of iron ore, but we also exported eight million tons of finished steel products. In 1979, we imported fifteen million tons of iron ore and we also imported about twenty-five million tons of finished steel products.

I know this audience appreciates the implications of interdependence. Treasury Secretary Regan wrote earlier this month that exports of goods and services as a share of U.S. Gross National Product doubled between 1970 and 1979, accounting for about 12 percent of GNP. Today we see about 20 percent of all goods produced in this country and 40 percent of our agricultural production go into export. I share Mr. Regan's assessment that the time is long past when economic dislocations in a foreign country will not impact the United States. Henry Kissinger was quoted in *Time* magazine last month, "In a world of many perils, continuing economic weakness is likely to undermine the democracies' ability to conduct an effective foreign policy or to maintain their collective defense."

We see changes in our domestic economy, with a shift from capital-intensive, heavy industry to highly specialized, short-run manufacturing involving sophisticated technologies. One by-product of this so-called post-industrial society has been an entirely new industry of collecting, processing, and disseminating information—and, the members of the press notwithstanding, all facets of the communications revolution are equally startling. I am here tonight at the request of my friend, John Nichols, from the Illinois Tool Works. He and I and many of you know that this country is moving away from whole categories of security-relevant enterprises—including machine tools, heavy foundry fabrication, and shipbuilding to name a few.

Our world has grown far smaller. In the same number of days that it took me to make my first trip from New York to the British Isles in 1942, I recently visited a NATO headquarters in Italy, visited our troops in Lebanon, spent a couple of days with our naval forces in the Mediterranean, visited Egypt and our troops in the Sinai, spent a week at the NATO meetings in Brussels, worked a week in Washington and took a long weekend holiday.

This world of ours is also a dangerous place. One popular weekly news magazine noted a few years back that in the time since World War II there have been 150 wars at a sacrifice of 25 million people. Conditions have not improved since that estimate. Unfortunately, I need only call your attention to continuing strife in Iran-Iraq, Lebanon, Kampuchea, the Somali/Ethiopian border, Namibia, or Central America; the brutal suppression of Afghanistan's *mujahideen*; or the specter of the threat of aggression posed by Libya, North Korea or any number of Soviet proxies to remind you of that fact.

Clearly, it is not a perfect world that we live in. The Good Lord didn't promise us a perfect world, but it is the only world we have. I believe our job is to make the best world out of it that we can, not just for ourselves but, more importantly, for those who follow us. Our national security requires economic, political, social, military, and spiritual health. They are all interconnected, but tonight let's talk about military health.

The principal reason that the United States needs military health is the threat posed by the Soviet Union and its military forces. The most significant and certainly the most dangerous trend over the last 25 years has been the unrelenting growth of Soviet military power. The Soviets have armed themselves to the teeth. They continue to do so at a rate far in excess of legitimate defense needs. We need not theorize regarding their motives.

In his acceptance speech on assuming the duties of Secretary-General of the Communist Party in November, Yuri Andropov said, "We well know that peace cannot be achieved by begging from the imperialists. It can be defended only by relying on the invincible might of the Soviet Armed Forces." Mr. Andropov failed to mention that the battlegrounds of their "defense of peace" have included Hungary, Czechoslovakia, Cuba, Nicaragua, Afghanistan and Poland, to say nothing of those "imperialist" nations of Estonia, Latvia and Lithuania.

I find it difficult to believe that anyone could want war. Yet we know that the Soviets are building the forces they believe are needed to achieve their war objectives. This relentless Soviet quest for military superiority achieved new levels during the *past year* across all areas of strategic and conventional forces. To cite several examples by way of illustration:

- The Soviets began test flights of a new land-based, solid-propellant Intercontinental Ballistic Missile while continuing to modernize their SS-17, SS-18, and SS-19 missiles. The Soviets in 1982 fielded more MX-quality warheads in their forces than we are *asking* to deploy in our *entire* ICBM modernization program. Soviet preparations to begin testing of other new ICBMs continued—we'll probably see them next year. You know the sad dilemma we face trying to surmount opposition to the MX program.

• Test flights were flown by their new strategic, manned bomber, the BLACKJACK—larger than our own B-1B. Our own B-1B will not deploy until 1985, after years of R & D, false starts, and acrimonious controversy.

• More than 80 mobile SS-20 Intermediate-Range Ballistic Missile launchers with three nuclear warheads each were added to Soviet forces so that more than 330 launchers and reloads are now arrayed against Western Europe, Japan, and China. We have *no* comparable systems.

• Three Soviet KIEV-Class aircraft carriers now conduct Atlantic, Pacific, and Indian Ocean operations; a fourth ship has been launched. Development continues on a newer, larger class of aircraft carriers. Their navy took delivery of several new classes of submarines. While we maintain an edge of superiority in these areas, it is decreasing year to year at an alarming pace.

• They continue development of a new long-range heavy-lift transport aircraft. The prototype, just completed, is closely comparable to our own C-5.

• The Soviets' high-energy laser program ran at three-to-five times the U.S. level and is geared to the development of specific laser weapon systems, including land-based and sea-based air defense.

• They've shown a new approach to combined arms combat with the introduction of special, high-speed, tank-heavy raiding forces. The Soviets continue to increase the number of modern T-64, T-72, and T-80 tanks facing NATO.

We are not talking about unsophisticated weapons systems. The Soviets have begun deployment of a MIG variant, the FOXHOUND, their first interceptor with a true look-down/shoot-down capability. Two more fighters with this capability are in development and will probably enter service soon. The trends are clear. Foy Kohler has written that this Soviet military investment and their view of science and technology are so fully intertwined as to make them indistinguishable. You members of industry and science know that the Soviets pursue the acquisition of our technology through legal and illegal sales, Third-World transfers, and a highly organized espionage system. Customs Commissioner William von Raab wrote last year that the Soviets "... have come to depend on the U.S. electronics industry as a major source of both components for their own military systems and for manufacturing equipment with which to develop new systems." Let there be no doubt about the quality of our own systems. But, never expecting to outnumber our potential enemies, we now find the qualitative edge we once enjoyed dissipating at an alarming rate.

We must deal with the reality of Soviet military power. Their forces are large—about 5 million active in contrast to our 2 million. Their forces are also well-organized, well-trained, and well-equipped for a full range of military operations. Soviet leaders continually say that they don't want war, yet when we look at the forces they've built, the threat of war seems very real.

As we in the United States go about our business in this world of nation-states, we don't want to be coerced by Soviet power or to have our friends coerced. We don't want war, but as we pursue the political, economic, social and cultural objectives that "We the People" choose to pursue, we don't want to be paralyzed by the fear of war.

The strategy of the United States is the prevention of war. Let me state unequivocally (just in case there is any doubt in your mind) that neither the Chairman nor any member of the Joint Chiefs of Staff wants war, not a conventional war and certainly not a nuclear war. On the contrary, we are in the business of "waging the peace." The modern jargon word is "deterrence," dissuading one's potential enemies from starting a war by making it self-evidently clear that their war aims cannot be attained—that the cost will be too great. Many people have suggested that we announce a "no-first-use" policy for nuclear weapons. President Reagan restated our policy in 1981 and it was reaffirmed last year by the NATO Ministerial Council: "No NATO weapons, conventional *or* nuclear, will ever be used in Europe except in response to an attack." Our fundamental strategy is defensive.

Our strategy reflects a global perspective, centering on *alliances* and forward-deployed forces in East Asia and Europe; strong naval forces to control sea lanes from our island nation; a *central reserve* of flexible land, sea, and air forces comprised of active forces and reserve units; the necessary *strategic mobility* capability; the command and intelligence systems; and on the North American continent and in the oceans of the world the most important ingredient in our ability to prevent nuclear war: *our strategic nuclear forces*.

We want to make it clear that we can and will retaliate to a Soviet nuclear attack by destroying Soviet forces in such a way that guarantees that their war aims will not be achieved. To do so, the United States must and will maintain a modern strategic triad (intercontinental ballistic missiles, submarine-launched missiles, and strategic bombers) with the required readiness, accuracy, warhead effectiveness, warning systems, and command arrangements. Modernization of our strategic nuclear forces to counter the dangerous and growing nuclear warfighting potential of the USSR is essential for deterrence and peace now and for the hope of strategic arms reduction talks and a more stable peace in the years ahead.

The Joint Chiefs of Staff firmly support the President's arms control initiative for substantial reductions in strategic nuclear arms. Our support for the reductions recognized that, with both sides at lower levels of forces, any disparity in the quality and capabilities of the forces would be even more pronounced than at today's levels. Therefore, the Chiefs support for the reductions was given with the understanding that all three legs of the TRIAD would be modernized. As we seek these significant reductions in strategic armaments, modernization will be an essential element in preserving our deterrent at reduced force levels.

The capabilities of United States forces are improving. Clearly, they are stronger now than at any time in the recent past; many needed programs have been set in motion. The readiness of our own forces is improving and has improved dramatically in the last several years. Probably the most important reason behind these readiness improvements is the improvement in the people situation in our Armed Forces. In 1982, all the Services met their recruiting goals and their reenlistment goals. About 86 percent of the recruits that entered the Services were high school graduates and about 85 percent of those were average or above average in the mental categories. The retention of well-trained officers and non-commissioned officers has improved markedly. The Services are well on the way to solving the serious NCO shortages that have plagued them over the past few years.

Other things have contributed to readiness improvements—a lowered maintenance backlog for equipment, an increase in flying hours and steaming hours for airplanes and ships. Our exercises and maneuvers have been expanded and improved. Training is vastly better. A concerted investment in new training methods is paying off. The accelerated delivery of modern weapons has begun to reach the forces this year, and will make further improvements in readiness. It is important to maintain the momentum.

I would, at this point, like to interject a note on a topic that has attracted considerable attention in the Nation's press over the past year—the role the Joint Chiefs of Staff play in the formulation and execution of our national defense policy.

Broadly speaking, the tasks of the JCS fall into two general areas: to provide military advice to the Secretary of Defense, the President and the National Security Council; and to provide the strategic planning and direction for the Nation's forces and to oversee the readiness and capabilities of the forces to carry out the war plans.

You are probably familiar in at least a general way with the calls over the past year to reorganize the way the JCS do their business. One of the things I did on my first day in office last June was to agree with the other members of the JCS that we personally, not staff officers, would make a thorough examination of our organization and our way of doing business.

We also agreed that, because the JCS relationships are with the Secretary of Defense, the President and the Commanders of the unified and specified commands, we would work out the problems—real and perceived—with those people directly, and not debate the issues in the press. We agreed on criteria to be used for judging the changes that had been proposed by others and by our own members. We also agreed that if any of the changes we could make within the present law made sense, we would go ahead and implement them. We have done that. We also examined a list of suggested changes which might require changes in the law or in our instructions from the Secretary. This personal review by the Chiefs was completed last November and we forwarded our recommendations to the Secretary of Defense. Since he and the President are not finished with their review of our suggestions, I am not going to tell you what they are. I will say that from our point of view our suggestions would belie the claims by some that I am prepared to do no more than "tinker" with the present mechanism.

The present set of Joint Chiefs believes that the duties outlined in the law are the right duties and at the heart of those duties is giving the Secretary and the President good, timely military advice. Our concept of timeliness is that they ought to get the advice before they know they need it. We have developed a close working relationship with the Secretary and we consult regularly as a group with the President. In fact, in the past eight months we have met with the President as a group more than has occurred in any recent four year Presidential term. The relationship between this particular group of Chiefs and their civilian supervisors seems to me to be exactly what the law implies it should be.

JCS organization simply cannot be viewed in isolation when one explores the conduct of our national security affairs. God forbid that this nation will be forced to fight another war; but, if we do, it will be fought by the Commanders of our unified and specified commands. The Chiefs are paying increased attention to the views of those commanders and we are incorporating their views in our strategic guidance. We also recognize the need for better integration of the efforts of the Services—the Army, Navy, Air Force and Marines—and we're working hard to emphasize greater integration of effort to expand our total combat potential. Can we do more? Can we do it better? Of course we can! And we will as we go about trying to provide the best and most defense available for every dollar in the defense budget.

Over the last three weeks, I participated in more than thirty hours of Congressional hearings on the defense budget. The debate about the size of the budget has been sharp and spirited. The questions raised are questions that deserve to be explored and answered for the citizens of our country. The key question is how much is enough? The strategy that I outlined involves forces far smaller than those of the Soviet Union and involves close cooperation with friends and allies around the world. The defense budgets of the last year and projected for the years ahead, when expressed as percentage of the Gross National Product, are well below those of the average for the peacetime years between the Korean War and the War in Vietnam.

Earlier this evening, I said that this Administration came into office pledged to restore our defenses. They were backed by an overwhelming public majority. Have Soviet actions or international events changed so profoundly that the pace or scope of our defense effort should be slowed or redirected? The answer, clearly, is *no* and it is on this point that the current debate *must* focus.

The question of how much is enough for defense is sometimes translated into tradeoffs: defense or full employment, defense or social programs, or what is a "fair" allocation of resources and funds between defense and other areas. Certainly, none of us are happy if anyone who wants a job in this country is unable to find work. The citizens of the country need to pay attention to the social infrastructure of the Nation. But, we must remember that only the Federal government can provide for the common defense. What we pay for defense with a strategy of deterrence is the price of peace for us, for our children, and for generations to come. If our strategy fails, either because it was wrong or because we failed to devote enough of our efforts and treasury to it, we will pay in a different coin—the blood of our citizens.

Is there waste in our defense program? Yes. Show me any organization or social grouping—from your family to the corporations whose headquarters grace the shoreline of this city—and there will be waste. It is, I suppose a sad reflection on the shortcomings of fallible humans. I want to tell you that there is no Federal endeavor which receives greater scrutiny than Defense. Many man-years are spent by the military Services and by the Defense Resources Board in developing and revising each year's program. It is thoroughly reviewed and modified by other Executive Branch offices before it ever reaches the defense, budget, and appropriations committees of the Congress.

Can the defense budget be cut? Yes! Can you do it without affecting the defenses of the country either in the short run or in the future? The answer is no! Cuts of the magnitude proposed in some quarters would have an absolutely disastrous effect on our defenses. Herb Stein, in a very fine article in the *Wall Street Journal* on February 11, 1983, correctly labeled such proposals "unilateral disarmament."

Some years ago Henry Kissinger said, "Henceforth the adequacy of any military establishment will be tested by its ability to preserve the peace." I agree with this statement but would add that in the event deterrence fails, adequacy will be measured by the ability to win.

The natural and understandable longing for peace sometimes undermines our ability to prepare for war. And I believe it is precisely that lack of preparation that will tempt our enemies and lead to the very war we seek to avoid. This phenomenon was explained very well by John F. Kennedy in his 1940 book, *Why England Slept.* He wrote, "A boxer cannot work himself into proper psychological and physical condition for a fight that he seriously believes will never come off. It was the same way with England. She so hated the thought of war that she could not believe it was going to happen" As Bobby Knight, the Indiana basketball coach once said, "Everyone has the will to win, but few have the will to prepare to win."

We can thank Herman Wouk and ABC-TV for refreshing our memories of World War II. There are some parallels between the world of the late 1930s and the world of the early 1980s. In those days just before World War II, many people in England, France, and the United States also considered defense appropriations far too high. They weren't dishonest or disloyal, but they were dead wrong. I hope we are not so judged by history.

Remarks at the
NAVAL RECRUIT GRADUATION REVIEW
Naval Training Center
Great Lakes, IL
25 February 1983

Graduating companies. I speak not only to you graduating recruits but also to you parents, girl friends, wives, and friends. I think I have learned a few things during my service in the Armed Forces of the United States—I guess it will be 44 years come this next May—and I'd like to pass on a few of them to you recruits. I have also been the parent of a recruit. So, I have learned something about that, too; and I want to pass on a few tips to you parents.

The first observation I have is that these 400 or so recruits probably came in for 400 different reasons when they joined the Navy. But, there's only one reason from now on for them to stay and that's because they've taken an oath of enlistment to serve their country and to obey the orders of the President of the United States and the orders of the officers appointed over them, according to the Uniform Code of Military Justice.

And they have taken that oath because "We the people" of the United States decided that we needed to defend our country from whatever threats may face it. These young men don't work for the Navy. They serve in it. And there's a great difference. Some of you work for various companies around here. Working for a company carries with it some loyalty to the company, some duty to the company; but, you also have the opportunity to quit whenever you want and go wherever you want to go. That isn't the case for these young men. They're going to go where the Navy wants them to go and they're going to do what's needed to be done to defend this great country of ours.

One of the things they'll learn—whether they stay in the Navy for an entire career or whether they leave it at the end of their first enlistment to go on to some other civilian pursuits—is that the most important thing about the Navy is teamwork. It's not a one-man show. It belongs to everyone, all the men and women who are in the Navy.

There are no unimportant jobs in the Navy or the Army or the Air Force or the Marine Corps. When it comes to doing what we want to prevent but have to demonstrate that that we can do in order to prevent it—that is to defend the Nation and to be prepared to fight in its defense—you get to something that requires more trust and confidence in your fellow human beings than in any other business or profession in the world. It makes no difference what the color of the man's skin is who fights next to you, what state he came from, what his religion is, what his ethnic background is, whether he is rich or poor. What counts is what's in his head, what's in his heart and what he can do with his hands to help the team get its job done. Your buddies depend on you. You depend on them. Learn to get along with them. *Learn to make the team work.*

For you parents, I would say these young men are going out to a very difficult duty. They'll be asked to do extraordinary things—some things that you can't imagine the difficulty of. We have ships sailing in the Indian Ocean; and there's a task force rounding the northern tip of Norway today. If you think it's cold here; imagine what it's like on the deck of those ships out in the far north of the Pacific or what it is like under the seas for days on end. Those people will be expected to participate in those activities and fulfill the jobs assigned to them. And I'm confident that they'll do it well because they're top-notch young sailors in the United States Navy.

As you graduate today. I know you too are top-notch. And, it is important that you are the best because the security of the Nation depends on each sailor doing his duty. My best to all of you. Good luck. Good sailing.

Remarks at the
GENERAL MARK CLARK VOLUNTEERS
42ⁿᵈ Annual Banquet
Charleston, SC
19 March 1983

I can't tell you what a big honor it is for me to be here with you tonight, General Clark. General Clark had a lot of American volunteers serve for him during the almost 66 years since he was commissioned, notably those in the First World War and World War II and Korea. But I'm particularly proud to say that I served under General Clark in his 5ᵗʰ Army—the 5ᵗʰ Army will always be "General Clark's Army"—and in his 15ᵗʰ Army Group. I served through the entire Italian Campaign, and I had the good fortune to serve under him both as an enlisted man and as an officer.

Among my mementos is a short 5ᵗʰ Army radiogram appointing me and one other 34ᵗʰ Division Sergeant to be 2ⁿᵈ Lieutenants. It was signed simply "Clark." Today, I get more than a little bit of pride out of looking at that radiogram when I dig it out. It changed my life dramatically, and that seems to be quite obvious. I can tell you very honestly, General Clark, that at the time I wasn't all that enthusiastic about it. I had a very neat job as First Sergeant of a Field Artillery battery, and that radiogram arrived on the 6ᵗʰ of May of 1944, a few days before the breakout from the Anzio Beachhead. What it really meant was that I was going to be a Forward Observer for an Infantry company rather than be back in the battery position. By the time we reached the Alban Hills a few days after the breakout, we were only a few miles from the beachhead and I was the only one of those guys still on the rolls of the Service. So, General Clark's talk about the seriousness of the fighting certainly brings back the same sort of memories to me.

Many years later, well over 30 years later, I walked from a change of command ceremony to my new office as Commander in Chief of the United Nations Command in Korea. And outside the office door was a brass plaque engraved with the names of the former commanders including, of course, General Mark Clark who was the commander during that historic period—the last year of the Korean War and the signing of the Armistice. At that time I couldn't help but wonder if General Clark really knew what he had wrought when he signed a routine order for a National Guard Sergeant to be a 2nd Lieutenant back in 1944.

I congratulate Captain Lybrand, Sergeant Raines, and the men and officers of the Mark Clark Volunteers. I want to tell you that you have a very proud name, but you also carry a great responsibility to live up to that name. So, do your job well.

One of the things about this job of mine is that you find yourself compelled to read the newspapers in Washington, as well as those from New York, every day. That may be one of the reasons that the life expectancy for former Chairmen of the Joint Chiefs is not very long. They die of gas pains after having read the newspaper every day. I'd like to talk to you about a few of those articles. The articles talk about the state of the Nation a lot. One of the articles that I read in the paper as I rode down in the airplane this morning was an article about the defense budget being too large and about the necessity to cut the defense budget. Now, I want to say to you that there's only one reason today to spend any money for defense at all and that is because there are threats to the Nation's security. We live in a very complicated world of nation-states. The economies of these nation-states have become more intertwined as we've gone through the years. For example, the year I joined the Minnesota National Guard, the United States was the net exporter of oil—about 20,000 barrels a day. Forty years later, we are a net importer of oil—about 6 million barrels of oil a day. In the year that I took the oath of enlistment, we imported one million tons of iron ore. But that same year we also exported 8 million tons of finished steel products. Forty years later we imported 15 million tons of iron ore, but we also imported 25 million tons of finished steel products.

The world is growing a lot smaller, too. I remember my first trip overseas in the early months of 1942—we sailed to North Ireland. And I remember the length of that trip. In exactly the same number of days I recently did the following: I visited the NATO Headquarters in Italy, I visited our troops in Lebanon, I spent a couple of days with our naval in the Mediterranean, I visited our Infantry battalions and saw our peacekeeping mission down in the Sinai in Egypt, I spent a week at the NATO meetings in Brussels, I worked a week in Washington, and I took a long weekend holiday. So, you can get to a lot of places a lot faster than you could 40 years ago.

The world is also a more dangerous place. One of the most popular weekly news magazines a few years back said that since World War II there have been 150 wars at a sacrifice of 25 million people. Conditions haven't improved since that estimate. And all you need to do is look around the world—at Iran, Iraq, Lebanon, Kampuchea, the Somali-Ethiopia border,

Namibia, Afghanistan and at the threats posed by Libya, North Korea, or any number of other Soviet proxies, including Cuba in our own backyard—to recognize that the world is a dangerous place. Yet, the principal reason that the United States needs its military health and a defense budget is the threat posed by the Soviet Union and its military power. The most significant and certainly the most dangerous trend over the past 25 years has been the unrelenting growth of Soviet military power. The Soviets have armed themselves to the teeth, and they continue to do so at a rate far in excess of any legitimate defense needs for themselves or their allies.

Now, I find it pretty difficult to believe that anyone would want a war in these days. Yet, we know the Soviets are building forces that they believe they need to achieve their war objectives. In this relentless quest, the Soviet military superiority continues even today, in every single area of military power. They've built up a vast force of strategic ballistic missiles. They've continued to test new bombers that are larger than the new B-1 bomber that the United States is trying to add. They've added a vast force of intermediate-range nuclear missiles to threaten the nations of Europe and Asia; and, they've added greatly to their naval power that permits them to go into all corners of the earth. They've maintained large ground forces since General Clark was trying to take them out of Austria many years ago, and those ground forces have continued to grow and be modernized with some of the best equipment in the world, and certainly the greatest numbers. When you look at 50,000 tanks, you're talking about a staggering number of tanks.

We in the United States must deal with the reality of Soviet military power. Their forces are very large—about 5 million in the active force and with millions to be called in their reserves, while we sit here with 2 million in our active forces and about another 1 million in the reserves and National Guard.

The United States has a defensive strategy. We want to go about our business in this world of nation-states and conduct our business peacefully. We don't want to be coerced by Soviet power, and we don't want our friends to be coerced by Soviet power. We don't want a war, but as we pursue the political, economic, social and cultural objectives that "We the People" have set for ourselves, we don't want to be paralyzed by the fear of war either.

Twenty-five years ago, when the Soviets started this tremendous buildup, this nation had unquestioned nuclear superiority. Yet, we believed it necessary to maintain an army that was 30 percent larger than today's active Army, and a Navy of well over 700 ships in contrast to today's 500 ships. And we were willing to spend over 7½ percent of our Gross National Product for defense.

Yet, today—a time when our economic interdependence with the rest of the world is far greater than when the Soviets started this buildup, when the Soviets have at least achieved nuclear parity and continue to extend their influence far beyond the area they influenced 25 years ago and when they are spending 15 percent of their Gross National Product for defense—we're telling ourselves that we can't afford to spend 6 ½ percent of our Gross National Product for defense. I tell you we need to think that through very clearly. I understand the need for reducing the deficit, and I understand the need for fixing the social problems of this country; but, I want to remind you that our strategy is defensive. We're not going to start a war, but we're going to have to defend ourselves. We want to prevent a war if at all possible.

This business of preventing war reminds me of the ads that you see in the newspaper from the Independent Insurance Agencies—it's a very good ad. The ad shows a picture of a house burning down and the announcer says, "When's the worst time to find out you had the wrong insurance coverage on your house?" Well, exactly the same is true for defense because if we don't prevent a war we will pay for it not simply with dollars; we'll pay for it with the blood of our citizens. So, I tell you that the defense budget that the President has asked for is not too small. It is exactly what is needed. In fact, if anything, it is not big enough. The Soviets have outspent this country for defense by close to $500 billion in the last 10 years. We cannot afford to let our defenses continue to fall farther behind.

The next myth I want to talk about also comes from an article I read in a newspaper on the way down here. The article said that modern equipment is too complicated for you, the people who are in the Armed Forces of the United States today. They say that you can't handle high technology; the equipment will break down and you won't know how to make it work on the battlefield; and besides that, what this country really needs to do is buy more, cheaper equipment instead of buying modern, technologically sophisticated equipment.

Well, that's another myth that needs to be destroyed. In the first place, this country has valued its manpower more than any other country. We have made up for the expenditure of manpower by buying modern, sophisticated equipment, and we needed to do that. The modern equipment that we're buying today will do just exactly that.

General Marchant talked about the Air National Guard squadron being the first to get the F-16s. During August of 1944, the Allies broke out of the Normandy beachhead. To do that, 3,000 heavy bombers of the 8th Air Force flew more than 18,000 sorties. Something like 30,000 air crewmen were exposed every time one of those sorties was flown. When 18,000 were flown, 30,000 airmen were subject to the enemy air defenses. With today's technology, you can take 800 F-16 fighters with 800 crewmen, instead of 30,000 crewmen. You can take the same number of bombs to the target in far less time than it took the 8th Air Force to do it, and you can get those bombs there a lot more accurately.

In North Vietnam, there were 872 bombing sorties flown against Thanh Hoa Bridge, all unsuccessfully. Eleven aircraft were lost, and 22 American air crewmen were killed trying to destroy it. On the 27th of April, 1972, eight sorties were flown using modern, laser guided bombs. The bridge was destroyed and no aircraft were lost. And, in my view, that's an example of what happens when you use high technology correctly.

The same is true when you have great sea power in our Navy today. The new AEGIS Class Cruisers have a crew of 319. The AEGIS replaces cruisers that once had a crew of 1,600 men; and the firepower and capability of those cruisers far, far surpasses anything that the older cruisers had.

The same is true for the new submarines. The LOS ANGELES class submarine can search through 10,000 square miles of ocean in a 24-hour period—nearly 10 times the area that its predecessor could do. The TOMAHAWK cruise missile, which is just entering service, can strike targets 250 miles away, far exceeding the 8-mile reach of old submarines.

Now, the same is also true of land power. The same is true for the people with the Infantry; the battalion of the 118th Infantry here today will be expected to cover an area about 40 to 50 times greater than its predecessor, the World War II battalion, covered. You can do that simply because you're supported with better firepower; you've got better mobility yourself; and you've got better communications and firepower in your own hands and among the troops that support you. My youngest son is an attack helicopter pilot in the Army. When I think what those attack helicopter pilots are going to have to do when they go out there and face those 50,000 Russian tanks—and they're going to have to get a lot of them—I don't want him out there flying some cheap helicopter. I want him out there flying the best ones that this country can afford. I don't want any of you out there either flying around in cheap equipment, or firing cheap guns or cheap anti-tank missiles. I want you to have the best that this country can have because, in the first place, that's the way we'll prevent war and, secondly, that's the way we'll win if we have to fight.

I am very pleased to see that the 169th will be the first of the National Guard squadrons to get the F-16s. I am also pleased to learn that the 1-263rd Armor will begin training on the M-60A3 tank this summer—a very modern tank that will make that tank battalion able to fight both in the night and the day and to engage targets at much greater ranges than in the past. The North Carolina National Guard will be equipped soon with the M-1 Abrams tank. In fact, they'll get it a lot earlier than many of the active Army get it.

The importance of the Guard and Reserves today can't be overemphasized. I was out here at the air base today and looked at the 437th Active Military Airlift Command Wing and sat there with the Commander of the 315th Reserve Wing. Those two work hand-in-glove and they typify the relationship between the Active force and the Reserve Components today. I want to tell you that neither the Active Components nor the Reserve Components will be good unless they have modern equipment. The idea that we can buy more cheap equipment and not give our men the best and most modern equipment that we can afford to buy is a myth that needs to be destroyed.

The third myth that I read about in the paper on the way down here today was the myth that the United States is the one that is being intransigent in trying to negotiate the nuclear weapons reduction agreement with the Soviet Union. I read an article that suggested that maybe President Reagan was preparing to fight a nuclear war, and that he might even be building a first-strike nuclear force. That's utter hogwash, and every citizen of this country ought to recognize that. And, certainly, the leadership of the Soviet Union knows that. They're the ones that have built the first-strike nuclear force. What we need to do is modernize ours because it's old and desperately needs to be modernized; and then we need to make it very clear to them that they need to reduce their nuclear forces. The President of the United States has made a very sensible proposal in both the Long-range Intermediate-range Nuclear Force negotiations and the Strategic Arms Reduction Talks in Geneva. But it is, in fact, the Soviet Union that is being intransigent in saying that we're being unfair to them because we want them to make very substantial reductions in those nuclear weapons.

The fourth myth is that we could reduce the probability of nuclear war by voting a nuclear freeze in this country. The Soviet Union has, in fact, modernized their nuclear forces, and if we vote a freeze that involves us not modernizing our own nuclear forces, we vote ourselves into a permanent disadvantage with the Soviet Union. We would play right into their hands and, certainly, there would be no incentive for them to negotiate seriously with us for reduction of nuclear arms.

Now, those myths need to be destroyed. I'm very pleased to see your remarks, General Clark, about the importance of modernizing our own nuclear forces while we try to negotiate an agreement with the Soviet Union to reduce nuclear arms.

The last thing I want to mention to you officers and men of the Combat Support Company of the 1st Battalion of the 118th Infantry is that you have a great outfit here, and I'm very pleased to be here with you. You have a lot of new people who come into this outfit every year. Train them well and take care of them. I'm delighted to hear of the Mark Clark Volunteers Association and the work that it does in trying to make life more pleasant for those new members of the unit. I want to tell you officers and NCOs of this Combat Support Company: take care of those new soldiers because you're going to build a company with them, and that company is going to be part of a battalion, and that battalion is going to be part of the Army that we build to keep together to defend this nation.

It's been a great pleasure to be with you, and it's been a great honor to be with my old commander, General Clark. Thank you.

Interview in *US News and World Report* 28 March 1983

The strategic balance continues to shift in favor of the Soviet Union. We deterred war yesterday and we are going to deter war today; but the margin of assurance for that deterrence is dissipating.

*   *   *   *   *   *   *   *   *   *   *   *   *   *   *   *

Question: Why should the MX be considered so important?

Answer: The Soviets have built a nuclear force to achieve their own war objectives. Whether or not that signals a willingness to go to war is certainly a debatable point. I would think that it's hard to find a sane man in today's world who would want such a war.

Nonetheless, we have to design a strategic force that will make it clear to them that they cannot achieve those objectives, that we will frustrate them. The MX is a vital part of that goal. As we seek significant reductions in strategic armaments, it will also be essential in preserving our deterrent at reduced force levels.

Question: If the best strategic minds in the Pentagon are having such a hard time finding a place to base the MX, doesn't that suggest that it may be an idea whose time has come and gone?

Answer: No, the time of the land-based ICBM has not come and gone. The accuracy, the high-readiness rates and relatively low operating costs of the modern ICBM continue to make it an important part of our strategic deterrent force. The quarrel over the basing system for the MX is really an argument about the relative vulnerability of the missile. It is important, but that should not be the most critical issue. What is most important about the MX and ICBM modernization is at the business-end of the trajectory, a capability that we do not now have in the inventory. It is the capability to attack hardened Soviet command bunkers and missile silos quickly. Only the MX—or some weapon like it—will give us the ability to do that. So, even if you took the MX and erected it right our there in the parking lot, we would be far better off than we are today.

To the extent that you can add survivability beyond my "parking-lot" version of the MX, so much the better.

Question: General Vessey, why does the Pentagon give America the impression that Russia produces near-perfect weapons and goes from strength to strength while the United States always has trouble with its weapons and is constantly plagued by problems in its defense buildup? Is the military situation really that bleak and lopsided?

Answer: If the picture we have painted appears that grim to the public, then we have painted it inaccurately. It's fair to say that the Soviets have all the same problems in producing high-technology weaponry that we have— maybe more. Besides, their troops are inferior to ours.

And while we in the United States are choking on the question of whether or not to spend 6.3, 6.4 or 6.5 percent of our Gross National Product for defense, the Soviets are spending 15 percent of their GNP for defense. That alone has got to give them great social and economic problems—and it clearly does.

But having said that, we must also recognize that the Soviets are continuing to build an enormous military arsenal. They are building far more than they would ever need for legitimate defense—and that concerns me.

Question: Are you saying that in a war today the Soviets could inflict defeat on the United States?

Answer: That's a very tough question to answer. We would do extraordinary things to keep them from inflicting a defeat on us. I guess the best way to express it is this: I could not feel very comfortable about the outcome if we had to go to war with Russia tomorrow, but neither could the Soviet Union feel comfortable about the possible outcome.

Question: One final question about this country's defense burden: Given the problem of maintaining a high level of military spending over a long period, would it make sense to cut back some of America's global commitments—for example, in the Persian Gulf or the Far East or even Europe?

Answer: We've given a lot of thought to that. I don't see that you can do that in this world today.

There are two great military powers—the United States and the Soviet Union. The United States has economic, social and political connections with the rest of the Free World, all of which are important to our society today. I don't believe we can abdicate those responsibilities even if we wanted to. The chances are that we would find out later that we made a mistake, and we'll pay a much higher price than we are being asked to pay today, and the coin in which we pay may well be the blood of our people or the loss of our freedom rather than simply dollars.

Statement before the
HOUSE ARMED SERVICES COMMITTEE
On Strategic Nuclear Force Modernization
21 April 1983

Mr. Chairman, members of the Committee. Thank you for inviting us to testify on the important subject of strategic force modernization and to give our views on the report of the President's Commission on Strategic Forces.

Because the Joint Chiefs of Staff were unanimous in their latest recommendations to the President on the Strategic Force Modernization Program and because our views are unanimous on the report of the President's Commission, my colleagues have asked that I deliver a single statement on behalf of all of us.

In December of last year, the President asked the Joint Chiefs of Staff to review our strategic forces modernization program, and to report back to him in February with the results of the review. We did so. We also reviewed the report of the President's Commission and provided our recommendations to the President on that report on the 4th of April. Today, Mr. Chairman, we report to you that the Joint Chiefs of Staff, working independently of the Commission, arrived at conclusions about the land-based ICBM force which are fundamentally the same as those of the President's Commission. We report to you, as we did to the President, that we are unanimous in our support for the report of the Commission.

Through the years, the Joint Chiefs of Staff have examined strategic nuclear force issues in great detail. This particular group of Chiefs has continued the examination. Since last Fall, we have met 48 times to examine strategic nuclear force issues. We have looked at our entire strategic nuclear force, examined its effectiveness, survivability, the need for modernization, and the arms control impacts of our programs. We have looked at the Intercontinental Ballistic Missile force, with particular emphasis on MX, its contribution to our total force, and the alternate basing modes for the MX. We have heard reports from recognized authorities from both inside and outside the government; we met often with the Secretary of Defense on these issues; we met twice with the President's Commission; and, since the first of the year, we have met twice with the President on strategic forces issues. We have spent a great deal of time and effort studying the problems.

The need for our defense forces stems from the threats this country may face. This Committee has a good understanding of the Soviet threat. Therefore, we will not spend a great deal of time in reciting the specifics of that threat. We would simply point out that the Soviets have made massive strategic deployments in the past decade. In the last six years, they have deployed operational missiles among the most accurate in the world, and those missiles are based in the world's hardest silos. In the last year, as part of the further modernization of those missiles, they deployed over 1,200 modern, hard-target killer warheads—more than we intend to deploy in our entire ICBM modernization program.

For the past several decades, the United States has relied on deterrence through strength to counter the growing Soviet threat. We have tried to make it clear to the Soviets that they would not be able to achieve their aims through war. Our strategy is to deter war. The Joint Chiefs of Staff believe that deterrence and stability come from establishing significant doubt in the minds of the Soviets that their war aims can be achieved. We also believe that, from the military point of view, the entire range of U.S. and allied forces—strategic nuclear forces, theater nuclear forces, and general purpose forces—all contribute to deterrence. Strategic nuclear forces are a major part of that deterrent, and it is the modernization of those forces, especially of our ICBM forces, that we wish to discuss with you today.

In considering the modernization of our strategic forces, we must recognize that accelerating Soviet modernization and our own lack of modernization in the past two decades have left us well behind the Soviet Union in several important measures of military capability. We have not deployed a new ICBM since the early 1970s. We have deployed only one new ballistic missile submarine since 1967. In fact, under the provisions of SALT I, the Soviets are dismantling ballistic missile submarines that are newer than our newest POSEIDON boats. We began to deploy cruise missiles only in December of last year. On the other hand, during this same period the Soviets tested and deployed several new types of ICBMs and new and improved submarine-launched ballistic missiles. The Soviets have had cruise missiles deployed on submarines since the early 1960s.

The present body of the Joint Chiefs of Staff has consistently recommended the modernization of the entire strategic nuclear TRIAD to restore an adequate margin of safety in the immediate future. The President's Commission has made the same recommendation, confirming the need for the modernization plans including strong support for improvements in our vital strategic command, control, communications, and intelligence capabilities. We reaffirm our own strong support for that modernization.

On the 11th of February, the Joint Chiefs of Staff briefed the President on the results of their review of strategic forces and recommended:

—Continued strong support for the TRIAD, and continued support to modernize the TRIAD. We believe that the combination of land-based ICBMs, sea-based ballistic missiles, and bombers with air-launched cruise missiles provide a broad range of capabilities whose synergism complicates the Soviet planning, provides us flexibility and provides an important hedge against technological surprise by the Soviets in neutralizing any particular leg of the TRIAD.

—Continued highest priority support for improvements in command, control, communications and warning. Because our strategy is one that does not include a first-strike, the ability of the command and control and intelligence system to survive an attack and provide the wherewithal to retaliate is key to deterrence.

—Fielding MX in MINUTEMAN silos. The accurate, prompt, hard-target attack capability of the MX is needed now and will add greatly to our deterrent strength.

—Continued research and development for survivable land-based ICBM systems, to include research on small, mobile ICBMs.

—Continued research to resolve the uncertainties about hardness of fixed bases for ICBMs.

—We also recommended that the President set a new direction for the future and announce increased research for active defense against ballistic missiles. We pointed out our recognition that there was no near-term solution for defense against ballistic missiles, but that technological developments on the horizon could give hope to our own people and to our Allies that we could use our technology to provide defenses which, when supplemented with arms control agreements, could move us away from sole dependence on the threat of retaliation.

We agree with the Commission that deployment of MX as soon as possible is necessary to counter the increasing Soviet advantage in hard-target-kill capability, to replace an aging ICBM force, to provide a leverage in arms control negotiations, and thus to improve our deterrent posture.

The Commission pointed out that it is the survivability and effectiveness of the entire TRIAD, and not of any single leg, on which deterrence must rest.

Strategic modernization must deal with the combination of land-based ICBMs, sea-based ballistic missiles, and bombers with air-launched cruise missiles, which provide a broad range of necessary, complementary and mutually supporting capabilities. The synergism of these capabilities complicates Soviet planning and provides us flexibility to threaten various forms and levels of retaliation against the Soviet Union. It also provides an important hedge against technological surprise which might lead to neutralization of any leg of the TRIAD. The accurate MX warheads will let the Soviets know that their missile silos, their leadership, and associated command and control are placed at risk, and that their ability to achieve their war aims is seriously in doubt. Deterrence will be improved.

I told the Senate Armed Services Committee on the 8th of December that the Joint Chiefs of Staff fully support the deployment of the MX but that there were differing views on the basing mode. Today, we have reported that we all support basing MX in MINUTEMAN silos. Now, some will ask what has changed our views since the President's 22 November 1982 recommendations on deployment. To set this issue to rest, we think I should provide you some of the details of our November recommendations to the President.

On 8 November we told the President that we believed he was being forced into a final basing decision prematurely and that his first decision to field MX in MINUTEMAN silos while searching for a better mode was a good decision. Three of the Chiefs believed then that we should deploy the MX in MINUTEMAN silos due to technological and cost uncertainties with the Closely Spaced Basing mode. General Gabriel and I, considering the early Congressional rejection of MX in MINUTEMAN silos, recommended going ahead with deployment in the Closely Spaced Basing Mode and recommended a vigorous research and development program to resolve the uncertainties of Closely Spaced Basing. We believed that most of the uncertainties could be resolved and that uncertainty itself has deterrent value. Central to both viewpoints was unanimous agreement on the importance of deploying on schedule. After considering the intervening political development and in reconsidering the arguments on technological uncertainty, the Joint Chiefs of Staff have unanimously concluded that the crucial need for an advanced, highly capable ICBM can best be met by the deployment of MX in MINUTEMAN silos.

The Commission correctly looked beyond the specifics of an MX basing mode and, more importantly, did not consider the ICBM force in isolation. They saw that, in the mid-term and beyond, our goal should be to increase stability. We endorse their recommendation that research on a small, single war-head ICBM begin at once. Development of such a weapon may offer the prospect of continued deterrence with even greater stability in the future. We also strongly support the recommendation for continued research to resolve uncertainties about silo or shelter hardness. The Commission's report gives us a formula that makes sense both militarily and fiscally. The Commission has performed a great service for the country, and the Joint Chiefs of Staff unanimously support their recommendations for modernizing our ICBM force.

Following the Commission's recommendations will provide effective deterrence. The deployment of MX will help redress the imbalances that have developed over the past decade. In the future, adding the small, single-warhead ICBM coupled with an aggressive arms control effort offers the prospect of increased stability. We believe that these steps, coupled with the President's long-term goal of effective defense against ballistic missiles, provide a blueprint for deterrence well into the next century. We understand the Commission's concern over the technical difficulties associated with defense against ballistic missiles in the immediate future. Therefore, we agree with the Commission that, for the near-term, deterrence must continue to depend on strong offensive forces.

Before concluding, we should mention arms control. As the Secretary of Defense noted in his FY 1984 Annual Report, it is the policy of the United States to maintain the lowest level of armament compatible with the preservation of our security and that of our Allies. The Joint Chiefs of Staff have concluded that the preservation of that security urgently requires deployment of MX and continuation of the strategic modernization program. But we are united in strong support for meaningful, effective, and verifiable arms reductions. Such reductions will occur only if we make it clear to the Soviets that we have the resolve to maintain an adequate strategic deterrent force. Approval of the President's recommendations is an essential first step toward greater stability and genuine arms reduction.

All of us share a common desire to provide for our national security in the most effective and most economical way. Soviet goals and objectives are not a reflection of our own, and the capability that might deter the United States does not necessarily deter the Soviet Union. The Joint Chiefs of Staff are firmly convinced that the program outlined by the Commission and endorsed by the President will deter aggression and represents a balanced approach to providing the forces necessary to provide for the common defense. A strong, modern deterrent coupled with aggressive arms control policies will provide for stability and ensure national security. The President's decision has the unqualified support of the Joint Chiefs of Staff and deserves the full support of the Congress. We urge this Committee to lead the House of Representatives in this most important undertaking in providing security for the American people and the Free World.

Address at a Prayer Breakfast
Bloomington, MN
9 May 1983

God intended golf to teach us something about life. In our relationships with Him, God will forgive us for our bad shots. He'll let us be guiltless to play the next one. But another thing you must remember is that in this world of human history, He won't let us go back to the tee for a mulligan. In the world of history, we're going to play the next shot from where the ball lies. If we've hit the last shot into the rough or the bunker, that's where the ball is and from there we must play it.

Address to the
MINNESOTA MEETING
St Paul, MN
9 May 1983

It is a distinction to be here and participate in the Minnesota Meeting's first year of activity. Certainly a laudable activity. The need for all of us to be informed of the difficult and important issues that face our country today seems to be self-evident and the Minnesota Meeting will certainly help do that here in Minnesota. I was pleased to see that my boss, Secretary Weinberger, was here last year to inaugurate your series.

About a year has elapsed since I assumed my duties as the tenth Chairman of the Joint Chiefs of Staff. Some of you may wonder when we're all over why generals aren't good orators. As I told the group this morning, I have three basic speeches. One's on tank maintenance, one's on helicopter maintenance and the third one's on reenlistment. I got this job a little bit by accident. Actually, I had no idea I was being considered for the job. I had come back from a trip to South America and I was asked to see the Secretary of Defense. I went to see him and I had all my notes from my trip to South America where I had met with a number of Latin American leaders. He said, "Come on. We've got to go see the President. We have an appointment in five minutes." And I said, "Alright." So I thought, "Boy, the President's going to ask me about South America." We got in the elevator and Mr. Weinberger said, "The President wants to settle this JCS Chairman business and you're pretty high on a short list." And I said, "Stop. I can't go over there. I've just built a new house in Minnesota. My wife thinks that we're going to retire. I've put in my retirement papers. I couldn't say 'yes' even if the President asked me." Mr. Weinberger said, "Come on. You'll just have to tell that to the President."

Well, we got over there and I explained the astronomical cash flow problem I had with a 19½ percent construction loan on my house and I told him of my wife's views; and the President said, "Well, you just get some advice and go home and tell your wife because I want you to take this job." So, I went immediately to Fort McNair to explain it to Avis; and, as I explained what the President had said, a tear rolled down her cheek. I said, "How in the world do we get into things like this?" She said, "You lied about your age to get into the National Guard, and God is punishing you."

But it's an interesting job. People ask me how I like it and I tell them I'm too busy to ask myself that question and, besides, I might not like the answer. Hardly a day goes by that I don't read some new account asserting that this country lacks a coherent defense strategy; that we are throwing money at the military Services; and that our weapons are too costly and too sophisticated for our fighters to operate. It doesn't surprise me at all that our citizens are sometimes confused about some of the things one reads about the state of the country's defenses and about our national security. And I'd like to share some of my observations with you based on some 44 years of wearing this uniform.

As I survey the range of enormously complex security issues that confront our elected officials, our civilian appointed leaders, and our uniformed leaders, I get mixed emotions. On the one hand, I know that the state of our own military health is better now than I have seen it at any time in the 44 years that I've been in uniform. Many needed programs have been set in motion to correct the shortcomings of recent years. There's accelerated procurement of new equipment on the way. I see some Minnesota National Guardsmen out here in the audience. I know that you're getting some of it now. We see much better readiness as a result of years and years of research that we've put into training. We understand much better how to train soldiers, sailors, airmen and Marines. We see better leadership as a result of the improved education and training for the young leaders that we have. We see greater recognition and respect for our uniformed people by the people of this nation.

I am buoyed by my first-hand observations of the Army, the Navy, the Air Force and the Marine Corps. You can be proud of the forces that you have out there, both Active and Reserve. They are all over the world, under the oceans and in the skies, doing remarkable things and doing them very well. And by doing so they are reducing the risk of war for this country. And let there be no doubt in your mind on that account. The peacetime strategy of the United States is the prevention of war.

My awareness of the strides we are making to improve our forces contrasts with some concerns that I have about our willingness and commitment to provide for our future security. We inherited the liberty and freedom that we enjoy in this world, the unprecedented liberty and freedom we enjoy in this world of ours, from the work of our Forefathers who did take care of our security.

As I look to the future, I can see some primary challenges for us:

—An already dangerous world will become increasingly more so during the remaining years of this century.

—The political and economic interdependence of our global family of nation-states will continue to grow.

—Our principal military threat will continue to be the unrelenting growth of Soviet military power.

And despite our standing around and beating our breasts and rending our garments about our own growth in military power, I see no abating in the growth of Soviet military power.

—The Nation must remain united in its determination to provide for the common defense if we're going to secure the blessings of liberty for our posterity.

It seems very trite to observe that this world is a dangerous place, but that reality is often overlooked as we look at what we're trying to do with our budgets to solve the problems that this nation has. One popular weekly news magazine noted a few years back that since World War II; there have been 150 wars at a sacrifice of 25 million lives. Conditions haven't improved much since that estimate. If you adopt the criteria that a war may be defined by a significant loss of life and the employment of regular armed forces, there are 20 wars of one variety or another going on in the world today—in the Middle East, in Africa, and South Asia and right here in our own hemisphere. Add to that 20 or so other hot spots where conflict is likely—either for religious, or social, or political, or economic reasons—and you can see why the Secretary General of the United Nations said the world is "perilously close to a new international anarchy."

At the same time that international stability is so seriously threatened, the economic interdependence of the world has grown astoundingly. When I joined the Army, the United States was a net exporter of oil—about 20,000 barrels a day. Forty-three years later, last year, we imported five million barrels of oil every day—and that was down a million barrels of oil from the two years previously. Comparable statistics, as you businessmen know, apply to almost every area of business activity. We're dependent on foreign markets, on overseas resources, and on global lines of communication. It is not necessary to look to distant horizons to seek manifestations of that interdependence or of the brutal consequences of armed aggression in the world today. It's a reality that's very close to home here in the United States.

The President asked us to turn our eyes southward to the fourth border here a week or so ago—to the Caribbean Basin. We see Latin America's importance to the future vitality of Western society steadily growing, not only in terms of its strategic resources and expanding industrial base but also because of its strategic importance geographically.

In his address to Congress last month, the President reminded us that Central America's economic and military importance to the United States is often understated. We're well aware of our close ties to our European allies. Yet half of the NATO supplies we would need to reinforce Europe would come from our Gulf Coast and go through the Caribbean. Equally important, 44 percent of all foreign tonnage that comes into this country and 45 percent of all our crude oil imports pass through the Caribbean. The Caribbean Basin is our fourth largest market for exports. We have vital interests in the region, and we have to look seriously at the legitimate security concerns of the United States.

During the weeks preceding Easter, you may have seen photographs in the papers here in Minnesota of Navy F-14 jet fighters escorting Soviet BEAR bombers off the East Coast and down into the Caribbean to their bases in Cuba. Those Soviet aircraft serve as a reminder of the foreign presence here in our hemisphere—a presence that is growing year to year. In the decade between 1970 and 1980, there was a thirteen fold increase in Soviet naval activity in the Caribbean. Soviet influence and presence in Cuba have grown dramatically in recent years. The stream of Soviet military assistance to that small nation has been incessant—totaling more than a billion dollars in security assistance in 1982 alone.

The struggling governments and people in the Caribbean and Central America region need our strong support, not only because of our traditional cultural and economic ties with the region but also because of the strategic imperatives that we face today. That entire region is facing a crisis, with social and economic change aggravated by subversion in almost every country. It is American policy to offer an integrated program of economic and military assistance. The need to seek social, economic, and political progress is clear. For some countries, El Salvador in particular, there are pressing reasons why they must have military assistance in order to get security in the country so that the other internal reforms can take place.

Consider what a freely elected government in El Salvador faces today; it's the challenge of 7,000 armed insurgents trying to shoot their way into the government. I say that that shouldn't happen. Leftist guerillas have responded in a predictable manner to this country's call for democracy, reform, and human freedom. Their latest slogan being broadcast to the farmers there in El Salvador today is "Plant and Die." Electric power plants and bridges have been destroyed to disrupt the economy. Clearly, the leftist were repudiated in last year's election; but, despite that, they continue their violent intimidation. Since that time, armed guerillas have ransacked a third of the country's mayor's offices in attempts to preclude future elections.

I want to tell you very clearly that neither I nor any of the other uniformed military leaders of this country nor any of the civilian leaders in the Department of Defense advocate introducing U.S. combat forces or trying to implement an American military solution to the problems of Central America. But insurgencies such as those in El Salvador must be handled by a combination of political and military and social efforts. What we seek to do is give El Salvador the training and the military assistance that they need so that they can solve the problem themselves, and so they can establish the security that's needed for economic growth. I frequently read in the newspaper "The

American-backed" or "American-sponsored" El Salvador Armed Forces. The forces we have trained, if you took the total of the people that we have trained in El Salvador, amount to about 10 percent of the Armed Forces of El Salvador. They are the best-trained units, and have been subjected to almost continuous combat, but those forces amount to only about 5 percent of the armed forces that are extant today.

The regional and world situation today drives the United States strategy. Our strategy has evolved from the experiences of two world wars and the political realities of the post-war era. Our peacetime strategy is defensive. It reflects our global perspective. It's built on our economic interdependence. It's centered on our alliances—strong alliances in Europe and in East Asia. We strengthen those alliances by having troops stationed in those particular areas, both to give military strength to the alliances and to give political unity to those alliances—to let those people know that we and they share a common future and common security problems in the world today.

Another element of our own strategy is strong naval forces because we are, in fact, almost an island nation here when separated from our East Asian or European allies. We need to control the seas in order to be able to communicate with them. We have a central reserve of ready and flexible land, sea, and air forces which are comprised not only of active forces but also of strong National Guard and Reserve forces. We have the necessary strategic mobility to be able to move those forces. Our forces are considerably smaller than those of the large forces we would expect to oppose. Consequently, we need to be able to move faster and we need to have the command and control and the best intelligence in the world to make those smaller forces effective. And here on the North American continent and in the oceans underneath we've got that other key ingredient of our national strategy, and that is our strategic nuclear forces—the forces that we need to prevent a nuclear war.

Our strategy calls for the use of American technology, America's strong point. And we rely on technology because we value human life a lot more than we value things. I constantly hear people say why not buy more cheap weapons because we can buy a lot more of them and give those to our forces. And then if you lose them you won't have lost so much. You'd just have more of them. Well, I don't know how many of you have children in the Armed Forces. I have one and I don't want him out there with cheap weapons.

From a military perspective, the most significant and certainly the most dangerous trend over the last 25 years has been the unrelenting growth of Soviet military power. The Soviets have armed themselves to the teeth and they continue to do so at a rate far in excess of any legitimate defense needs by any measure—theirs or ours. The plain fact of the matter is that, in the last 10 years, Soviet military investment in hardware alone has exceeded ours by some 500 billion dollars. We are forced to contend with the raw military power that the Soviets have acquired and I have seen the face of battle enough in my military career to find it difficult to believe that anyone could want a war. Yet, we know the Soviets are building the forces they believe are needed to achieve their war objectives. This relentless quest for power and military superiority by the Soviets has achieved new levels during this last year in almost every area of strategic and conventional forces. Certainly, the Soviets have a host of problems. They're not 10 feet tall. They do some very dumb things. They are a one-dimensional power. They are a great power militarily only. And they've got some other strategic problems in the world. As I often say, they're the only country in the world surrounded by hostile communist neighbors. But certainly their power must be recognized. We never expected to outnumber our potential enemies. But now we find that qualitative edge that we once enjoyed dissipating at an alarming rate. In areas where we once had an advantage, we see the Soviets closing the gap. Those trends simply can't be ignored.

As we here in the United States go about our business in this world of nation-states, we don't want to be coerced by Soviet power. And we don't want our friends and allies coerced by Soviet power. We don't want a war as we pursue our political, cultural, economic and social objectives in this world— those that "We the people" choose. Those are our objectives and we want to pursue them. But we don't want to be paralyzed by the fear of war as we go about pursuing those objectives.

Nuclear deterrence and the role of our strategic nuclear forces have commanded a great deal of public attention recently and rightfully so. The issues are debated exhaustively on moral, political, and military grounds. And I think it's important for all citizens to understand the complex issues, since the prevention of war and the preservation of our way of life are inextricably linked to the deterrence of war. I know that Secretary Weinberger discussed his views on these issues with you last Fall and I'd like to go over, perhaps, some new points.

We call our strategy "deterrence." And that means simply that our potential enemies must realize that the losses they'll suffer from our retaliation won't be worth the advantage they might gain by attacking. They realize that, if they attack, they cannot achieve their wartime objectives. The United States built the first strategic nuclear capability in this world. We did that in the 1950s not in response to Soviet nuclear power but in response to Soviet conventional power. We did it because we and our allies were unwilling or unable to match the vast conventional forces that the Soviets maintained on the borders of Western Europe and elsewhere in the world. That conventional threat that the Soviets posed at the time is still there. It is considerably larger now than it was at that time. And it's much more modern today than it was then. In addition, the Soviets have amassed a remarkable nuclear capability. We can't wish that threat away. It simply won't go away with wishes or hopes for good will. The U.S. is striving for deep reductions in nuclear arsenals, but with nuclear proliferation in the world a sad reality, I think it's unlikely that the nuclear genie will be stuffed back into the bottle.

Some will argue that the conventional forces alone should suffice to deter man's regrettable tendency to destroy one another and all those things that we hold dear. And I would say to you that history tells us otherwise. Liddell-Hart, in his landmark history of World War II, compared the opposing forces and revealed some things that some of us may have forgotten. He wrote that in

1939 it was doubtful Germany could long withstand the pressure of prolonged conflict given the country's shortage of war products and resources. Hart argues that Germany's early spectacular victories did not result from an overwhelming superiority of arms and weapons. In fact, the German army and navy were not prepared for war in 1939 and were not superior by many of the indices we now hold when compared with the forces of Great Britain and France. What they did possess, of course, were some new ideas about warfare and an ideological commitment that brought them to the brink of victory. Indeed, Nazi Germany was not deterred by the combined superiority in conventional forces arrayed against her. On the other hand, there's no denying that with the possession of strong nuclear and general purpose forces in the hands of a coalition of free and democratic governments, the continent of Europe has enjoyed one of its longest periods of uninterrupted peace.

There is an article of great insight that was published in the *National Review* here on the first of April. The article was "Moral Clarity in the Nuclear Age," written by Michael Novak—and, if you haven't read it, I strongly urge that you read it. Novak said, "Deterrence is sometimes judged against ideals and not against recent history." And there are certainly moral arguments and specific actions to support that point.

In the past six years, the Soviets have deployed among the most accurate operational missiles in the world, and they put those missiles in the world's hardest missile silos. In 1982 alone, as part of that modernization of their strategic nuclear missile force, they deployed over 1,200 modern, so-called hard-target-killing warheads—more than we intend to deploy in our entire Intercontinental Ballistic Missile force modernization. And they did the same thing in 1981 and they will probably do the same thing again in 1983.

The Soviet Union has deployed and tested a number of new ICBMs and new and improved submarine-launched ballistic missiles. The Soviets have had cruise missiles on their submarines since the 1960s. Now, we simply have to recognize that the accelerating Soviet modernization and our own lack of major improvements in the past two decades have left us well behind in some very important measures of strategic military capability.

We as a nation simply must deal with the reality of Soviet military power and the destabilizing consequences of the Soviet actions. Salvador de Madariaga, the great Spanish historian and philosopher who worked on the League of Nations Disarmament Council for many years, said that nations don't distrust each other because they're armed. They're armed because they distrust each other. And that's a very important point for us to remember.

We must be clear to the Soviets if deterrence is to work. We must be clear that we can retaliate to a Soviet nuclear attack by destroying the Soviet military forces in such a way that guarantees their war aims will not be achieved. Someone said they heard George Brown here some years ago, my predecessor twice-removed. George said when General Ogorkov, Chief of the Soviet Armed Forces, went to see Brezhnev and Brezhnev said, "Now. Is now the time?" he wanted Ogorkov to say, "Not yet." Well, that's exactly what I want General Ogorkov to say to Mr. Andropov, too. "Not yet."

Now, to do this we must simply modernize our strategic nuclear forces. And it's essential for deterrence. It's essential for peace. And it's essential for any hope of strategic nuclear arms reductions. If Mr. Andropov can look at this country and Western Europe and see us dismantling our own modernization program through the western political process, there's no need for him to go to the negotiating table to reduce nuclear arms.

Many loyal and intelligent Americans have advocated a so-called nuclear freeze in the hope of reducing the risk of nuclear war. There is a very strong surface appeal for such proposals, but the sad fact of the matter is that a freeze is more likely to increase—and not decrease—the chances of war because it'll undermine the very foundation of deterrence. A freeze would prevent this country from correcting the deficiencies that I've described would perpetuate Soviet advantages that exist today. It would not guarantee that the Soviets wouldn't continue to build on those advantages by either clandestine programs or by technological improvements which are difficult to verify. It would not prevent Soviet improvements in passive and active defensive measures which could further degrade our own deterrent posture. It could well nullify our determination to reach meaningful arms reductions during the negotiations that are going on.

The potential destructive power of nuclear weapons is awesome. But is any weapon "immoral" in and of itself? I believe we must consider the ends that are to be achieved by their possession. Mindful that there will be no "winner" in a nuclear war, we have to do all we can to prevent one. Together with our European allies, we've pledged that *no* weapons, conventional *or* nuclear, will ever be used in Europe except in response to an attack. The greater moral good that we seek to achieve through deterrence must take into account the actions of our adversaries and the conditions that we face in the world today. Peace must be tended. It must be nurtured. It must also be protected. To do otherwise would be morally incorrect.

De Madariaga, at the same time, in that same quotation, said that the problem with disarmament was that it has looked at the problem of war upside down and at the wrong end. That is to say that you have to come to some fundamental agreements between the contending nations before you can expect disarmament.

The natural and understandable longing for peace and domestic prosperity sometimes undermines our ability to prepare for the war we seek to prevent. But George Washington said, "There is nothing so likely to produce peace as to be well-prepared to meet an enemy."

In the days just before World War II, many people in England, France and the United States considered defense appropriations too high and an adequate defense too difficult to maintain. They weren't dishonest. They weren't disloyal, but they were sure dead wrong. I hope we are not so judged by history.

Extract from Remarks to the
NEW ORLEANS CHAMBER OF COMMERCE
New Orleans, Louisiana
13 May 1983

The health of the Armed Forces is like fresh bread—you have to make it fresh every day or it gets stale. Just as you can't leave bread on the shelf forever and expect it to be fresh when you ask for it; military readiness requires daily attention.

*   *   *   *   *   *   *   *   *   *   *   *   *   *   *   *

Our strategy calls for the use of American technology—America's strong point. We do that because we value human life more than we value things. At the same time the taxpayer deserves a fair shake. He deserves to have us buy sensible equipment whose value is worth the price.

*   *   *   *   *   *   *   *   *   *   *   *   *   *   *   *

I am certainly not the first Chairman of Joint Chiefs faced with questions about the adequacy and costs of our defense. In April of 1950, the first Chairman of the JCS, General Omar Bradley, was describing the problems of defense to an American radio audience. "The problem," he said, "is to provide enough military strength during the peace years—so that we will never have to pay the cost of war, either in lives or dollars." The defense budget under consideration that spring was 13 billion dollars. This great American soldier went on to tell his listeners that the Second World War had cost the United States close to a hundred billion dollars a year. Two months after the radio talk of General Bradley's 60,000 North Korean troops, spearheaded with Soviet-built tanks, invaded the Republic of Korea and plunged the world and an unprepared America into another bloody conflict. The proposed defense budget of 13 billion dollars climbed to more than 60 billion dollars by the following year. But those 60 billion dollars were not the real cost. The real cost was the 33,000 Americans killed in battle and the more than 70,000 lost from the Republic of Korea. When we have not stayed strong enough to prevent war, history has shown us that we paid with a price and a coin that is far more precious, the blood of our citizens. This and other examples remind us of the wisdom of George Washington's counsel that, "There is nothing so likely to produce peace as to be well-prepared to meet the enemy."

We simply cannot afford to disregard the advice of men like Washington and Bradley. We have learned the bitter experience that the terrible costs of war and the price of peace are great. On this Armed Forces Day, we should resolve to give our men and women in uniform and their civilian leaders not just our appreciation, but our pledge of continued support. In so doing, we will provide our nation the strength that it needs to preserve the peace.

Remarks at the
U.S. SOUTHERN COMMAND
CHANGE OF COMMAND CEREMONY
Howard Air Force Base, Panama
25 May 1983

It is an honor for me to be in Panama again. I am pleased to participate with you today in the passing of command of U.S. Southern Command from General Nutting to General Gorman. I am pleased that General Nutting's achievements and talents are being recognized with promotion and reassignment to another important command, the one most directly responsible for supporting SOUTHCOM. I bring General Gorman to this command with mixed emotions. I am sorry to see him leave his last job because he served very ably as my assistant, but I am delighted to see his talents recognized by promotion and assignment to this important command. I am also pleased to see the President of the United States recognize the importance of the command by making it once again a 4-star General post.

On 27 April 1983, President Reagan made it clear to the Congress, to the people of the United States, and to the world that Central America is a vital interest to the United States, closely linked to our security and well-being and vital precisely because how people live and work here is a matter which affects each and every one of our citizens. The region is important for its proximity to our shores. But there is another and more fundamental reason that this area is important. The region is comprised of independent and proud people who share with the people of the United States a love of freedom, a trust in democracy, and a hope for peace. President Reagan has recognized the importance of our obligations to the people of the region. He has established four goals for U.S. policy in the region:

1. We will support democracy and human freedom.
2. We will support economic development. By a margin of three to one, U.S. aid is economic. We recognize that military assistance is complementary to other essential national development programs.
3. We will support the security of the region's threatened democracies.
4. We will support dialogue and negotiations, both among the countries of the region and within each country.

This ceremony today is a clear signal of our continuing commitment to fulfill the President's goals.

Unhappily, some countries in Central America are not as fortunate as Panama. They are torn by violence or beset by terrorism. To economic problems and the stress of modernization has been added the specter of Marxist totalitarianism. Foreign military power is being thrust upon the region by the Soviet Union and by its puppets in Cuba, Libya, and the Warsaw Pact.

These governments seek to spread totalitarianism by exploiting instability in the region. They give arms and training to misguided extremists who seek to gain by violence what they have failed to gain by democratic process.

Secretary of State Shultz put it very well in speaking of El Salvador: "Unable to win the free loyalty of El Salvador's people, the guerillas are deliberately and systematically depriving them of food, water, transportation, light, sanitation, and jobs. And these are the people who claim they want to help the common people."

The missions of U.S. Southern Command (USSOUTHCOM) accord with our concerns for the security and stability of our friends in Latin America. USSOUTHCOM stands as an embodiment of our good will—supporting our nation's stance as a full partner in this hemisphere, not as a patron.

Chief among the missions of the Command is the defense of the Panama Canal, a facility whose security is important to all nations in the region, not only the United States and Panama. Today, more than ever, defense of the Canal is a vital regional concern, and its security is unavoidably affected by the stability of all countries in the region. It is, therefore, even more important that the United States continue to implement the Panama Canal treaties, to work with Panama in defense of this vital waterway. It is heartening to note that the success of the recent canal-defense exercise, "Kindle Liberty," was due in large measure to the cooperation of the government of Panama, General Paredes, and the National Guard. In the years ahead, cooperation between Panamanian forces and U.S. forces must continue to grow as Panama assumes, in accordance with the treaties, greater and greater responsibility for the defense of the Canal.

Secondly, as the focal point for inter-American military cooperation, USSOUTHCOM will continue to assist in providing a shield against subversion and insurgency. The command serves to assist our friends to act in their own defense so that sovereign governments of the region can develop economically, politically and socially.

Today, USSOUTHCOM says farewell to its commander of over three years. General Nutting made far-reaching and lasting contributions to the security of the region. He played a key role in the development of our policy for Latin America at a time when subversion, insurgency and open hostilities threatened the peace and security of the region. His support for security assistance has led to many improvements in the forces of El Salvador, Honduras, and other regional countries. In Panama, General Nutting played a critical role, in cooperation with General Paredes, in the development of innovative methods to improve combined training and to enhance the effectiveness of U.S. forces and those of the Panamanian National Guard. His work has resulted in closer cooperation between our two countries. His distinguished service and extraordinary skill are duly recognized in his promotion to General and assignment as Commander in Chief, U.S. Readiness Command.

I have asked General Gorman to continue on the path set by General Nutting. I am sure that he will prove equal to the task. I have known and worked with General Gorman for many years. He is an officer with great talent and with a demonstrated understanding and respect for the people of Central and South America. You fine soldiers, sailors, airmen, and Marines who will serve with him know that he is a proven combat leader, a true soldier-statesman, an officer with a record of extraordinary achievements in peace and war, and a top-notch commander in whom the President, The Secretary of Defense, and the Joint Chiefs of Staff have great confidence. His promotion to the rank of General is richly deserved and accords with the broad range of important responsibilities he will assume as your new commander. I know you will serve him well.

Finally, I bring to you special greetings from Secretary Weinberger who regrets his absence today. On his behalf and for all the members of the Joint Chiefs of Staff, I extend to you, General Nutting and to General Gorman, best wishes for your continued success in the challenging days ahead.

Interview
Armed Forces Journal
May 1983

The issue is not JCS reorganization. The central issue is making the key man in this whole national security establishment as effective as we can possibly make him—that's the Secretary of Defense.

Address to the
NATIONAL DEFENSE UNIVERSITY FOUNDATION
Fort McNair
Washington, DC
10 June 1983

I am very pleased to be here at this meeting of the Foundation. I am a graduate of two of the colleges of the National Defense University; I wasn't smart enough to get selected to go to the other one. The meeting of the Foundation here is important to the National Defense University. It's important because of the goals you've set for the Foundation. It's important to the University—to the work of the University—and will certainly make the University a better place and a more valuable place for the Nation. I know that you members of the Board have taken on a lot of extra work. Certainly, the Joint Chiefs of Staff and I thank you for the work that you are doing.

Getting the Foundation underway is an important step in the National Defense University's history. As you know, NDU itself was established in 1976 but it actually had its beginning here in 1903. During that 80-year history, the University has evolved and matured into what it is today. But I think that what it has come to be was fairly well-envisioned by President Teddy Roosevelt when he laid the cornerstone out here for the building that is now called Roosevelt Hall. He said the lesson to be learned by our people was ... "that the Army, like the Navy, will do well in war mainly in proportion as it has been well-prepared in peacetime."

The concept of having colleges to train our officers to prepare for war has not always been popular. As a matter of fact, when the British established their staff college in the early 1800s, the Duke of Wellington said: "By God! If there's a mutiny in the Army—and in all probability there will be one—you'll see that it's these new-fangled school masters that will be at the bottom of it!" Now, having come here to all schools of the College as a lecturer and to listen to the students' questions after my lectures, I'm inclined to believe that that may be so today. But there are other views of what the College is and might be. As a matter of fact, somebody said in 1982—and I will let him remain nameless—that "It was the war college system that got the job of justifying government decisions *ex post facto*—far from serving as the basis for development of national security, the function of the war colleges now is to put icing on previously established policy."

That's a grave charge. The Joint Chiefs have invoked General Pustay on a number of occasions to answer that charge or to make certain that the charge cannot be supported. I can tell you from frequent visits to this University and also the nature of the University's product, that such is really not the case. NDU is a unique source of knowledge and education for both military and civilian leaders of this government. It is under the direction of the Joint Chiefs, as you know. It has an experienced military and civilian staff, and it provides education on national security issues that is probably broader by a sizeable factor than one can get anywhere else in this country. It treats national security issues in the fashion that President Eisenhower meant for them to be treated when he proposed in 1958 the last major reorganization of the Joint Chiefs of Staff and to the defense Reorganization Act of 1947. At that time, President Eisenhower said there would be no more uni-Service battles. The Navy could not fight by itself, the Army could not fight by itself and the then-new Air Force could not fight by itself. The National Defense University honors that point and has made certain that the officers who attend here understand.

NDU serves as a lubricant for the defense decision-making process of the government. In addition to providing graduates who serve on the higher-level staffs, it also conducts studies and research projects for the Joint Chiefs of Staff and for the Secretary of Defense. It delves into worrisome civil and military problems that we can't or don't have the time to deal with because of the press of day-to-day activities. I cite my own time here as a student. I was here in the Industrial College in 1965. My seminar did a study of logistics

60

support for Southeast Asia. Our seminar was one of those chosen to address the session of the two colleges, the National War College and the Industrial College, and to present our findings. In the audience at that time was the Deputy Secretary of Defense, the Assistant Secretary of Defense for Logistics, and the Assistant Secretaries of the Army and the Air Force for Logistics. There were 11 members of our seminar who worked on that report. When we finished our report, we were then asked to meet with those Assistant Secretaries. We did and before the day was out, nine of the 11 members of that study group had their orders changed to be sent to implement the recommendations which they had made. Fortunately, or unfortunately, there was a little pop quiz and I spelled "logistics" with a "J". So I was not one of those who had his orders changed. I went directly on to a combat unit in Vietnam, but I was able to enjoy the fruits of the work of my fellow students.

NDU also provides an atmosphere of reflection that is a little bit insulated from the fire brigade urgency of day-to-day governmental work. I have to go to a JCS meeting a little later on this afternoon. Certainly, that is the plight of other leaders in government, both civilian and military. We are "meeting" people.

The University also serves as a sort of neutral ground where civilians who are not connected with the government can meet with military leaders and civilian leaders in government to examine political and economic problems as well as military problems that face our country. That is important because, certainly, our national security doesn't rest on military strength alone. It rests on our economic health and political health, our social health and our spiritual health. Hence, sponsoring such conferences as you are engaged in here is an important activity of the University.

For me, as the JCS Chairman, I find the University particularly useful. When I signed on to this job last year, I worked out an agreed menu with the other members of the Joint Chiefs of Staff and with the Commanders in Chief of the unified and specified commands. And, at the top of that menu was war planning, or military planning. And it's an important thing for those of us who are in this business to be involved in. As I told the Chiefs at that time, we could blame the Congress if the defense budget was too low; we could blame the society or the school principals or the parents if the recruits were not smart enough to do their jobs; we could blame the defense contractors if the equipment didn't work; but, if the war plans were no good, the finger points only at us. And, whatever the difficulties were, we had to have realistic plans for the defense of this nation. It was our responsibility and ours alone. Now, I think we have most of those knots reasonably well-tied together. Certainly, they are not as well-tied together as they ought to be, and we are using the National Defense University to help us.

As many of you old warriors out there in the audience know, war plans tend to grow like mold in the basements of headquarters. They sometimes never see the light of day. We think it is our job as the Joint Chiefs of Staff to tell the people how to make plans—to give those plans the right direction in the first place with some guidance from the top. In many places in the world, our

Commanders in Chief are out there with yellow foolscap, pencils with erasers, and hand-held calculators trying to make the war plans while we have the vast computer resources and analytical agencies, many of which are at the war colleges helping the students study the hypothetical problems. The fellows out there who solve the real problems don't have the support that they need. So, the other thing that we've tasked the President of NDU to do is to harness that capability that we have in the colleges that makes up the entire education establishment of the Armed Forces and make that available to the Commanders in Chief of the unified and specified commands to help solve their problems in their global planning responsibilities.

These then are some of the important ways that NDU has evolved since President Roosevelt gave the college its start in 1903. In looking back to that time, I see a number of familiar crises that faced our nation. When the University had its beginning in 1903, the Army was struggling with the Philippine insurrection and simultaneously trying to reform itself under that great reformer, Elihu Root. The Navy was mustering its strength at that time under President Roosevelt and was soon to embark on a trip around the world to show the rest of the world that the United States did have a "blue-water" Navy. The Marines were also involved in activities outside our shores. The whole of the Marine Corps, a battalion, was posted in Central America at that time. The Air Force, of course, wasn't far away because the Wright Brothers made their first flight in that year. With those events as a backdrop, Teddy Roosevelt stood on the steps of the building that was about to have his name and he said:

> "As a people, whether we will or not, we have reached the stage where we must play a great part in the world. It is not open to us to decide whether or not we shall play it. All we have to decide is whether we shall play it well or ill .... This nation, by the mere trend of events, has been forced into a position of world power." And then he added, "It cannot bear these responsibilities aright unless its voice is potent for peace and justice, as its voice can be potent for peace and justice only on one condition ..., that we ask peace, not in the spirit of the weakling and the craven, but with the assured self confidence of the just man armed."

I would say to you that those words President Roosevelt pronounced on that day in 1903 ought to be handed out on cards to Congressmen who are going to vote on the defense appropriations bill this year—and to those who are going to decide whether or not to modernize our strategic deterrent as well as seek arms control negotiations and to those who will decide whether or not we are going to continue to keep this nation a healthy, global power, as indeed we must be. We cannot avoid the responsibilities we have in the world. I say to you that this new National Defense University must play a major role in keeping this nation a just nation justly armed. It must play its part in the preservation of peace. The quality of the education that the officers and civilian leaders get here will have a great deal to do with the defense decision-making in the years ahead. And we hold them to the responsibility of giving an adequate education, one that will help our nation maintain its security and the peace and freedom of the world.

For those reasons I applaud you of the Foundation for the work that you're doing because it exemplifies that the country has always been a country of free citizens willing to help do the job themselves.

Statement before the
HOUSE ARMED SERVICES COMMITTEE
Subcommittee on Investigations
On the Organization of the Joint Chiefs of Staff
14 June 1983

Mr. Chairman, members of the Committee.

Thank you for asking me and my colleagues to return here to testify on the very important topic of improving the effectiveness of the Joint Chiefs of Staff. You will recall that General Gabriel, Admiral Watkins and I presented our views on July 28, 1982, roughly one month after we assumed our duties. You may remember also that General Myer and General Barrow had already preceded us in their testimony. Since then, the Joint Chiefs of Staff have studied proposals for improving the way the JCS contribute to national defense. I would like to discuss with you the conclusions we reached and to describe the changes we have set in motion to improve the way we do our business. The Chiefs have asked me to report the findings of our review.

Early last summer, the Chiefs and I agreed that we would undertake this review of our organization and our way of carrying out our responsibilities. As a basis for our review, we recognized that the effectiveness of the JCS is a direct function of the relationships the JCS maintain with the Secretary of Defense and the President, with the Commanders of the unified and specified commands, and with each other. Accordingly, we decided to address the issues personally rather than have staff officers do the work.

We agreed on criteria we would apply to all proposals for change. I described these in some detail last July, but I want to repeat them today:

- Would the change improve our ability to wage war if we're ever forced into one? The ultimate test is the ability to transition from peace to war and to fight the war to a successful conclusion should deterrence fail.
- Would it provide the President and the Secretary of Defense better and more timely advice?

- Would it better ensure that the requirements of the commanders in the field, the Commanders in Chief of unified and specified commands, are met? These Commanders in Chief, the "CINCs," are the ones who will execute the war plans and fight the battles; and their needs were a key part of our review.
- Would it improve the ability to allocate national security resources more wisely and efficiently—helping the President and the Secretary of Defense to meet their difficult responsibility of getting the most security from our limited budget?

The Secretary of Defense asked us to add a fifth criterion,

- Would the suggested changes maintain our national legacy of civilian control of the military? We added and used the criterion.

As the starting point for our examination, we used the duties of the JCS prescribed in Section 141, Title 10, U.S. Code. Our examination of those duties outlined in the law confirmed for us that those are the correct duties and responsibilities for the JCS. Further, we concluded that the existing law gives us most of the latitude we need to improve the effectiveness of our own operation. We are working to do that now in cooperation with the Secretary of Defense and with the commanders in the field. We believe improvements are underway. There is improved personal communication among the JCS, the President and the Secretary of Defense; we are placing emphasis on the timeliness of JCS advice to the President and the Secretary of Defense; there is increased participation by the CINCs of the unified and specified commands in the program and budget decisions; and we believe we are sharpening the JCS focus on strategic matters.

We agreed last summer to call in the Commanders in Chief of the unified and specified commands, asking each to brief us personally on his most demanding war plan and his concept of operations. We learned a great deal and have set in motion the mechanism for better planning guidance to those commanders. The CINCs have become more active participants in defense resource planning and in global operational planning; and the Secretary of Defense has asked that I, as the Chairman, become their spokesman on operational requirements. As a result, the advice of the CINCs has become increasingly influential in the development of joint warfare requirements and programs.

We have taken measures to assure continuity between the Chairman and the JCS member acting in my absence by assigning an Acting Chairman on a quarterly basis.

Service schools continue to emphasize joint planning and operations; and, a training program for officers of the Joint Staff is being prepared. Our system of colleges under the National Defense University is giving new attention to joint strategies and operations at theater and global levels.

In the conduct of our review, we learned something that probably should have been obvious from the start. The challenge for any "reorganizer" is to enhance the effectiveness of the Secretary of Defense. The Secretary of Defense is the key man in the defense establishment; and reform must focus on improving how he uses the JCS, his military advisors, as part of the entire DOD organization. We determined that an important part of his effectiveness depends on how well the JCS carry out the duties prescribed for them in the law and on the effectiveness of three, interdependent relationships.

The first relationship is that among the Chiefs and the Secretary of Defense and the President, a relationship which stems from duties specified in Section 141, Title 10, U.S. Code. In the performance of these duties, we've developed a close working relationship with the Secretary and we consult regularly as a group with the President. The relationship between this particular group of Chiefs and their civilian superiors seems to me to approach what the law indicates it should be.

The second relationship is the relationship among the Chiefs as a corporate body. We must have trust and confidence in one another. Each Service Chief has responsibilities as the senior uniformed officer in his own Service, responsibilities different from those duties he performs as a member of the JCS. These other duties uniquely distinguish each Chief as best qualified to advise on the capabilities and limitations of his Service. The close relationships developed within this group of Chiefs ensures that this expert advice is heard.

The third relationship, which I addressed earlier, is that among the Joint Chiefs and an important group of nine—the commanders of the unified and specified commands. The JCS as a body and the Chief of each of the Services must ensure the requirements of the CINCs are heard and acted upon.

These relationships are fundamental elements in any consideration of how we do our business. JCS organization cannot be considered in isolation. The functions of the JCS can only be considered in the light of the larger mechanism for building our defenses. In this respect, the effectiveness of the JCS is a function of understanding and of mutual respect within each of the relationships I outlined. The relationship must be tendered by all the people involved.

Nevertheless, our review has led us to conclude that some adjustments of Department of Defense organization and procedures are indicated—necessitating changes in the law. This is so for a number of reasons. Past experience shows that military advice on strategy, on force requirements, and on measures for the transition of our defense posture from peace to war can best be provided by the JCS. However, the JCS need to improve our ability to provide the analytical basis for military strategy; force structuring, joint tactics, techniques, procedures and related training; and joint logistics. Further, the staff working for the Joint Chiefs of Staff, the Joint Staff, is not now best structured to assist the JCS on major decisions relating to force requirements or to weapons system choices. Accordingly, the Joint Staff needs to be strengthened. Finally, in the interest of aligning our peacetime and wartime functions, the law also should be amended to place the Chairman in the chain of command to the unified and specified commands.

I would like to amplify on these needed changes as contained in two basic recommendations for new legislation made through the Secretary of Defense and submitted to both Houses on April 18, 1983.

First, we recommended that statutory restrictions on the size of the Joint Staff and tenure of its officers be changed to augment and strengthen their support to the Chiefs. The changes are necessary so that the size of the Joint Staff can be adjusted when necessary to ensure it has the number of experienced officers needed to assist the JCS and the Secretary of Defense in carrying out their assigned responsibilities.

Second, we recommend that Title 10, U.S. Code, Section 124, be amended to place the Chairman in the formal chain of command. The Chairman presides over the Joint Chiefs of Staff; and he communicates, at the direction of the President or the Secretary of Defense, orders to the Commanders of the unified and specified commands. The proposed legislation would make explicit the Chairman's functions as a link between the Secretary of Defense and the unified and specified commands, an arrangement which already works well in practice.

In sum, the Joint Chiefs of Staff believe that these changes to the current organization are necessary for a more effective JCS. Other proposals which were advanced for changes to the organization of the JCS were given a thorough examination by the Chiefs. We have told the Secretary of Defense that we believe that other improvements can most probably be made within the boundaries of existing legislation. And, we have recommended that we work together to develop and test those changes.

We do not believe it is necessary to specify that the Chairman is the principal military advisor. This is adequately provided in existing law and the proposal would serve only to disrupt or confuse the flow of advice from the other members of the JCS. We believe the Chairman does not require a full-time, 4-star Deputy Chairman. The system of quarterly rotation of an acting Chairman is working well. Similarly, the JCS gave careful consideration to the concept of a National Council of Senior Military Advisors apart from the Chiefs of the Services, but we believed that the proposals already outlined provided the opportunity for us to improve the military advice to the Secretary of Defense. Nor is it necessary or appropriate to revise the law to subordinate the Joint Staff specifically to the Chairman. The Chairman is already responsible for the management of the Joint Staff and its Director on behalf of the Joint Chiefs of Staff.

Mr. Chairman, the Joint Chiefs of Staff have completed the review of the various proposals to change the organization of the Joint Chiefs of Staff. Our recommendations, concurred in unanimously by all the Chiefs, have been submitted to the Congress through the Secretary of Defense; and we recommend their approval.

Remarks at the Graduation Ceremony
EMPIRE STATE MILITARY ACADEMY
Camp Smith
Peekskill, NY
24 June 1983

The Army's a great leveler. The enlisted men and women come from a multitude of backgrounds—different family backgrounds, different economic backgrounds, different skin colors, different sexes. But those don't mean a thing when it comes to the Army. It's what's in your head, what you can do with your hands and what's in your heart that counts and makes the team work. It builds that trust and confidence in each other.

*   *   *   *   *   *   *   *   *   *   *   *   *   *   *   *

There are some constants in military success. Today, as in times gone by, success on the battlefield demands not only technical competence but trust and confidence of the highest order in each other—trust in the skill of one's comrade, knowing that the fellow next to you, the fellow in front of you, and the fellow behind you, whether from another Service or from your own outfit—trust that the other fellow on the team is going to do his job and do it correctly. Trust and loyalty, courage and willingness to share the burden. Those relationships and that teamwork can be built only with discipline— organizational discipline that comes from such things as drill as well as individual discipline and the self-discipline that comes from the ability to stand out there at attention or at ease, with the sweat running down your nose and a fly on your ear, and be able to continue to stand at attention. Because in battle, you'll have to do things that are a lot harder than that.

Von Steuben had some good guidance for officers. He said that "The first duty of the Captain is to gain the love and confidence of his men by treating them with every possible kindness and humanity, inquiring into their complaints and, when those complaints are well-founded, seeing them redressed," and that the Captain should know the men by name as well as character. Now, that does not mean fawning or mollycoddling. It means the highest duty is teaching one's men and women to know their duties on the battlefield so that they can build that trust and confidence in each other.

Address to the BREAKFAST of the
25TH DIVISION OFFICERS AND MEN
Schofield Barracks, HI
30 June 1983

The United States has extraordinary responsibilities in the world today. There are many in our population who would like to have us evade those responsibilities or renege on those responsibilities. Unfortunately, that is not possible. There are many in the world today who would like to "uninvent" nuclear weapons. That is not possible. The Good Lord didn't promise us a world without troubles or a perfect world. But He gave us the only world we have and our job is to make the best we can out of that world. I think we as Americans have the duty to make that world as safe as we can—first, for our own citizens, to protect those rights and liberties which our Forefathers pledged their lives, their fortunes and their sacred honors to protect. Second, we have a duty to make life as safe and as good as we can for our friends and allies in the world.

One reason I want to talk to you today is that I hear a lot of talk in the newspapers which says we don't have a strategy. Well, I want to tell you that's a lot of baloney. We do have a strategy. It's a very sensible strategy. Our strategy is one of preventing war by making it self-evident to our enemies that they're going to get their "clocks cleaned" if they start a war with the United States.

Our strategy counts on a couple of things. It counts on alliances. You see that if you go to Korea—it's sort of the anchor of our alliances in East Asia. And we have our alliances in Europe. Many of you have served there.

Another part of our strategy is forward-deployed forces to reinforce those alliances. We have forward-deployed forces for two reasons. The first is to make sure that the alliances have military strength enough to make it self-evident to our enemies that we're ready to fight. Second, by providing American forces in those forward-deployed military units to countries that are part of alliances, we provide political strength to the alliances. We let those nations know that we're with them. That's important because we need them and they need us.

There are some other parts of our strategy and they tie into the 25th Division. We don't have large forces. You people who go out to Korea face the North Korean forces across the Demilitarized Zone. The North Korean Army is about the same size as ours. It comes from a country of about 18 million people. We come from a nation of 225 million people. So, you see, we don't have nearly as many of our people in uniform as they do. We have a large Navy and Air Force which they don't have. Nevertheless, our forces are not large in comparison to the military commitments that this nation has. So, we count on three things, three key ingredients, to make our forces more effective.

The first is extraordinary good intelligence. We spend more money than anybody else in the world on intelligence. We have better intelligence than anybody else in the world. The second thing is good command and control. We can send forces to the Egyptian desert and I can send an order to the task force commander and get it there in no time at all. And, the third ingredient is extraordinary mobility. We can move forces to other parts of the world better than anybody else. Nathan Bedford Forrest wasn't the first to recognize that when he said, "Get there 'fustest' with the mostest." But, he was the first to put it in truly good American English. Certainly, that's something that was recognized by Sun Tzu, Genghis Khan, Alexander the Great, Napoleon, Washington and all those strategists before him. If you want to make smaller forces effective, you have to be able to control them, let them know more about the enemy than the enemy knows about them, and then get them where they need to be in a hurry. That translates into how you do your job, as well as what you see going on in the Armed Forces today.

The Army is involved in its greatest modernization program of all time. People ask me what I got the most satisfaction from in my career. I think I got the most satisfaction out of my career when I was Vice Chief of Staff of the Army, as the guy who was in charge of getting Army procurement programs moved through the bureaucracy of the Pentagon. I take pride in saying that while I was Vice Chief of Staff, the Army went into production with the M-1 tank, the M-2 Bradley Fighting Vehicle and the PATRIOT air defense system. We aren't in production yet but we have permission to go into production with the AH-64 APACHE helicopter, the BLACKHAWK helicopter and the Multiple Launch Rocket System along with modernizing both our 155mm and 8-inch cannons. In addition to that, we have a whole range of electronic warfare equipment and command and control equipment that is modernizing the Army. The whole purpose behind that modernization is not to make life easier on the battlefield but to make you more effective on the battlefield—to be able to do just exactly what I outlined in the larger sense for the Nation, and for you as part of the Division. That is, to be able to know more about the enemy, to be able to move faster for the Division Commander, and to control our forces in the fashion that makes them as effective as they can possibly be on the battlefield.

Now, what does that say to you? That says to you—as officers; as Brigade Commanders, Battalion Commanders, Company Commanders, and as noncommissioned officers: Sergeants Major, First Sergeants, Platoon Sergeants, and Squad Leaders—that you inherit an extraordinary responsibility to the taxpayer of this country, to the citizens of this country, to make your forces effective. We're buying a tank that costs the taxpayer around 2 million dollars apiece. That's a lot of money by anybody's standards. It has a jet engine in it. It has a solid state computer, a laser rangefinder, and ammunition that costs about $1,000 a round. It's there for one reason and that's so you can get out there and punch holes in a whole bunch of Russian tanks if you have to. Fortunately, if the Russians recognize that we can do it and will do it, we'll probably never have to do it. That's the best possible outcome. It means that you and I have to do our job to make the equipment as effective as we possibly can.

Having spent many, many years in armored divisions—I can snipe at the armored divisions here when I'm talking to an Infantry division—I always went around to the tank crews and said, "Tell me how you got your tank driver's license?" Well, I want to tell you that we've had a lot of tank battalions through the years which weren't as strict with tank drivers' licenses as the State of Minnesota is for driver's licenses for cars. We can't afford to do that anymore. I rode over here in a helicopter this morning. It cost the Army about a quarter of what that tank costs the Army. We sent those two warrant officers through six months of training. We give them standardization rides frequently. We do all sorts of things to ensure their proficiency. The same sort of thing needs to be done with this modern, very good equipment that you're going to get or that you're already getting. We need to be as strict with that equipment as we are with things like helicopters to make sure that they are run properly and that we get the most out of them.

The second thing that we need to do is take care of ourselves. That fire control system in the M-1 tank or in the M-60A3 tank costs the taxpayers a quarter of a million dollars. The effectiveness of that equipment is dependent on the eyeballs and the hands and the brains of the soldier that goes behind it. If he doesn't take care of himself, if he's not in good physical condition, if he's not eating the right things, if he's boozing, on drugs, or something like that, that quarter of a million dollars is down the drain. It won't do any good at all. Leaders have the duty to see that all members of the Armed Services stay in good physical and mental condition so that we're ready to do what we have to do.

The third thing I'd like to bring up are the tactics involved with the new equipment that the Army is getting. When you take a company of those AH-64 helicopters and hang the HELLFIRE missiles on them, and if you say, "I'm going to get the same reliability, the kill probability, that we got in the operational tests from each of those missiles with that one company of helicopters, you've got a whole Russian tank division's worth of tanks—dead. With the test results we got with the HELLFIRE missile, that's how many tanks a company of attack helicopters would kill—a whole Russian division worth of tanks by one company of helicopters!

That means you, the commanders, have to think through the tactics properly to take advantage of that capability. You don't dribble those things away. You don't send that attack helicopter company out chasing one or two tanks. You don't send it out to do cavalry missions or something like that. Create conditions on the battlefield so that you can get a division's worth of tanks. Now, when you face a division of enemy tanks, you know Murphy's Law will operate. Somebody will screw up. Some guy will fly in the wrong direction. Somebody will forget the proper Army techniques for some of the missiles. But, even if you only get 75 percent of the tanks of the Russian tank division, you have destroyed that tank division for all intents and purposes. What I'm saying to you is that it requires a quantum leap in the tactics of the United States Army to take advantage of the equipment we have now purchased and to take advantage of the soldiers that we now have.

The job for you and me, the leaders, is to make sure that we put those ingredients together, including the proper functioning of the new equipment, the tactics that take the best out of that equipment, the care and feeding of those soldiers, sailors, airmen and Marines so that they are in good physical condition and have the right mental condition to do the job that they have to do. If we do that, there won't be any war. The Russians will know it and I believe they know it now. But we can't afford to be sloppy or they might draw the wrong conclusions. If they draw the wrong conclusions, then we will have to fight; and, if we are already sloppy and have to fight, then we're in serious trouble.

The last thing is the training techniques. We have put a lot of money into the science of training. We know more about how to train soldiers so that we won't have those catastrophic first-day-in-the-battle casualties that we've had in recent wars. What we have to do is take command. Have you got the "MILES" here? (Yes, sir.) How's it working? (Great.) Good. The greatest thing that's come along. Are you going to get an opportunity to go to the National Training Center, Bill? (No, sir.) You ought to complain about that. Try and get it. If you don't get to go there, build your own out here so that the operator gets some very realistic enemy tactics.

If we do all those things, the world will be a safer place.

I would leave you with this. The United States does have a strategy. It's an effective strategy. We have strong forces. We're getting stronger. The people in this country are a little nervous about what's being spent for defense. You read stories in the newspapers everyday about how the procurement system is fouled up, and how we want to wish away nuclear weapons. Just cool it; do your job; be effective. The truth will come out and the citizens of this country will do what they have to do.

**Remarks at the Opening Ceremonies
For the 22nd Class of the U.S. Army
Command Sergeants Major Academy
Fort Bliss, TX
5 August 1983**

What we have to do is think through these modern tactics and not be in the Stone Age with our tactics. We must make sure that we're not sending one helicopter off to fight one tank or some such thing as that and that we don't violate the principles of mass and surprise .... We are training people to do the jobs that absolutely have to be done. We're training them in a way that will avoid those catastrophic casualties that can occur in the first days of combat because training has been inadequate.

And it is up to you, the senior noncommissioned officers, to make sure that the most precious thing the unit has—the most precious commodity aside from the men and women in uniform themselves—training time, is used effectively.

If we do all these things, I'm absolutely convinced that the Soviets will know what we have done and that there will be less danger of us having to fight them. Your skills are important, in fact, essential; but it's the combination of skill, integrity and character that will make the difference in your fighting organization. Your job is to build an Army and to see that it stays built and stays in good condition.

Remarks to the
VETERANS OF FOREIGN WARS,
84th NATIONAL CONVENTION
New Orleans, LA
16 August 1983

Thanks for the welcome and thanks for inviting me. It is nice to be with fellow Veterans and fellow members of the Veterans of Foreign Wars. I bring you greetings from my fellow members of the Joint Chiefs of Staff and from the men and women of America's Armed Forces. The people in the Armed Forces today appreciate very much the support that the VFW has given, and we appreciate its reputation for supporting a strong national defense and for supporting the veterans of the Armed Forces. On behalf of all those members of the Armed Forces, I want to thank you for that support.

I was introduced to the VFW long before I became a veteran. My dad was an Infantry squad leader with the Rainbow Division in the First World War; and, after the war he helped to organize the Oscar and John Soberg Post 210 in Lakeville, Minnesota—I think he was the second commander there. Just as the VFW does today, that post was a very important influence in our community. Among other things it did was sponsor the first Boy Scout troop that I joined. Even to this day, my mother, when she wants to dress up or show off a little bit, puts on her Ladies Auxiliary Past President's pin.

These conventions, too, have a great reputation. They provide the forum for serious reflection and an opportunity for you to hear a lot of very important people—and some of us not so important—and at the same time I'm sure they give you an opportunity to have a little fun. I remember my dad saying that when he went to the VFW conventions and talked to my mother over the telephone, she could smell his breath over the phone.

I know you have listened to President Reagan, Senator Glenn, and Secretary Weinberger. Incidentally, I want to thank you for honoring "Cap" Weinberger here last night. He is a good and courageous Secretary of Defense.

I know they have told you a lot about their views on national security, about the threats we face and the need to sustain the revitalization of our forces. I am glad you had the opportunity to hear their important views. I am a little bit apprehensive about being fourth behind those heavy hitters, and I'm sure I'm not supposed to be the clean-up hitter; but maybe we are at the tail end of the batting order here now. I guess I was invited because I'm an old soldier. I will warn you in advance that, except for probably MacArthur, old soldiers aren't necessarily good speakers. I remember a tale about General U.S. Grant who was once presiding over a court martial of an old soldier. Grant heard the defense lawyer say that the old veteran had been through many, many campaigns. "Well," Grant said, "And so has that mule over there but he is still a jackass."

I want to tell you a little bit about what I see from the foxhole that I now occupy and some of the concerns those sights give me. In this country today, we spend a lot of time being concerned about defense budgets and hardware and defense policy. But, I don't have to tell this group that the most important ingredients in our national defense are the individual soldiers, sailors, airmen and Marines who serve in those forces—tomorrow's veterans.

People are the heart of our defenses. No matter how advanced our technology or how devastating our weaponry, the skill of the men and women in uniform is going to be the key to the success of our arms. The effectiveness of modern weaponry, either for preventing war in times of peace or for ending it successfully in times of war, depends on the minds, the eyes, the hands, the skills, the spirit, and the hearts of those Service men and women who operate the equipment. No matter what degree of sophistication we get for the tools of war, there will always be, on some remote battlefield, two soldiers with a flashlight, huddled underneath their ponchos, soaked to the bone, trying to coordinate their forces in a battle that occurred by chance on some map sheet they were never issued. And I can tell you that right now, out there today, there's a high probability some fancy piece of gear is being fixed by some innovative serviceman with bubblegum and bailing wire.

It is very much as General Creighton Abrams said: "People aren't in the Armed Forces; people are the Armed Forces." We've relearned that lesson about twenty times in the past 207 years of our history. The lesson is that if you want good defense forces, the cornerstone is people, good people.

I have spent a good part of my time as the Chairman visiting our operational forces throughout the world. In the process, I have had the opportunity to see soldiers, sailors, airmen, and Marines operating in deployed forces in all sorts of circumstances—most of them difficult. I want to report to you that those forces are in good shape and the people manning those forces are among the finest we have ever had. Today, the Armed Forces are getting and keeping very good people. The recruiting and reenlistment for the first six months of this year were better than last year, and last year was the best it ever was. Eighty-nine percent of all the new recruits have high school diplomas. That is better than we had at any time during conscription.

What's more important, though, is that all the Services are keeping top-notch men and women to fill the very important non-commissioned officer jobs and the jobs requiring high skills. And I'll tell you that the more I look at our armed forces, and the more I look at the Soviet Armed Forces, the more I believe that the difference between us—the difference that will allow us to be successful on the battlefield—is the fact that we have more, very good, professional non-commissioned officers.

We have the image in this country of Sergeant Bilko and Sergeant Snorkel as typifying the Armed Forces over the years. Two weeks ago I visited the Army's Sergeants Major Academy. The class was made up of students from all four Services and from both Active and Reserve Forces. Two hundred and thirty-eight of the 255-man class were First Sergeant rank or the equivalent in the other Services. The average age was 39. The average time in service was 20 years. The range of their special skills was as long as my arm. They are Rangers and Special Forces, and tankers and infantrymen and submariners, and air crewmen. Half of them were parachute-qualified. They were all in top-notch physical condition. And, if that doesn't destroy—or help destroy—the "Sergeant Snorkel" image for today's armed forces, let me tell you about their education: one of them had a PhD., six of them had Masters Degrees, another sixteen had Bachelor Degrees, twenty-two had Associate Degrees; sixty-six had completed some college; and all were high school graduates.

If you look back at the average age and the average length of service, you have to come to the same conclusion that my survey of that group did—every hour of that college work they got at night during their off-duty time. I say to you that America can take pride in its armed forces but, more importantly, it can take pride in the people in them. Certainly, the support they receive from organizations—in particular like the VFW—is crucial to help Americans realize that service in the Armed Forces is honorable duty; and that helps us get high-quality people and keep them.

Sonny Montgomery has questioned whether or not the All Volunteer Force works. Is this the final answer for providing manpower for the Nation's Armed Forces? I don't know, but I do know it is working today. In time of war, we know we will need compulsory military service. As the economy continues to improve, will we be able to continue to get good people in the right numbers to man the Armed Forces under the volunteer system? I don't know. But, I say to you that whatever the Nation has to do, it should watch very carefully and make sure that it does get good people in the right numbers—and we must do that whether it's the draft or increased pay, or whatever it happens to be.

In the past three weeks, I have visited Army units in primitive camps in Central America. I have seen the Marines in Beirut. I have visited naval units off the coast of Central America and off the coast of Lebanon. I gave seen Air Force units manning early warning sites in Greenland and Iceland, and I have visited our missile units out in Wyoming. And I'll say to you that in those three weeks, I have seen a tremendous number of skilled people doing a wide variety of difficult jobs under arduous conditions. The point that impressed me most in seeing those people is that I didn't see a sullen soldier, sailor, airman or

Marine in the crowd. Their spirits were high. The more difficult the job they were doing, the better they seemed to like it; and I say to you that is a very good sign for America and a very good sign for our armed forces.

Not too long ago, I visited an Infantry battalion that we have doing peacekeeping duty in the Sinai. If you have never been to the Sinai, it is nothing surrounded by nothing. These guys are stretched out from the head of the Gulf of Aqaba down to Sharm El Sheikh on the peninsula, the tip of the Sinai Peninsula. They are in squad positions because it's really a squad leader's job. And they're doing a terrific job. I had dinner with an infantry company one night and I said to one of these soldiers, "What do you do when you are not out on those squad positions?" He said, "Well, last weekend 62 of us from our company climbed Mount Sinai." Then he said, "I learned something, too, Sir." I said, "What did you learn?" He said, "Old Man Moses was really in good shape."

Well, as I look out over here—and particularly towards the delegations from my home state of Minnesota—I see faces of comrades in arms who have been in places like those I have described, who have been huddled under those ponchos, or who have been cramped in cockpits, or on ship's bridges. And, I must tell you that we in uniform today feel a special link to you patriots here today. You served as we serve now; you know the meaning of the word "service." You know firsthand that our people in the active forces, and in the Reserves and National Guard do more than simply work for the Armed Forces; they serve in the armed forces. That concept of service is an altogether different concept than simply being a member of a work force. It is a mark of a special obligation taken by members of our armed forces, a mark of people who are ready to surrender some of their own personal liberties to take special risks so that their fellow citizens can be secure. These people in our military forces are going to go where the citizens of this country want them to go. They are going to fight the wars that the citizens of this country want them to fight. They are going to do whatever the citizens of this country want them to do. They are prepared to do that, whatever the risk. Keeping these people ready for their tasks requires a continuous commitment from the citizens of the Nation. I have heard it said that the health of the Armed Forces is like fresh bread. If you want fresh bread, you have to make it fresh every day or you just have stale bread. I'll tell you that the same is true for military forces. If you want good military forces, you have to give them daily attention. Soldiers, sailors, airmen and Marines are going to lose their proficiency if they don't work at their trade regularly.

The members of the Joint Chiefs of Staff understand that point; and, I want you to know that we do battle with the budgets to see that our forces get the money they need to keep them ready. Our people in the Armed Forces are dedicated and they serve unselfishly; but, it is important that we continue to make it attractive and rewarding for good people to stay in the Services, particularly when they become skilled. The pay and the other emoluments must be adequate. The rewards for military service have to reflect the unique nature of military service. Funds for training and supplies and for the other aspects of readiness have too often been looked on as "slop buckets" that can be dipped into at will. And I want to see that the people we have in uniform get proper treatment, and that they get the equipment and training they need.

Just as the Armed Forces have a duty to the Nation I believe the Nation has a duty to our people who serve in uniform—those who have served, those who now serve, and those who will serve in the future. The liberty that our citizens enjoy today has been secured by those who have served in the past—including those who are sitting in this room, the members of the VFW.

We are not at war today. One of the reasons we are not at war is because of the service of those men and women in the Armed Forces today. We have to remember that it is their willingness and their readiness to fight for this country that are an important part in keeping the Nation out of war. They are out there today doing very tough, sometimes dull, but often very dangerous work, in very dangerous places. They are doing that to keep this nation at peace. Very much a part of that willingness and readiness to defend the Nation is the certain knowledge among those members of the Armed Forces that the citizens of our country—during peacetime, during combat and after the wars are over—will take care of them and their families: that we will give them good equipment, good training, and take care of their families if they have to march off to war; that we will pick up our wounded and give them good medical care; that we will pick up our dead and give them reverent and dignified treatment for their remains and their graves; that we will do whatever is necessary to get back those who become prisoners of war and we will account for all the missing in action; and that we will honor those who gave their lives by helping the living veterans, as the motto of this organization so eloquently and simply states.

Anyone who joins the Armed Services to get rich has to be faulted for bad judgment; and, I don't believe you will find any members who expect to get rich. However, those who do serve deserve to be able to feed their families, and feed them without the use of food stamps, and to educate their children and be rewarded somewhat reasonably for the skills and the extraordinary service they give the Nation. The pay and the emoluments and the retirement system have to continue to attract good people or we simply won't have good armed forces.

They deserve good equipment, too—top-notch equipment, equipment that works and equipment that gives our people an edge over our potential enemies. Our strategy calls for the use of American technology, one of America's strong points. We do that because we value human life more than we value things. I frequently hear some misguided people say, "Why don't we buy cheaper weapons because then we can buy a lot more of them and give them to our armed forces? We won't feel the loss so greatly if we lose them to the enemy." The problem with that philosophy is that when you lose the equipment, you also lose the men who operate it. I see many of you out here who are my age and I know that many of you have children in the Armed Forces. I have a kid who flies attack helicopters for the Army and I don't want him or any other young American out there with bargain-basement, cheap, ineffective weapons.

In that respect, I am happy to say to you that the Reserve Components of our Armed Forces are beginning to get a sensible share of modern equipment.

We have finally begun moving very good equipment into the Reserve Components. And that is very important because the Reserves and the National Guard figure more importantly in our strategy than ever before. I say to you that continued support for the National Guard and the Reserves from all the people in this country, and particularly from their employers, is important to the security of the Nation.

At the same time, it is very important for us in uniform to recognize that the taxpaying citizen deserves a fair shake in this whole exercise. He deserves to have us buy sensible equipment whose value is worth the price—equipment that's effective but not "gold-plated." The members of the Armed Forces and all the taxpaying citizens deserve to have a fair shake from American industry and from American labor by having them produce quality equipment. As Secretary Weinberger pointed out recently, the Nation deserves the highest levels of integrity and honesty from industry in seeing that a fair price is asked.

All these factors lie at the heart of our military health—good equipment, good people, good training, dedicated leadership and support from the populace and industry. As I said earlier, I am buoyed by the progress that I have seen in my frequent visits to the field. Yet, at the same time, I am concerned about our willingness to provide for our future security. There is a great debate going on in this country today: "How much is enough for defense?" "Are we spending too much for defense?" "Can we get by with less?" "Can we avoid modernizing our strategic nuclear deterrent forces?" I say to you that this debate turns the whole issue of national security on its head because the real question is, "What must we do to provide for our security?" I don't need to remind the people in this room that we inherited our liberties from our Forefathers. They, at their particular time in history, didn't hesitate to do what was needed to be done. They paid for our security by pledging "their lives, their fortunes, and their sacred honor." We today reap the benefits of that commitment and of their sacrifices. And our burden is the privilege of doing the same now for our posterity.

President Reagan said to me when I took this job last year, "Keep us strong, keep us ready, so that we can keep the peace." Indeed, it's clear to me that that's the essence of our strategy; keeping the peace by deterrence. And that's a fancy word which simply means making it plain to the other guy that we're going to kick the tar out of him if he tries to start a war.

The job for me and the other members of the JCS is to make sure that our forces are as ready as the defense budgets will permit—that we tell the Secretary of Defense and the President what is needed to defend this country and to carry out its strategy; to see to the welfare of those soldiers, sailors, airmen and Marines so that they can be trained and equipped properly, that they are in good physical condition, and have the right mental and spiritual health to do the job that they have to do.

I want to take just a minute to reassure you that the advice of the Joint Chiefs of Staff is being sought and heard by the President and the Secretary of Defense. We meet regularly with the President of the United States; and this group of Chiefs has met more with the President of the United States than any group of Chiefs has with the last four Presidents. I meet daily with the Secretary of Defense, and he meets regularly with the Chiefs as a body.

I can tell you that all those four Service Chiefs are addressing in a business-like fashion the jobs that the citizens of this country have laid out for them to do in the law. We have a good body of Joint Chiefs right now—Admiral Jim Watkins, Chief of Naval Operations; General Charlie Gabriel, Chief of Staff of the Air Force; General John Wickham, the Army Chief of Staff; and P.X. Kelley, the Commandant of the Marine Corps. They are all respected, battle-proven veterans. They are true experts in their own Services. And, I want to tell you that they are working diligently to improve those Services.

I can tell you also that they are officers of broad strategic vision who understand that the defenses of this nation are only as good as the ability of all four Services to work closely together. Those four Chiefs understand that President Eisenhower was right when he told the Congress in 1958 that wars in the future could only be won if the four Services worked closely together under unified command. In fact, all of those Chiefs have experience in unified commands. I want to tell you also that I hear a lot about reorganization of the Joint Chiefs; and I tell you that the Chiefs have examined their own organizations. We have made recommendations to the President for some changes in the law. We have made recommendations to the Secretary of Defense on better ways to do our business. And, we have set about the task of cleaning up our own act to make sure that we can do the job as well as the Lord will permit us to do it.

According to stories that I read in the newspapers and hear on television and radio, I am supposed to see quite a lot of inter-Service "bickering" among those Joint Chiefs of Staff. In fact, according to some of the stories, I take part in that "bickering" myself. Those Chiefs don't always agree; and I don't think you would want them always to agree. Occasionally, when they do disagree, they disagree on matters of policy and they make those points very clear. Now, by law, I am charged with explaining their disagreements to the Secretary of Defense and the President and I am happy to have those disagreements made clear.

I want to thank you for having me here today and giving me the opportunity to tell you a little bit about how I see the Armed Forces. I know that you understand what the price of liberty is. My colleagues on the Joint Chiefs of Staff understand the very special duty that we have to help preserve the peace and liberty for our country. Sunday night, perhaps some of you did as I did and watched "Bataan, the Forgotten Hell," on television. Certainly, that tragedy was a reminder of America's lack of preparedness in the past.

I recall being at Fort Sill, Oklahoma in 1950. Early that year, we were cutting up lard in the mess hall, cutting it off the meat, so we could make soap. At that time, General Bradley, the first Chairman of the Joint Chiefs of Staff, had the job I now have. I heard General Bradley in a radio broadcast tell the American people about the defense budget. He said: "The problem is to provide enough military strength during the years of peace so that we will never have to pay the cost of war, either in lives or dollars." The defense budget that was under consideration that spring was woefully short of what was needed; it was 13 billion dollars. Two months after that radio broadcast, 60,000 North Korean troops, spearheaded with Soviet-built tanks, invaded the Republic of Korea and plunged an unprepared America into another bloody conflict. The proposed defense budget of 13 billion dollars climbed to 60 billion dollars by the following year; but, more importantly, this country paid in another coin, a coin a lot more precious, and that was the blood of our people.

If we want peace and liberty, every lesson I see in history tells us that we should have an adequate defense force in peacetime and we should be ready to help other free people protect their liberty when threatened—whether that threat is from Soviet SS-20s aimed at our NATO allies or from communist guerillas in Central America. If we don't, we will probably have an unholy peace without any liberty, such as the peace in Poland today; but, even worse, we could probably lose both the war and the peace and liberty. I say to you that is not necessary, and it is also very un-American.

And I say to you that with the help of God, and with the readiness and spirit of selfless service of Americans serving in our armed forces, with the support of the American people, especially outfits like the VFW, and with support from the President and the Congress, we can, in fact, preserve both peace and freedom, not only for ourselves but for our posterity. It is nice to be with you. God bless you all.

Extracts from Remarks at the 88th
ANNUAL NATIONAL CONVENTION,
JEWISH WAR VETERANS OF THE
UNITED STATES
Atlanta, GA
17 August 1983

Thanks for the welcome. I am very pleased to be here and have the opportunity to address this distinguished, patriotic group at its 88th Annual Convention. I bring you greetings on behalf of my fellow members of the Joint Chiefs of Staff and on behalf of the men and women in the Armed Forces of the United States today.

As the oldest active veterans' organization in our country, you enjoy a great reputation. Certainly, these conventions also enjoy a great reputation as well—a gathering of comrades in arms who address important issues of the day but also to reminisce a little bit about the past, and perhaps even to have a good time.

Your outfit has come a long way from that small meeting of the Hebrew Union in 1896—a meeting that was gathered together to answer the slander that American Jews were reticent in the defense of freedom. General Omar

Bradley, who was the first officer to hold the job that I now have, said that "The military achievements of the men of the Jewish faith are part of the proud record of American fighting men." When he said that, he was addressing principally service in World War II and Korea; but, he simply echoed what General "Blackjack" Pershing had said about American Jews after World War I when he said, "No one had served with more patriotism or with higher motives." Certainly, the record of both World Wars stands as a clear testimony to the patriotism of American Jews. In World War I, the Jews in the United States served in the Armed Forces at a rate two and a half times their numbers in the population as a whole. And, in World War II, they served at a rate that was over 30 percent higher than their numbers in the population.

Your organization has long since gone beyond the original goals of the Hebrew Union. Today, you are well-known for your service to all veterans and for your community involvements, particularly your concern for maintaining liberty and justice and for promoting brotherhood among all our citizens.

I personally believe that the promotion of brotherhood in the battle against bigotry is an appropriate task for all veterans' organizations. There's no greater leveler than service in a combat organization. The observant veteran knows that, when the chips are down, the color of a man's skin, his religious and ethnic background and his economic and social status all get washed away. It is what's in his heart and soul and what he can do with his mind and body that counts.

I am convinced that all of us in our nation share with all the free peoples of the world a hope for liberty and justice and a common responsibility to prevent wars—not just nuclear war but all wars—while, at the same time, containing the threat of totalitarianism. We have to confront both those issues if we want to walk properly the path toward peace and liberty for us and for our posterity. And, certainly, peace without liberty is empty.

We should not shrink from our obligations to sustain the necessary effort to preserve peace and liberty in the face of the challenges of the Soviet system, a system which is the very antithesis of our own values. Even while we negotiate and try to work with them to reduce the risk of war, we absolutely have to do what is needed to be done to ensure the adequacy of our own defense.

In Secretary Weinberger's speech to the American Jewish Committee of New York in May of this year, he noted the unity found in King David's words from the 29th Psalm where it reads, "The Lord will give strength unto His people; the Lord will bless His people with peace." And I say to you that strength and peace are bound together. It is a recognition in this world that only a free nation which is also strong can deter the enemies of peace and justice.

Those words imply two parallel ideas that contribute to peace. The first, that we be sufficiently strong to deter war and also the threat of war. We don't want a war but we also don't want to be paralyzed by the fear of war. By deterrence, we seek to preserve peace and freedom and to protect our vital interests by making it self-evidently clear to any potential enemies that they cannot achieve their aims through violence or the threat of violence.

Secondly, we must seek by every reasonable means to reduce the risks of war and the dangers of war. Certainly, arms control negotiations is one of the means that we need to pursue. But, we also need to work to reduce the misunderstandings that lead to war. Salvador de Madariaga, the great Spanish philosopher and historian who worked for many years on the League of Nations Disarmament Commission, said, "Nations don't distrust each other because they are armed; they arm because they distrust each other." And that is a very important point for us to remember. We need to reduce the distrust among nations.

Our objectives in this country have been relatively constant over the years. The world itself has changed and the threats to our security have changed. In the 1950s and the early 1960s we clearly had strategic nuclear superiority; and, our conventional forces, although they were outnumbered by our potential enemies, were technologically superior. Since that time there has been a general shift of power. We arrived at a point early in this past decade where the security of our nation and that of our allies could no longer be assured for the future—in spite of the great strength of our forces and those of our allies.

Global instability threatened Western interests abroad and endangered our own national health here at home. Moreover, the unrelenting growth of Soviet military power became an overriding concern. Today, after two decades of uninterrupted buildup by the Soviets and almost a decade of neglect on our part, our nation is now working hard to restore the degree of military power necessary to maintain the peace.

The relentless quest for military superiority by the Soviets has achieved new levels during this past year. Certainly the Soviets aren't 10 feet tall. They have problems of their own. They are really a one-dimensional power—a military power. You don't see a lot of people trying to escape to the Soviet Union, or clamoring for Soviet blue jeans or Soviet computers or Soviet automobiles. Their policy has no moral authority. Their economy is in serious trouble by Mr. Andropov's own admission; and their ideology is laid bare even to their friends as being militant and aggressive. I often tell people that they are the only country in the world surrounded by hostile communist neighbors. But, their power has to be recognized.

The Soviets have deployed strategic missiles which are among the most accurate in the world. They have placed those missiles in the world's best-protected missile silos. And, they have aimed those missiles at us. In 1982 alone, as part of this modernization program, they deployed over 1,200 modern so-called hard-target-killing nuclear warheads. That is more than we intend to deploy in our entire Intercontinental Ballistic Missile force modernization program. I want to tell you they did the same thing in 1981 that they did in 1982. They deployed another 1,200 this past year and there will probably be another 1,200 this next year. They have developed a new strategic bomber that is comparable to our own B-1 and they have new, modern ballistic missile submarines. We simply have to recognize that the accelerating pace of Soviet modernization and our own slow pace in improving our strategic forces have left us well behind the Soviets in some important measures of military capability.

We as a nation must deal with the reality of Soviet nuclear weaponry and its destabilizing consequences. We have to make it clear to the Soviets that they cannot threaten nuclear war, or any war, without understanding that we can and will respond in such a way that guarantees that their war aims will not be achieved. If that is clear to the Soviets, I am confident that there will be no war.

The President's Bipartisan Commission, the Scowcroft Commission, has made some very sensible recommendations. The Commission said that we must modernize our strategic nuclear forces to counter this dangerous trend and the growing power of the Soviets. The modernization of our strategic forces, including the PEACEKEEPER missile, the Trident submarine, the B-1 bomber, the cruise missiles, but more importantly, the essential command and control—the warning systems—are all necessary and they are necessary right now to ensure deterrence and keep the peace. In addition to this modernization, our negotiation strategy is tied very closely to our modernization in order to seek verifiable arms reductions. And we shouldn't be deluded at all. If we give the Soviets the hope that they can wait out the West's political process in order to limit our arms, they are simply not going to negotiate with us at the negotiating table.

Up to this point, I have concentrated on the nuclear balance. But you have to know that the Soviets have good reason for increased confidence in their conventional forces as well. They are fielding a sophisticated range of capabilities on land, in the air and on the seas. And all of these challenge our own forces and the forces of our allies. In the past 15 years they have added 30 divisions to their army and that takes them up to more than 180 divisions—on the other hand, we have only 24 in the Army and four more in the Marine Corps. Of those, seven are in the Reserves. Their air power is massive and sophisticated; and, for the first time, they have developed a very strong blue-water navy. Increasingly, their influence has spread well beyond their borders. Their naval power, their airborne forces and, most significantly, their use of surrogates, such as the Vietnamese and the Cubans in Third World conflicts, seek to outflank our traditional alliances, to threaten our strategic materials and to endanger our long-standing friends and allies.

The Soviet Union isn't our only problem; but, certainly, they stand ready to capitalize on every other problem in this turbulent world. It is a world which the Secretary General of the United Nations characterized as being "perilously close to a new international anarchy." Since World War II, there have been 150 wars and 25 million people have been killed in those wars. If you use the criteria that a war is an activity involving significant loss of life, with the use of regular armed forces, there are 20 wars going on in the world today.

At the same time that international stability is so seriously threatened, the interdependence of nations in the world has grown astoundingly. We have close cultural ties, religious ties, moral ties and political ties with many nations of the world. We have friends and allies—such as Israel—with whom we have longstanding commitments, and they have longstanding commitments to us.

We are dependent on foreign markets, on overseas resources, and on global lines of communication to keep our economy going. The year that I joined the Army, the United States was a net exporter of oil. We exported about 20,000 barrels of oil a day. Forty-three years later, we import five million barrels of oil every day and that was down about a million barrels from what it had been a couple of years earlier. The day has long since passed when we can close our eyes to conflict outside our own shores. And, I want to tell you it is not necessary to look very far beyond our horizons and beyond our shores to see that interdependence and consequences of armed aggression in the world today. That reality is very close to home. In April, and again last month, the President asked all Americans to put their attention to the desperate need for aid for our neighbors to the south. The President made it very clear that we have vital interests in Central America and the Caribbean and we have to look very seriously at our legitimate security concerns and those of our friends. We live in this hemisphere. Peace, liberty, security for democracy and economic health for our American neighbors will certainly help us maintain the same benefits for ourselves.

What may not be so well-recognized is the way conflict in one part of the world affects everyone else. Take the example of the turbulent African continent. Last Tuesday night, I listened to ABC News and I heard Peter Jennings sum up his broadcast by saying, "There is a nasty little war in a thoroughly inhospitable place. What has been going on until recently in northern Chad has been a civil war. The trouble is there aren't any wars anymore which don't somehow involve the major powers."

Now I would say to you that Mr. Jennings is only partially correct because any war anywhere affects not only the major powers but every other nation. Libya, for example, which is involved in Chad, has gotten itself involved deeply in Africa, and in the Middle East. Its mischief has recently surfaced in this hemisphere, in Central America. For instance, in Nicaragua, Libyan support and PLO extremists are active in training and supplying the Soviet-supported Sandinistas.

I return at this juncture to my basic point of peace and strength. Just as peace and the preservation of liberty remain our unending objectives, there will be those whose only instrument is force. It is, therefore, essential that we see to the health of our own military strength, to deter conflict and to act as a shield for more peaceful resolution of differences. Our job is to meet the challenge and make our strategy of deterrence work. We must recognize that our willingness to rebuild our strategic forces and our willingness to strengthen the conventional forces all send signals to those who would threaten peace. We must tend to our national power—and not only to the military dimensions of that power but also to our diplomatic power, our political power, our political strength, our economic and our moral health as well.

I am heartened today to see more consensus in this nation toward that end. We saw, at last, a favorable vote in the Congress to support the recommendations of the Scowcroft Commission for the modernization of our strategic nuclear forces. But that still hangs very much in the balance and there are a lot of other votes to come. You need to tell your Congressmen that they need to support that if we're going to remain a strong nation.

We also are beginning to see a growing awareness and concern for the welfare and security of our Central American neighbors. We are seeing the continued strengthening of our own armed forces. I listen to the news last night and heard from a Nicaraguan spokesman who said that our own military maneuvers in Honduras would cause that part of the world to break out into war. Now, I am not sure how that is going to happen, because, certainly, we are not going to start a war. We are simply down there with some forces helping train a friendly, free democratic nation. If the Nicaraguans can't figure out that those forces down there make it very unhealthy for them to start a war, I cannot possibly see how war is going to start.

I recall what President Reagan said to me when I took this job last year. He said, as he announced my appointment, *"Keep us strong, keep us ready, so that we may keep the peace."* Indeed, it is clear to me that the essence of our strategy is keeping the peace by keeping strong. We keep the peace by deterrence. That is a fancy Washington word. What it really means is we're going to make it clear that we're going to kick the tar out of anybody else if they start a war.

If our nation provides properly for its military health, for its economic and political health and, above all, for its spiritual health, there won't be any question as to our capabilities or our resolve. Our potential enemies will know that we're ready and I believe they know that now. Every lesson of history that I see tells us that if we want to preserve both peace and liberty, we had better stay strong. If we want to be satisfied with peace alone, we may well lose not only the peace but we will undoubtedly lose our liberty as well. We had better be strong.

I want to thank you for having me here today. My colleagues on the Joint Chiefs of Staff know that we have a special duty to work very hard to help protect that peace and the liberties that we all enjoy. We want to thank you for the support that you have consistently given for a strong defense to this nation. I say to you that with the support from the President, the Congress, and the people of this great nation of ours, we will preserve both peace and liberty, not only for ourselves but for our posterity. My very best wishes to all of you.

Interview with Newspaper
USA Today
September 1983

Question: Is there one rank that sticks out that you have enjoyed more than another?

Answer: I think the toughest job I had, and the one I remember as having more personal responsibility than any other, was being a first sergeant in combat. That was a *good* job also.

Remarks before the
UNION LEAGUE CLUB OF NEW YORK
4 November 1983

I understand very clearly the duty of those people in the media who inform the American people. But I want to tell you that I also understand the need for conducting military operations successfully. I think the Grenada rescue operation is the way you want military operations conducted. I understand the need for surprise when one conducts military operations, and I understand the need for saving American lives.... So, we kept that operation secret from a lot of people in order to have surprise and to have that operation be a success, and to reduce the casualties involved.

We had a potential hostage situation until the end of the second day. At 5:30 at the end of the second day, we finally freed all of the students, the American students at the St. Georges Medical School. The next day we let the press in. So, I just want to tell you this—for those who might have been misled by motives that were imputed to those who kept the press out of there—that we were doing it for two reasons: one was to make the operation a success; the second was to make sure that we successfully got those American students out.

Mr. Monroe: General Vessey, will you sum up for us, please, how the Grenada operation went from your point of view? Did everything go as expected? Did anything go wrong? And how would you describe our gains from it?

General Vessey: That's a lot of question, Mr. Monroe. We planned the operation in a very short period of time, in about 48 hours. We planned it with insufficient intelligence for the type of operation we wanted to conduct. As a result, we used more force than we probably needed to do the job, but the operation went reasonably well, considering those factors. Murphy's Law operated, as it does in almost every military operation or in almost anything else that human beings undertake. Things did go wrong, but generally the operation was a success. The troops did very well.

Mr. Monroe: How would you describe our gains from it from your point of view?

General Vessey: We went in there for political gains. We had Americans that were potential hostages in a country that was undergoing great unrest. We also had a request from the East Caribbean States to help them establish order in one of their member states. But there are some other gains: I think we exposed what happens to countries that come under Cuban and Soviet domination.

Mr. Monroe: Do you have any retrospective thoughts about the extent to which reporters were excluded from that operation in the first couple of days and then restricted for another two or three days?

General Vessey: Well, there's a lot to be done in that particular field. We kept reporters out and a whole lot of other people out of that operation because we needed surprise and secrecy to have any chance of having the operation be a success under the terms that we'd set out for ourselves, and, those were minimum casualties, not only for our own people but also for the people of Grenada.

Up until about sundown on the second day, we still had a potential hostage situation. We hadn't freed all the students from the Grand Anse Campus. The morning of the third day, we had the press in there.

Mr. Kalb: Thank you, General. I'm sorry. Did you have more to say on that, sir?

General Vessey: Well, there's obviously a lot more to say on military operations and the press. I think we need to work together to find ways to inform the public, but without endangering the military operation of our own people.

Mr. Halloran: General, let me turn your attention to Lebanon, if I could. Has the United States been able to discover who caused the truck bombing that took so many Marine lives two weeks ago? Can you tell us who did it?

General Vessey: No, I can't tell you who did it. As you probably know, several different outfits have claimed credit for it. I really don't know who did it. I wish I did.

Mr. Halloran: Sir, the senior officials of the Reagan Administration have talked openly of having retaliation against those who did it, or some other form of retaliation. Do you think the United States should retaliate? And if so, how?

General Vessey: I think that the United States should certainly protect its forces from that sort of activity. I also believe that we should be pro-active in pursuing international terrorism. And that's what it is. It's terrorism used as a political weapon. Retaliation, that's another question.

Mr. Halloran: Well, let me put it this way, then. If the United States does not retaliate, won't that be a signal to terrorists all over the world that they can attack American forces without fear of some kind of response?

General Vessey: I think we should attack the terrorists, Mr. Halloran.

Mr. Kraft: General Vessey, in response to Mr. Monroe's question, you said there was a lot more to say about relations between the military and the press. Is there anything you are contemplating? Any steps?

General Vessey: Yes. I have asked retired General Si Sidle, whom some of you may know—long in the public affairs business—to try and head up a panel for me of experienced newsmen to help us decide how we can conduct military operations and protect the operation—protect our own people—and still inform the American people—how to do it in this modern age of the television camera and instantaneous communications around the world.

Mr. Kraft: A panel's been appointed to look into the responsibility for the Beirut incident, let's call it, the terrorist attack. There was a panel that looked into the Desert One thing; and, as I recall it, we got a kind of bureaucratic answer that diffused responsibility.

My question is whatever became of command responsibility, identifying the responsible officer and court-martialing him?

General Vessey: Well, I think that certainly still exists and if court-martials are in order for whatever commanders are responsible, we'll have court-martials.

Mr. Kraft: If we did take action in Lebanon, would you favor cooperating with the Israelis?

General Vessey: The Israelis are in Lebanon in a different position than we are. The Israelis are at war with the Syrians. We came in as a peacekeeping force to try and help re-establish Lebanon and get both the Israelis and the Syrians out. Their retaliation comes from a different background than our own does. We need to find the perpetrators. We don't need to be siding with either the Israelis or the Syrians in trying to re-establish Lebanon.

Mr. Reynolds: General Vessey, two questions on Beirut, one past and one present. In terms of the past, there's been a great deal of criticism about the United States not using Israeli medical facilities which were just thirty minutes away, in terms of getting wounded men to Haifa. And in terms of present, there have been reports of some of the radical Muslim groups slipping in missiles through East Beirut, which are capable of hitting the Marines. These are rockets and rocket launchers, and also possibly capable of hitting some of the ships. Do we have the capability to take some sort of action against that?

General Vessey: Well, concerning the medical treatment. The people on the ground knew that the Israelis had offered medical facilities. Mr. Arens called Mr. Weinberger a few hours after the incident. Mr. Weinberger called me and told me of it. I called the Deputy Commander in Europe and informed him. He said he already knew of it and had instructed the people on the ground to take advantage of whatever medical help they needed to get the job done.

Concerning new weapons, Lebanon is an armed camp and there are all sorts of weapons. Certainly, we're doing everything that we can do to understand where those weapons are so that our forces can protect themselves.

Mr. Reynolds: General, in terms of intelligence, both in the case of Beirut and also in the case of Grenada, is there a review going on of the kind of intelligence that is available to us in terms of human intelligence?

General Vessey: Well, there's a constant review of intelligence in Beirut and in Lebanon. That's a very difficult intelligence target and there are all sorts of reports that come out of Lebanon. Certainly, one has to look at the reports and also look at the source of the report. You almost have to ask yourself what sort of an axe does this guy have to grind who's giving us this report.

Concerning Grenada, we had the right sort of intelligence for what we were looking at beforehand, and in 48 hours we had to plan a military operation that we hadn't expected to have to plan.

Mr. Monroe: I'd like to ask your comment, sir, on a report in this morning's *Washington Post* from Loren Jenkins, who has been in Grenada for the last several days, interviewing U.S. military people—commanders, pilots and soldiers. And he says these interviews have now convinced him that the Pentagon exaggerated the degree of resistance in Grenada from Cubans. He says that there appears to have been only a minor force of Cuban advisers who offered brief resistance and there were no major ground engagements.

General Vessey: Let me say that whoever's been in Grenada the last few days interviewing troops on the ground *has not interviewed the troops who did the fighting.* I would suggest that he go to Fort Stewart, Georgia or to Fort Lewis, Washington and interview the Rangers who did the fighting or talk to the Marines who are now on their way to Lebanon. Those are the people who did the fighting. There may be a few from the 82nd Airborne there who did some of the fighting later on in the first day, and then the second and third days. But the hard fighting against the Cubans was done by the Rangers.

Mr. Monroe: Would you comment on Mr. Jenkins' conclusions, nevertheless, that the Pentagon exaggerated the amount of Cuban resistance and the appearance to him that there was only a minor force of Cuban advisers who offered only brief resistance?

General Vessey: I talked to the operations officer and some of the command element of the 1st Battalion of the 75th Rangers yesterday, and I have come to the conclusion that the Pentagon underestimated the resistance from the Cubans in the first stages of that operation.

Mr. Kalb: General, I'd like to pick up two points that were left hanging before. In terms of retaliation by the United States for what happened to the Marines in Lebanon—I was wondering what your own feeling was. Are you opposed to retaliation?

General Vessey: When American servicemen are killed and killed in any numbers, my gut reaction is to retaliate, Mr. Kalb.

Mr. Kalb: Then, beyond your gut reaction, are you planning any?

General Vessey: That would be inappropriate for me to answer that question.

Mr. Halloran: Sir, you said that Lebanon is an armed camp. Are the Marines—who are primarily an amphibious assault force—are they the right troops to be in that situation?

General Vessey: Our armed forces that are in Lebanon are not there to conduct a military operation to seek a United States military solution to that problem. Those people are on the ground as part of United States "earnest" to the government of Lebanon as they get on with the political solution. And perhaps that's the most irritating thing to us military people, the slowness in getting on with solving the problems politically.

Mr. Halloran: Those people have been in a somewhat indefensible position, as we've seen by the bombing that took place two weeks ago. Should they be moved to other positions? Should they be allowed to patrol out front more aggressively?

General Vessey: There's a ceasefire in Lebanon now between the government of Lebanon, the Druze, and the Syrian-supported people who are attacking the government of Lebanon. That ceasefire line is very close to where our Marines are. And I would suspect that if our Marines were to go out and try to get better positions, they'd have to engage in a battle with some of those people involved in the ceasefire.

Mr. Kraft: General Vessey, I'd like to expand this range of questioning a little. The United States is a superpower with military responsibilities that are global.

Isn't it really inappropriate of us to have forces present in what's a kind of U.N.-type peacekeeping operation? Isn't that the real lesson, that we make our forces hostage when we put them in that kind of a situation?

General Vessey: I don't think we'll learn the real lesson, Mr. Kraft, until some years from now when we see what happens in Lebanon. Using our forces in small numbers in a peacekeeping operation is, as you suggest, a little bit unusual for the United States. But Lebanon isn't the first place. We've got a battalion who's down between Israel and Egypt in the Sinai, and has been there for some years now, on a peacekeeping operation and doing very well.

Mr. Kraft: What lessons, General, would you draw so far? Would it be fair to say that we should think very, very hard about putting American troops in that kind of a situation, that, in general, the bias should be against it, strongly against it?

General Vessey: I think one has to think through very carefully putting American troops in any kind of an operation where we're using them as a political lever. And certainly, I would urge caution in any such operation.

Mr. Kraft: Did you urge caution this time?

General Vessey: I think it's fair to say that everyone in the military, and the Secretary of Defense, and everyone in the government urged caution and was concerned about doing what we're doing in Lebanon.

Mr. Reynolds: General, in terms of what's gone on in the past few weeks, the phrase "stretched thin" has been used pretty consistently. Not only stretched thin in terms of the number of troops, but also stretched thin in terms of available transport—Navy ships, and Air Force planes, and so forth. Do you think that we're stretched thin?

General Vessey: I don't think that you could have found anyone who's held this job of mine who ever thought we weren't stretched a little thin and we didn't have enough—except perhaps General Marshall, who didn't hold the job but in effect had it at the end of World War II when he had some nine million men under arms and no wars going on. But I would say to you that our strategy is one that involves being able to use mobility, good intelligence and good command and control, in order to employ relatively small forces wisely and quickly to do the jobs that the Nation needs to be done. And I would say that Grenada—a small operation—is a good example of how we built our forces and what we're able to do with them.

Mr. Reynolds: But, General, if something happened in another area of the world very, very soon and very quickly—for example, something that all of us hope does not happen, but if something flared in the Persian Gulf—would we be capable of reacting there, too, at the same time?

General Vessey: Yes, we would, Mr. Reynolds. In fact, I spent a few hours on the phone talking to the Commander of the Military Airlift Command to make sure that he was in a position to carry out some other contingency if we had to do it.

Mr. Monroe: Could you give us some specifics, General, about the Cubans in Grenada? How many of them appeared to be well-trained military people, what kind of arms, how much resistance they put up?

General Vessey: As you may know, we didn't really want to fight the Cubans when we went in there and we weren't sure whether the Cubans would fight. Our government had attempted to get to the Cuban government and tell them that we're not there to fight the Cubans, so please don't fight us.

When we came in at the Point Salines Airfield, the Rangers dropped at 500 feet in a very skillful and daring parachute drop. They were attacked immediately by anti-aircraft fire as they were dropping. When they got on the ground, they were attacked by ground fire and had to move quickly to clear that ground fire.

Now, I went through that area a couple of days later and you could see that there were two camps that the Cubans were in. One was very close to the airfield tower. It was a camp of people who did construction work primarily, but there were *arms racks* in the barracks. We found a roster that said, "1st Company, 2nd Company, 3rd Company, 4th Company, mortar battery and anti-aircraft company." That's the way they were organized to do the "construction."

And there was another camp which appeared to have been probably the full-time military people who were in charge of organizing these, perhaps, "construction engineers," as we would call them, and have them perform their military jobs. There was some very tough fighting there in the first few hours.

Mr. Kalb: General, you said, at the very top of the program, you had 48 hours to plan Grenada. Is that a good way, a prudent way, to launch an operation?

General Vessey: Considering the situation that existed, it was about the right balance. If we had waited another day to get more intelligence information we would have lost a lot more people.

**Remarks at the Banquet of the
KOREAN-AMERICAN ASSOCIATION
Seoul, Korea
22 November 1983**

I am very pleased to be here tonight. I left Korea four years ago and I have been back in Korea for only three days; but the only food that concerns me is the Western food. And I wonder what happens to "kimchi" and "bulgogi" and all those other wonderful things. It's nice to see this great progress in

Korea but I would hate to see good Korean food disappear with modern industrial society.

This year, with President Reagan's visit here two weeks ago, we marked the thirtieth anniversary of our Mutual Defense Treaty. And, last year, the United States and Korea celebrated the centennial of diplomatic relations between our two countries. Those of you who have studied the history of our relations over these past one hundred years know that it reads like a real drama, laden with tragedy, shifting moods and characters, heroes and villains, defeats, triumphs, and more recently, mutual trust beneficial to both our nations. The history of our relations doesn't read like the dull history of staid diplomatic relationships between so many other nation-states in the world. Security cooperation arrangements between our two countries have been very much a part of the great story; and, in fact, for the most active 40 percent of that century of relations, the mutual security relationships have been one of the central themes of our relationship.

The prelude to the establishment of diplomatic relations had a violent beginning. In 1866, the armed schooner GENERAL SHERMAN violated the seclusion of the Hermit Kingdom; its crew was executed and the ship was burned. It was not until 1882 that a treaty of peace and amity, commerce and navigation was signed. I believe it was the first arrangement that the Hermit Kingdom had made with any Western nation.

A year later, King Kojong asked the U.S. Government for the services of an American officer "to instruct and drill our troops," promising "to confer upon him the second highest military rank in the Kingdom." For those of you who think security assistance matters move slowly in Washington in modern times, I would point out that it took almost five years to answer that request. In December 1887, General Phil Sheridan, then Commander of the United States Army, appointed his friend and West Point classmate, Brigadier General William McEntire Dye, to the Korean post.

It is difficult to believe that General Dye could foresee the enduring and close military relationships that the two countries would come to have. The two nations were so different—Korea, with its homogenous population and 4000-year old cultural roots, and the United States, an upstart nation with its polyglot population and scarcely a century of history of independence. Yet, the affection General Dye was to develop for Korea and for the Korean people, and the respect that Koreans had for him, were harbingers of the relationships that were to develop in later years, and that we share today.

I would like to quote from a prophetic article which General Dye wrote in 1897. He said, "... Korea must develop not only in agriculture, but also in other directions if she will have a full measure of prosperity and especially in the military line if political independence is to be preserved .... For full development and protection, Korea needs manufacturing and commercial enterprise, improvements in her methods of agriculture, and a military awakening of her people, for she is embraced by the well-known law decreeing 'survival of the fittest'."

I think if General Dye were to see us here today, and to see Korea and the cooperation between our two countries—and particularly in the security field—I believe he'd say, "Well done!"

In fact, very well done indeed. Today, we see Korea as an emergent and mature nation on the world scene. The economy of Korea has risen from the ruin of the terrible war which only 30 years ago seemed irreparable. It is now hailed as an economic miracle and a model for all countries. You have a rate of growth which exceeds 8 percent of the Gross National Product every year and a low 6 percent inflation rate.

The achievement of the Korean people is not only economic. It is an achievement in the advancement of the well-being of the people of Korea. Your steady sometimes painful movement toward democratic institutions, balanced with respect for Korean society and culture, assure the stature of Korea as a responsible member of the Free World community. There are numerous examples: the prestigious International Parliamentary Union had its meeting here in October; the Asian Games will take place here in 1986; and the World Olympics are scheduled to take place here in 1988.

Unfortunately, this great history has not been without its price. The history of American-Korean security relationships from 1945 to the present is well-known to all of you in this room—many of you were intimately involved in that history; the establishment of the arbitrary line in 1945 to facilitate the Japanese surrender; Russia's callous acts which turned the line into an iron barrier dividing a historically unified country; the 1948 Constitution and the August 15th establishment of the Republic; the UN recognition of the Republic and Russia's hurried establishment of the communist puppet state in the North; then, the withdrawal of the US troop units and the beginning of the training for the peace-oriented, constabulary-like defense forces of the Republic, overshadowed soon by the Russian work to train and equip Kim Il Sung's army; the first Chairman of the JCS, my predecessor, General Bradley's fears of an attack from the North and Dean Acheson's January 1950 speech at the National Press Club; and the June 25th, 1950, attack by North Korea and the decisive response by the United Nations.

These were precursors to the bloody war which was to follow and the further development of the unique security relationships that now exist between our two countries. The war brought the Armed Forces of the United States and the Armed Forces of Korea and the people of our two countries very close. The United States sent 1.6 million men into the war zone during the course of the three years of the war; Korea sent thousands and thousands of soldiers, sailors, and airmen to the United States for training. The armed forces of the two nations fought side-by-side for three years of tough, bloody fighting. United States units were augmented by Korean soldiers, a unique practice which continues to exist today. It is probably the only place in the world where such a practice has existed.

The post-war years saw us grow even closer together: economic cooperation which helped the fantastic industrial growth and economic development in Korea, and Korea's historic support of the United States in Vietnam. All of you are very familiar with both of those.

Unfortunately, the most serious challenge to the Republic of Korea and the cause of so much tension and grief remains the unrelenting, mindless animosity of North Korea—a nation of only 17 million but with an army as large as the Army of the United States. Nevertheless, the extraordinary buildup of the North Korean forces in the 1960s and early 1970s escaped many Americans in the United States, periodically from 1945 on. Many Americans regarded the presence of U.S. forces on the Korean Peninsula as a very temporary situation. Many failed to recognize that all the same forces that converged on Korea in General Dye's time 100 years ago have now been magnified by the interdependence of the modern industrial world.

A critical point in the drama of U.S. forces presence in Korea came in early 1977 when President Carter announced a plan to withdraw U.S. ground forces from Korea while maintaining the general United States commitment to Korea's security. On the face of it, that announcement was a jolt for the security relationships; but, as I look at it and look at the ensuing events in retrospect, I believe the announcement may have led to a healthier posture for both our countries. Certainly, the announcement stirred a thorough examination of the situation and a heated debate in the United States. The North Korean military buildup was studied and the importance of Korea to the security of Northeast Asia and to the United States came into clearer focus. Serious study by respected members of the United States House and Senate, such as Mr. Stratton and Senators Nunn and Glenn, helped to illustrate the problem.

The result has been sensible plans for modernizing the Republic of Korea and the United States forces on the Peninsula. President Carter eventually suspended his plan for withdrawing U.S. ground forces. And, more recently, President Reagan, by his words and by his presence here two weeks ago, reaffirmed that United States ground and air forces would stay in Korea, and, in fact, would be modernized and strengthened. But, more importantly, new command arrangements have been worked out with the establishment of the Republic of Korea/United States Combined Forces Command. That happened five years ago this month. Those command arrangements provide for the closest possible integration of all facets of military operations and should serve as the model of "how-to-do-it" for any group of nations which want to band together for security purposes.

I don't want you to think I believe that our military relationships are the only important connections between our two countries. They're not. In fact, the economic, cultural, and social ties seem to have eclipsed our military ties in recent years, and it is right that they should. On the other hand, today's solid military security arrangements provide the necessary shield behind which the Republic of Korea can build up its unique heritage of a 4000-year-old culture and pursue new levels of economic health, of political maturity, and of social harmony and justice—and, hopefully, pursue a reduction of tensions, and permanent peace on the Peninsula, and the goal of eventual peaceful reunification of the country.

Those last goals require cooperation from North Korea and its friends, cooperation which for the moment does not seem to be forthcoming. President Pak and President Chun both made sensible calls for talks. They made them repeatedly and they were repeatedly and recklessly rejected by Kim Il Sung. The terrible tragedies of the past several months have weighed heavily on all of us; the atrocity in the skies over Sakhalin Island in which 269 lives were lost and the brutal murders in Rangoon—those murders in Rangoon confirmed by Burma as having been perpetrated by North Koreans. Those events have sorely tested this nation and shocked the world.

But the far-sighted actions of the Government of the Republic of Korea have demonstrated to the world the stark contrast between a mature member of the community of civilized nations and a renegade power which uses state terrorism as an instrument of national policy. The superb government officials, your friends and my friends, lost in that assassination cannot be brought back to life; but there is now no doubt in any part of the world that North Korea is a pariah state, a state to be isolated morally, diplomatically and economically.

President Reagan has pledged the United States to work with your government to censure North Korea for its brutality. But he promised something else. He said that the United States, as a Pacific power, is committed to the security of this region, that "... the United States will stand resolutely by you, just as we stand with our allies in Europe and around the world. In Korea, we have learned the painful consequences of weakness."

Weakness is provocative. As we enter the second century of our security relationship, we will do well to remember Secretary Dulles' words, "The Korean War began in a way wars often begin. A potential aggressor miscalculated." Even as we go about the tasks of seeing to our economic, social and political well-being, we must continue in our vigilance. There must be no miscalculation as to the durability of the United States and Korean resolve to provide for the security of the Republic of Korea. If our resolve and our vigilance are clear to potential aggressors, I am confident we have the prospect of many years of peace and progress for both our nations.

The security of the Republic of Korea affects the world far beyond the situation on this peninsula. Strategic geographic realities have been an enduring consideration. Korea sits in the middle of a triangle involving China, the world's most populous nation, the Union of Soviet Socialist Republics, one of the few military superpowers of the world, and Japan, one of the great economic and industrial powers of the world. The interrelationships of these three powers alone would make the security situation in Korea important. Beyond that, in the past twenty years the republic of Korea itself has become an important international economic and trading factor in the world. It has ties to the whole world, not just to East Asia. Security and stability in Northeast Asia and the Korean Peninsula are important to the whole Free World.

Outside my office, as many of you know, I have a large picture given to me by some Korean friends. It's a color photograph of my wife and me dressed in beautiful old costumes of the Yi dynasty royalty. Under the picture I have lettered the caption: "We support NATO, too." The lesson in that picture is that the freedom and security of the whole world is inextricably tied together. Those strategic realities will govern the security relationship of our two great nations in the years ahead. It has been a great honor for me to have had some small part in our security ties in past years. It is a great honor for Avis and me to return to the land that we consider our second home and to enjoy again the warm friendship of the Korean people. Thank you (in Korean).

1984

Selected Works

**Address to the WHITE HOUSE
OUTREACH WORKING GROUP
ON CENTRAL AMERICA
Old Executive Office Building
Washington, DC
4 January 1984**

Happy New Year! I look out across this audience, and I see that I am speaking on Central America as the thirty-second speaker in the series of experts on Central America. I look in the audience and see people who know more about Central America than I do. It reminds me of some years ago when, as a much younger officer, I was ordered to give a talk to retired Army generals. The subject of my talk was the strategy for the defense of Europe. In the audience were Dwight Eisenhower, Mark Clark, and people of that ilk; and I got up there and wondered what in the world I was doing standing up in front of that crowd.

As introduced, my topic is Central America in the context of our larger strategy for the defense of the United States. One nice thing about this job is that you get an opportunity to look at the global strategy of the United States from a unique perch. We live in a dangerous world. And we don't have to look much beyond the headlines of today's newspapers to understand that.

What we want to do is live in that world as safely as we possibly can, not only for ourselves but also for our friends and allies, because we know that the world has become inextricably intertwined. We can't escape that fact. We have a national strategy which is a natural strategy for a democracy. We want to live in peace. We don't intend to start any wars, but we want to make it self-evidently clear to those who would like to start wars with us that it would be costly for them to do that and thus unwise.

That strategy is global in nature, recognizing the intertwining of the economy and the social and political fabrics of the world. It rests on a series of alliances in various important places in the world. The major alliances that come to mind, of course, are our alliance with the North Atlantic Treaty

Organization, our alliance with the East Asian nations, and then we have a number of other smaller alliances and mutual defense treaties that are important to us and to the people with whom we have those treaties. Then, we have ties with nations, many nations, with whom we have no mutual defense treaties but our ties are traditional; and, there is an understood recognition that we are important to their defense and they are important to ours.

The military part of that strategy involves having forces in place in major parts of the world where those alliances exist and are immediately threatened by our major enemy, the Soviet Union, or some other major enemy. Those forces are there for two reasons: one is to lend some military strength to the alliances and, second, to help keep the political cohesion of the alliances—which is probably more important than the day-to-day military strength. The nations of the world, the civilized nations of the world, agreed to act in concert to maintain the peace and to maintain the fundamental liberties to which we ascribe.

We have small armed forces for the size of our country. For the years from 1976 to 1979, I commanded our forces in Korea. I looked across the demilitarized zone at the North Korean Army, an army just about the size of our army—which sort of puts the size of our armed forces in perspective. This means that we have to add some other ingredients to that strategy. Another ingredient is the central reserve of ready reinforcements that are able to go to any of these alliances or to other places in the world where trouble may be.

If you want to move forces someplace, you have to control the sea and the air in order to get the forces there. You need to have good command, control and communications in order to do that. And you need to have extraordinary good intelligence. Now, we can criticize our strategic mobility, our command, control and communications or our intelligence—and I probably do that every day—but, at the same time, we put our money in those things in order to make them as good as we possibly can; and they are good.

The recognition of where we sit on the Earth and where those key threats to us are is very much a part of understanding that strategy. One really needs a globe. Since I became Chairman of the Joint Chiefs of Staff, I generally ban Mercator maps of the world because I find that people have a "Mercator-projection mentality." Mercator projections fail to get across the point that the shortest way to the other parts of the Northern Hemisphere is not through the Atlantic or the Pacific but over the Pole.

And another thing—if we looked at a polar projection of the world, we would see the importance of the Caribbean to the United States and its ability to interact with the rest of the world. I brought along a map of only a small part of the world, the Caribbean and Central America—just to remind us of that—because, if we were to have a war with the Soviet Union, over 50 percent of our reinforcing shipping would flow through the seas that we see here, through the Gulf of Mexico, the Caribbean and out into the Atlantic.

If one looked at a plot of the sinkings by the German submarine force of allied ships in the first 6 months of World War II, you would see that well over half of the ships were sunk along our coasts, from the Virginia Cape to the south and through the Caribbean and the Gulf of Mexico. That gives you some idea of the importance of the region. And the Germans then understood that importance as well as we do today. The Soviets also understand the importance of the Caribbean and the Gulf of Mexico and Central America to us. The Soviets are opportunists and they will do whatever they can do in their power to make life miserable for us in peacetime and certainly lay the groundwork for making life very difficult for us if we should ever fight the Soviet Union.

Now, I say to you that we don't want to fight the Soviet Union, but making it clear that we are in a good position to fight them would be the best way to deter war in the first place. I don't need to recite to this group the efforts of the Soviet Union through the past 25 years since Castro took over in Cuba. I see many who are well aware of them and I know that you have heard about them from other speakers who have spoken here.

The real question is, "What do we do about the situation as it exists today?" Cuba is communist. The Nicaraguan revolution has not been true to its promises for democracy and freedom and, in turn, has opened the gates for Cuba and the Soviet Union to move into the mainland of Central America. There is a bitter fight going on in El Salvador today, with that country trying to stay alive. Honduras, between El Salvador and Nicaragua, feels threatened. Guatemala has an insurgency going on. Costa Rica feels troubled and threatened. And, certainly, the unease extends in both directions through Mexico and down through Panama and down to the northern coast of South America. So, the question is, "What do we do to clear up the situation that exists today?"

I would like to make two points. First, we need to clear it up. We need to clear it up for our own strategic defense to make sure we are not left in a disadvantageous position against our major enemy, the Soviet Union. Secondly, we really don't want to go to war in Central America. My sensing from talking to the people in that area is that they don't want us to come down there and do their fighting for them or bail them out. They are perfectly willing and ready to do that themselves, but they need some help to do it.

There are longstanding problems in Central America ... the economic problems for example. I think that those of us living in this hemisphere can't expect to live here with close neighbors whose per capita GNP disparity ranges about 6 to 1, 7 to 1, and not expect to have some abrasiveness with that part of the world. They need economic help; but, at the same time, recognizing that our help to that part of the world is 3 to 1 in favor of economic over military, I want to tell you that unless the security situation improves, all the economic help in the world won't help solve the problems down there. That was demonstrated this past week in the destruction of the one major bridge on the Central American highway in El Salvador. Certainly, a country that is faced with an insurgency where the insurgency is destroying the economic infrastructure has a very, very difficult time aiding its people to raise their standard of living and economic well-being. So, security is very, very important to those countries.

Now, what has been the strategy of the United States? It seems to me that we talked about part of it. One is aiding those people down there to defend themselves and to solve their problems, and also helping them at the same time to get on with solving their economic problems.

There are some problems inside the United States with aiding those countries. I would cite, for example, the problems of El Salvador in military assistance last year. The Administration went forward with the request to the Congress that was only about half of what the experts on the ground thought was needed. Then the Congress, in turn, *cut that in half*. Then, we had to deal that out in dribs and drabs which led the Salvadorans to do unwise things militarily and not only militarily on the ground but also economically in using their military aid. They ran out of ammunition so the President had to ask for emergency authority for more money so they could get more ammunition. Then, because they ran out of ammunition, we had to fly the ammunition down there at a transportation cost that was perhaps four or five or six times what it would have been if we could have shipped it in more orderly fashion by ships. So, that ate up the military aid.

This year we have started off in just about the same fashion. We are on a Continuing Resolution Authority for El Salvador and we are at about 25 percent of what any reasonable military and diplomatic team looking at the problem would say is needed; and I think the Kissinger Commission, when they finish, will affirm that it is probably even less than 25 percent—with restrictions on that, telling us that only a certain portion of that can be done until certain judicial actions are taken with regard to some of the murders that have taken place in El Salvador. I don't want you to believe that I am against holding a club over the Salvadoran Government to clean up its own act. I simply want to tell you that by February, we will probably be flying ammunition there again at some exorbitant cost because the government will not be able to keep itself alive and prepare for the elections in March without using up the ammunition it has on hand.

What do we need to do? We need to make it clear to Cuba and Nicaragua that it is not in their interest to interfere with those other nations. We need to separate the Nicaraguans from the Cubans and I would tell you that it seems to me the Administration has done a remarkably good job in getting that message across. We note here Daniel Ortega saying the right sorts of things. Most of the intelligence people say, "Well, his actions have not caught up with his words yet." But, at least we see some evidence of the Nicaraguans moving in the direction that President Reagan has said they must move.

The exposure of the involvement of the Cubans and the Soviet Union and the North Koreans and other assorted strange and unusual people on the little, innocent island of Grenada certainly ought to be a lesson for the rest of the nations in this hemisphere. It certainly should be a lesson to us—that the rest of those people are serious; they're serious in their attempts to make this hemisphere an uncomfortable place for the United States. So, we need to be serious about our efforts to abort their attempts. We need to follow through with the pledge to those people who have said, "We can defend ourselves if you will give us the help." We need to give them the help in reasonable amounts in order to do what has to be done militarily. At the same time, we have to give them some hope for solving their economic problems so they can solve the political problems which are all important to solving the military problems.

I went to the Simon Bolivar celebration in Bogotá last year and it was an interesting and enjoyable celebration to attend. At the same time, I got caught by some American press people who said that "Here are all these Presidents of South American countries saying unkind things about the United States, and about the military exercises in the Caribbean." And then, when I would go around to some of the other social events and I would see Vice Presidents or Ministers of Foreign Affairs or Defense Ministers of these same countries, they would sidle up to me and say, "Keep up what you are doing in Central America. It is the only way you will get the message to Cuba and the Nicaraguans. And you are being successful. We want you to know you are being successful." So, I would beard them with the point that our own press people had made to me: "If this is so, why are your Presidents making these speeches?" And, they'd look at me incredulously and say, "Certainly, you understand more about the history of this region than to ask that question. How can any of the leaders of this country stand up and make pro-United States speeches at this Simon Bolivar celebration? You simply have to recognize that and recognize that what you are doing is the correct thing and keep a steady course and go ahead and do it."

I would think that those words are the key for us—a "steady course and go ahead and do it." Remember that we are not going to solve the problems in Central America forever and turn and walk away from Central America this year or next or the year after. They are going to be our neighbors forever and ever, as long as we are here on the North American continent. We have an unending interest in that part of the world and we simply have to keep up the steady course and the commitment to solving those problems.

Opening Remarks before the
SENATE ARMED SERVICES COMMITTEE
On the FY 85 DOD Authorization
31 January 1984

Mr. Chairman and members of this Committee:

Secretary Weinberger has covered the major points of the budget. He has laid out very clearly the need for a strong defense and why this budget is a sound basis for that defense. He also stated that the health of our armed forces is being restored. In the interest of time, I will add only a few points to those made by the Secretary.

The health of our armed forces *is* good. This trend is most evident in the quality of the men and women in uniform. From my visits all over the world, I can tell you that the soldiers, sailors, airmen and Marines we have now are the best I've seen in my 45 years in uniform. The Congress and the Executive Branch have made this renewed strength possible. And, on behalf of the men and women in uniform and my colleagues on the Joint Chiefs of Staff, I want to thank you for your support.

We talk a lot about hardware, but people are the heart of our forces; and we are filling up the shortages in skilled manpower. Recruitment and retention are excellent. And, this nation needs to continue to make military life attractive or we simply won't have good armed forces.

The operational commanders in the field report renewed confidence in their forces. New, good equipment from long-delayed modernization is now coming into the hands of our soldiers, sailors, airmen and Marines where it counts most. Our forces are well-trained and well-led. In talking to military leaders of our allies and friends, I find that they, too, are reassured by the restored strength of American forces. These facts must serve as an incentive for Soviet restraint and the growth of our strength will eventually provide a climate for sensible negotiations.

I say to you that this nation should not slack off. This is a key year for the United States. Last year I reported to you that we were making progress in reversing the decline of the 1970s in our general purpose forces and that we were in the early stages of modernizing our strategic nuclear deterrent forces. In the face of what the Soviets are doing, it is important that we press on.

We should remember that while we are making progress the Soviets are not standing still. They continue to field increasingly capable equipment in their already large and modern conventional forces. This year they will conclude a significant phase in the modernization of their ICBMs while we haven't put even one PEACEKEEPER in a silo. And, they continue to fish in the troubled waters of the resource-rich Third World.

When I look at the Soviets' forces, I see forces which are very large, capable of offensive operations on a global scale, and increasingly capable of achieving their wartime objectives. And, I see they are willing to use their forces and those of their surrogates to achieve their aims.

When I look at U.S. forces, I see that our forces are essentially designed for deterrence. That has been our strategy, and it is a sensible strategy. We hope to make it clear to any aggressor that he can't achieve his objectives by war or the threat of war. Since World War II we have attempted to build and maintain the kind of forces that would, along with our allies, make our deterrent strategy work and preserve the peace and our way of life.

The Joint Chiefs have looked at the strategy and the threat and we believe that this budget will better assure the security needs of this nation. Our nation need not match the Soviets weapon for weapon or man for man. Nor should it neglect other elements of our power—our political, economic and spiritual health. But, this nation absolutely must continue to deal realistically with the unrelenting growth of Soviet power and with the realities of an increasingly interdependent and dangerous world.

I urge the members of Congress to remember that crises in this turbulent world come without much warning, and that reasonable preparation constantly carried forward is a sound investment in our future security, both to avoid defeat in battle and, more importantly, to prevent war in the first place.

Finally, I would like to quote the late Senator Henry (Scoop) Jackson's eloquent statement one year ago before this Committee:

> "I would hope ... that this would be a time of steadiness, a time when we go about our work in a manner and in a way which will demonstrate to the world that we can provide a very strong and steady hand in a very unsteady world. I think that is the challenge that we all face because the world looks to this country with only 7 percent of its population and the world expects at times bigger things than we are capable of providing, but above all else I think we need to provide a steadiness, not only in reality, but in appearance that will give confidence to others."

Statement before the
HOUSE ARMED SERVICES COMMITTEE
On FY 85 DOD Authorization
2 February 1984

Mr. Chairman and members of the Committee:

The U.S. military posture has improved from the low point of the 1970s. Commanders in the field report renewed confidence in their forces. The resources provided have permitted them to reverse the decline in the total force readiness and sustainability of existing forces. Moreover, these resources are a firm foundation upon which to continue to build the deterrent forces which, together with those of our allies, are necessary to protect the nation's interests for the remainder of this century. The Congress and the Executive Branch have made this possible. On behalf of my colleagues on the Joint Chiefs of Staff and the men and women in uniform, I thank you for your support.

The nation's military forces are good, and substantial progress is being made in overcoming past deficiencies. Many programs are beginning to show positive effects with the operating forces. Good people are the heart of our forces, and we're filling up the shortages in manpower. Recruitment and retention are excellent. New, good equipment from long-delayed modernization is now coming into the hands of our soldiers, sailors, airmen, and Marines where it counts most. Our forces are well-trained and well-led. In talking to military leaders of our allies and friends, I find that they, too, are reassured by the restored strength of American forces. These facts serve as an incentive for Soviet restraint, and the growth of our strength will eventually provide a climate for sensible negotiations.

However, the nation should not be complacent, nor accept the notion that these past three years can somehow erase the decline in real growth over the 1970s or eliminate the gap caused by the continued growth of Soviet power. Reductions in the President's requested budget this past year have slowed the momentum of revitalization. This slowed rate of growth in force capabilities will affect readiness and retard responsiveness in a crisis. The Joint Chiefs of Staff have looked at the threats to our nation's security and at our strategy. We believe this year's budget is sensible; it is a reasonable response to threats to national security and to the requirements of the military strategy of the United States.

Threat

The U.S. military posture—the ability to protect U.S. interests—is affected by many variables. Growing Western interdependence and Third World instability are dynamic influences on national security. While we were restoring our strength, the Soviets were not standing still. The momentum of the Soviet military buildup, unequalled in peacetime, will carry Soviet force expansion and modernization programs well into the 1990s. With this pace of modernization over the last ten years, the Soviets have produced three times as many aircraft and four times as many tanks and other tracked vehicles than has the United States. They also have deployed a large and powerful navy. Soviet conventional forces can dominate the Eurasian land mass, endanger our vital lines of commerce, and simultaneously threaten U.S. and allied interests in Europe and Asia. Even a limited confrontation with the Soviet Union immediately could have global implications.

The Soviets continue to modernize their strategic nuclear forces. In 1982 alone, they deployed over 1200 highly accurate intercontinental ballistic missile warheads. They deployed another 200 ICBM warheads in 1983, which will lead to the completion of a significant phase of their strategic ICBM modernization this year. All this is taking place and we have not yet deployed a single PEACEKEEPER missile. These Soviet missiles with a total of over 5000 warheads are being placed in the world's hardest silos and are linked with a redundant, survivable, and reliable command and control network to the Soviet leadership in well-protected sites. The Soviets have also strengthened their theater nuclear forces. Even as we negotiated, they deployed SS-20's at the rate of one a week and improved their theater nuclear forces in Eastern Europe. The Soviets claimed no nuclear weapons were in East Europe and that recent deployments to Eastern Europe were in response to our deployments of PERSHING and GLCM. The facts are that Soviet levels of new tactical nuclear systems reflect decisions made years before we deployed PERSHING II and GLCM.

Soviet military power impedes the peaceful resolution of Third World problems and contributes to regional instability in ways that could promote wider conflict. The Soviets are not the only source of turbulence in the world. In the case of international terrorism, there are many causes and sponsors. In Central America and Lebanon, centuries of injustice, poverty and violence have led to the dangerous situations that exist today. But the Soviets seek to gain from international turmoil. Together with clients and surrogates, the Soviets are attempting to weaken the ties between the United States and its allies and to establish their own patterns of influence throughout much of the Third World.

Strategy

The basic national security objective for U.S. Armed Forces is to help preserve the United States as a free nation with its fundamental institutions and values intact. This nation and its allies seek to provide security and protect our way of life by preventing war. Our strategy is defensive; it is based on deterrence. Should deterrence fail, the strategy is to restore peace on favorable terms, and at the lowest scope and intensity of warfare consistent with our objectives.

Strategy guides the development as well as the deployment of U.S. forces. Because of the great distances from the United States to areas of vital interests and the relative nearness of the threats of those interests, this nation has maintained forward-deployed land, naval, and air forces since the end of World War II. These forces lend political and military strength to our alliance strategy by a visible demonstration of the strength of the U.S. commitment—putting potential aggressors on notice that an attack will be met immediately by allied opposition that includes the United States.

We maintain a strong, central reserve of Active and Reserve forces in the United States ready to reinforce those forces forward-deployed with our alliances, and to protect U.S. interests in other regions where there are no forward-deployed forces or where friends ask for help.

Because U.S. forces will likely remain small relative to the requirements we have for them, they need to be as effective and flexible as possible. Superior training and superior equipment are required. Our forces must be fully equipped with modern equipment to give them the necessary technological edge over a numerically superior enemy. Our forces must be well-trained. Top-notch training is the decisive edge in combat effectiveness and it allows us to get the most out of our equipment.

U.S. commanders rely on good intelligence to warn and inform the forces and on effective and survivable command and control systems to direct their most effective use. As has always been the case, superior mobility and control of the key sea lines of communication will be essential to help make this strategy work. We have come to rely increasingly on space for command and control. However, because the Soviets have fielded the world's only operational anti-satellite weapon, space can no longer be considered a sanctuary.

Our non-strategic nuclear systems are essential to our deterrent strategy of flexible response. These systems deter Soviet aggression by our countering Soviet theater nuclear systems and by providing the capability to respond at whatever level of intensity necessary to prevent the Soviets from achieving their war objectives.

Over-arching all the components of our strategy, the strategic nuclear TRIAD and its associated command and control systems provide the strategic deterrent so essential to peace. We require modern, ready strategic nuclear forces in sufficient numbers to make it clear to the Soviets that their war objective cannot be achieved if they resort to strategic nuclear war.

Implications for Our Forces

The budget supports the strategy. Much of the budget is dedicated to the shorter-term needs of the existing forces, and supports the progress of the Services in restoring the vitality and the health of the total force. We urgently need to sustain that vitality. At the same time, the budget provides an effective, sensible program for modernization accompanied by modest growth in the size of our forces and appropriate R&D support.

The Joint Chiefs believe the proper balance has been struck—the balance between providing the present needs in readiness and sustainability and ensuring future capabilities through modernization. Inherent to this balanced approach is reliance on our technological base. The modernization programs are jeopardized by Soviet successes in acquiring Western technology. The nation urgently needs to protect the technology which gives us the qualitative advantages so necessary to give our forces an edge over potential enemies.

Force Readiness and Sustainability

Improving the warfighting efficiency of existing forces to deter and, if necessary, to fight at any level, intensity, and location remains top priority. We don't know when or if war will come. The forces must be ready. The success of this nation in battle depends critically on our ability to respond rapidly with well-trained, well-equipped, properly supported forces, and to sustain those forces. In turn, wartime readiness depends on how well the nation performs the peacetime functions of preparing for war.

Existing forces are now more capable of executing the strategy. Under this budget the Services will continue to provide new equipment to the forward-deployed forces and to those early-deploying forces in the central reserve in the United States. Priority is given to those first to fight, to include the Reserve Component forces. Many Guard and Reserve units are receiving first-line equipment—including the M-1 tank, the M-2 Fighting Vehicle, the F-16 fighter, the PERRY Class Guided Missile Frigate, and modern tactical communications equipment.

To tie these forces together, the Commanders in Chief of the operating forces and the Joint Chiefs are continually refining joint doctrine, combined training and exercises. Flying hours, battalion training days, and steaming hours will be increased over the FY 84 levels. A 16 percent increase in joint exercise funding will allow some 70 joint and combined exercises. The exercises are essential to readiness and to evaluate U.S. strategic plans. Such joint and combined exercises have the further advantages of showing our resolve and of improving the ability of the forces from the various Services to operate effectively with U.S. allies.

The capability of the forces of all Services to work together effectively and with forces of other countries is a major part of our coalition strategy. This strategic imperative is manifested in our unified command structure. The key players in implementing this strategy are the Commanders in Chief of the unified and specified commands, the CINCs. They are our operational commanders and provide oversight of our forces, as well as the direct interface with our allies.

Accordingly, the Joint Chiefs of Staff, in cooperation with the Secretary of Defense, are actively working with the CINCs to meet their needs. This is evident in the development of joint doctrine. The CINCs now have a direct role in the development of operational concepts. The CINCs have been deeply involved in creating this budget by personally presenting their warfighting and operational needs.

The CINCs need and have asked for a source of funds to meet urgent, near-term readiness and warfighting requirements. At present, when unforeseen requirements arise, the CINCs' only recourse is to seek funding through the Services—a lengthy process which may not be responsive. To satisfy unanticipated readiness problems, we propose a special fund. The fund would be managed by the Joint Chiefs who are in the best position to evaluate the urgency and priority of a request.

Another peacetime function essential to warfighting effectiveness is sustaining the forces. Sustainability gives our forces staying power both in peace and war. Forces that cannot be sustained can be outlasted, and deterrence gained by modernization and readiness becomes less credible. This budget will allow the Services to continue the progress they have made. Stockage levels are programmed to increase; and depot maintenance is improving, as are sustainability levels.

Supporting Our Alliance Strategy

We are working to encourage our friends to improve their ability to act in their own behalf or with us in the defense of common interests. In so doing, we make a contribution to our own security. In implementing our global strategy, allied Host Nation Support and security assistance stand as two of the most cost-effective measures. For example, better security assistance terms, and larger quantities, are urgently needed right now in Central America. Effective security assistance to this troubled region will help to improve the security situation so social, political and economic reform can progress.

Strategic Forces

The United States has placed a high priority on modernizing its strategic forces. This broad effort includes making command and control systems more responsive and survivable, improving strategic warning capabilities, and improving all legs of the TRIAD. The Joint Chiefs fully support the conclusions of the Scowcroft Commission that the nuclear weapons modernization programs are essential both for deterrence and to create the climate for meaningful arms reduction negotiations. The development and deployment of the PEACEKEEPER missile, TRIDENT submarine system, B-1B and Advanced Technology Bomber, air-launched cruise missile, and a new, small, single-warhead ICBM are essential programs to ensure the U.S. strategic deterrent.

This is a key year for the United States. This nation has delayed strategic nuclear modernization and we are now faced with the need to modernize all three legs of the TRIAD at the same time. The Soviets have built a strategic nuclear force capable of achieving their war objectives. We needs a force which will make it clear to them they cannot achieve those wartime goals. The TRIDENT submarine program and the D-5 missile will modernize our aging POSEIDON fleet. The PEACEKEEPER will upgrade our ICBM force to offset the imbalance caused by Soviet deployment of modern, hard-target capable ICBMs, while research proceeds on the small missile. The B-1B will provide a survivable, responsive bomber force able to penetrate Soviet defenses well into the 1990s. We need to go ahead with these programs to assure the credibility of our strategic deterrent.

A major effort to modernize our strategic command, control and communications (C³) systems continues in this budget request. In order to assure the capability to detect and provide warning of an impending attack, sensors, command centers and their supporting communications are being hardened against nuclear effects. Our C³ systems are being designed for increased survivability as well as redundancy and improved interoperability of key command facilities.

The Joint Chiefs support the President's initiative to have this nation employ its technological talent to seek an alternative to sole reliance on offensive retaliation. In consultation with our allies and with the U.S. scientific community, we are exploring means which provide the hope that we can end the dominance of offensive nuclear weaponry.

Nonstrategic Nuclear Forces

Nonstrategic nuclear forces are a key part of our strategy of flexible response. The modernization of our nonstrategic nuclear systems with the fielding in PERSHING II, modernized Field Artillery warheads, and ground-launched cruise missiles, as well as associated command and control, will improve effectiveness, reduce risks to allied territory, and improve safety and security. With the continued cooperation of NATO and the support of the

Congress, the new long-range systems will serve to counter Soviet SS-20 deployments and strengthen the credibility of our deterrent posture.

Chemical

The Joint Chiefs place great priority on modernizing the U.S. retaliatory chemical munitions stockpile. U.S. forces are improving their ability to defend against chemical attack, but the Congress must clearly understand that the lack of a modern chemical retaliatory capability will have our forces fighting at great disadvantage. Additionally, unless we take steps to modernize our own chemical munitions, we provide little incentive to the Soviets for a meaningful, verifiable arms control agreement prohibiting chemical weapons. This budget provides for long lead-time items and facilities in order to begin production in FY 86. We urgently need to move forward in the production of modern chemical munitions to make our chemical warfare deterrent credible.

Negotiations

The Joint Chiefs fully support efforts to gain genuine, mutual, equitable and verifiable reductions in armaments. Arms control and other related negotiations are being pursued with the idea that equitable and verifiable agreements can contribute to security at reduced force levels. Arms control should not be viewed as a substitute for force modernization; rather, arms control and other defense efforts should be mutually reinforcing.

Any agreement is only as good as the willingness of the signatories to comply with the obligations assumed. Soviet violations or probable violations of provisions of several agreements presently in force show a disturbing pattern of Soviet behavior. This behavior must be taken into account in the development of U.S. defense programs and approaches to arms control.

Conventional Forces

In this age of nuclear parity and with conventional and low-intensity conflicts widespread throughout the world, conventional forces are the mainstay of our force structure. In this budget, land forces are being reorganized to improve flexibility and to capitalize on the effectiveness of newly introduced weapons, such as the ABRAMS tank, BRADLEY Fighting Vehicle, APACHE helicopter, and Multiple Launch Rocket System (MLRS). Improvements to and modernization of Active and Reserve Army divisions, to include the new light division concept, will enhance global flexibility. Naval forces continue to build toward a 600-ship Navy with 15 carrier battle groups, 4 battleship surface action groups, modernized attack submarines, and amphibious lift for Marine forces. We are procuring the best fighters flying today. We need to continue to procure such aircraft and modernized munitions as we build and strengthen the Air Force towards 40 tactical fighter wing equivalents. Modern, survivable, high-capacity tactical communication systems are being obtained to provide adequate, secure and reliable information distribution systems. This budget will also improve the ability of Special Operations Forces to support the needs of the CINCs at any level of conflict.

Our strategy calls for a rapid-reacting central reserve and the transportation to move it. Budget requests for the Navy and the Air Force recognize the importance of supporting the other Services in deploying their forces. Progress is being made to improve sealift and airlift: the maritime Ready Reserve force fleet is expanding, the purchase of KC-10A is funded, C-5A improvements are underway and KC-135 re-engining and conversion of fast sealift SL-7s are well-along and need to be kept going. The Army and Marine Corps have taken measures to improve the capabilities of their forces to deploy. For instance, maritime pre-positioning for the Marines and the Army's light division will improve their mobility.

People

No matter how good the strategy or how excellent the equipment, good people will remain the heart of our defense forces. Well-trained, highly motivated Service members are fundamental to combat readiness. This nation has very good people in its Armed Forces today because of the nation's renewed pride and faith in those people and the willingness to pay the price for adequate security. The people in our Armed Forces are willing and ready to go wherever this nation asks them to go to protect our vital interests. Their tasks are difficult and dangerous. Very much a part of their willingness and readiness to do these difficult tasks is the sure knowledge that we as a nation will provide for their needs. The men and women in uniform need to know we will give them the best possible equipment and training for their difficult tasks, and they need to know this nation will provide reasonable pay and compensation for them and their families.

There are a number of proposals being studied now with respect to compensation and retirement. I urge the Congress in reviewing these issues to remember the unique demands of military service. The Armed Forces need to have confidence that trends will not be set in motion that will erode pay and other benefits or return the forces to the unstable personnel picture of the 1970s. In the case of retirement, it is not a pension system; it is an integral part of a lifetime, career compensation program. It is a means to shape the age and skill mix of the force. The military profession is still a young person's calling and the retirement system for the Active and Reserve Forces must account for that.

Conclusion

As the Congress considers the Defense Budget this year, I urge the members to remember that crises too often give little warning of their approach. Orderly preparation is not possible once growing tensions indicate immediate danger. An Army, Navy, Air Force and Marine Corps—in being and constantly maintained in readiness—support the other elements of our national power, give weight to diplomacy, and deter aggression.

The Soviets will not stand still. They will continue on the path they have begun, fielding increasingly capable forces on the land, on the sea, in the air, and in space. Our nation has no plans to match the Soviets weapon for weapon, and the Joint Chiefs do not suggest a neglect of the other elements of our national power. However, this nation simply must do what's needed to be done to counter the Soviets with forces which deny the utility of Soviet military power for coercion or war.

The Joint Chiefs of Staff believe that our strategy provides this nation with a sensible approach to preserve the peace and protect our national security. It is a strategy which makes it clear to potential aggressors they cannot achieve their goals by war or by the threat of war. The success of our strategy will continue to rely on the ability of the nation to provide ready, modern forces. The Joint Chiefs believe that the budget for FY 85 will do that. This budget provides the necessary resources to assure the revitalization of our armed forces and the continued effectiveness or our strategy.

Statement before the
HOUSE FOREIGN AFFAIRS COMMITTEE
On the FY 84 and 85 Security Assistance Program
9 February 1984

Mr. Chairman and members of this Committee:

Security assistance is an important instrument of U.S. foreign policy and an essential component of the U.S. coalition strategy. Effective and consistent security assistance relationships with allies and friends are fundamental to the achievement of our national security objectives. The success our nation has had in helping other nations help themselves through the security assistance program is due to the support of the Congress and the Executive Branch. On behalf of the Joint Chiefs of Staff, I want to thank you for your support.

This nation urgently needs to continue to support and enhance this crucial program. Further, our government needs to improve efficiency and flexibility in the management of the program. In doing so, we will more effectively improve the ability of our allies and friends to defend themselves and we thereby enhance our own security.

U.S. Strategy

This is a dangerous world. Turbulence in Third World countries and direct threats to global stability by the forces of the Soviet Union and its friends threaten the security of all free nations. It is a world of growing economic, political and social interdependence. U.S. security and well-being are inextricably linked to that of other nations—to our friends, allies and trading partners—as theirs are to ours.

We have a coalition strategy. In keeping with this coalition strategy, we maintain forward-deployed forces in key areas and a system of unified commanders with military responsibility for designated major regions of the world. To make our coalition strategy more effective, we are working to encourage our friends to do more in their own behalf or in cooperation with us in defense of our common interests. Security assistance stands among the most cost-effective means to achieve this.

The long-term influence of security assistance programs can be considerable. Security assistance programs were key ingredients in building the alliances we have today in Europe and in Asia. In the Third World, these programs have helped stabilize governments friendly to the United States, and they have helped contain the spread of Soviet imperialism. Professional military training has enhanced force development and influenced future military leaders who later serve in positions of leadership in many of the nonaligned nations.

Guidelines For Security Assistance

The Joint Chiefs believe security assistance is an important adjunct to other elements of our national power—our diplomatic, economic and political influence in the world. Security assistance should and does complement our strategic military objectives. In this respect, the equipment, services, and training provided under the security assistance program should do three things:
—Advance each recipient's ability to meet independently threats to its national security both from outside aggression and from externally supported groups bent on violent internal change.
—Foster the development of regional defense arrangements and cooperation that enable combined actions to deter or defeat regional incursions.
—Enable recipients to develop forces capable of operating with U.S. and allied forces in a collective security framework.

The Soviet Challenge

The Soviet Union realizes the value of security assistance as a low-cost, low-risk instrument for achieving political objectives. To this end, the Soviet Union has substantially increased its assistance programs over the past decade. Between 1979 and 1982, Soviet arms deliveries exceeded those of the U.S. by a factor of 3:1 in tanks, 4:1 in supersonic aircraft, and 7:1 in helicopters. The Soviet capability to deliver arms rapidly has kept pace with increasing sales. In 1982, deliveries were the second highest on record, and while all the data are not yet in, deliveries in 1983 promise to be as high. The

112

Soviets clearly have established an influential role in military sales to the Third World.

The Soviets frequently use surrogates as conduits for arms transfers to fulfill political objectives. Aid provided by Soviet surrogates is designed primarily to support guerilla activity in such areas as Africa, the Caribbean Basin and Central America. For example, among the many other arms and ammunition we found in Grenada were boxes from North Korea labeled "rice" but which contained ammunition. The Soviets are expected to continue to use direct and surrogate military assistance and arms sales to boost hard currency earnings and to gain influence and military access in Third World countries.

Soviet security assistance in the Mideast and Central America stands as a graphic example of Soviet use of such aid to gain geostrategic advantages, promote conflict, overthrow governments friendly to this nation, and thwart U.S. attempts to promote peace and stability. In Central America and Cuba alone, the Soviets provided military assistance deliveries in a six-month period through June of 1983 which outstripped our own by almost $9 million. They provide this aid, as they do worldwide, on very easy terms. We saw in Grenada how their aid is being used to overthrow governments and intimidate others. I want to emphasize that, had the Soviets and Cubans been successful in Grenada, they would have been in a position to threaten safe passage to and from the Panama Canal.

U.S. Programs And Legislative Initiatives

The Joint Chiefs do not suggest that we enter a security assistance race with the Soviets, or that this nation emphasize, as do the Soviets, the military element of our influence at the expense of our diplomatic, economic, political, and moral influence in the world. However, our adversaries place great emphasis on security assistance to achieve their objectives and there is a pressing need for assistance to our friends and allies. We should continue to emphasize diplomacy and economic influence as the preferred instruments of national influence. But, the U.S. security assistance program has a strong connection to our national security strategy and is often a prerequisite to effective diplomacy and economic aid. Further, our security assistance to many countries is essential to gain the basing, transit and support agreements we need to respond rapidly to crises worldwide.

About half of our security assistance funds goes to Israel and Egypt, and seven countries account for over 80 percent of the program. In addition to Israel and Egypt, major recipients are Turkey, Spain, Greece, Pakistan, and Korea. We need to continue to help these countries for a combination of political and military reasons. Nevertheless, by the time these seven countries are provided for, we have few resources left for other important strategic areas if the overall levels are cut. The Joint Chiefs urge adoption of the balanced program contained in the Administration's budget.

We must be concerned with the growing debt burden of developing nations. High-interest loans for security assistance exacerbate political, social, and economic problems on which revolutionary movements thrive. It is important to increase grant assistance substantially or ease the terms on which loans are extended. These better terms should be directed to nations whose survival and increased strength are in the U.S. strategic interest but are also in economic difficulty. This year and for the foreseeable future, this concern applies to a growing number of nations in Latin America, the Mideast and Africa.

Increases in grant assistance or concessional terms are highly recommended for Turkey and Portugal, the poorest among our NATO allies, where military modernization is key to strategic defense commitments. NATO depends on Turkey as the linchpin of the Southern Flank against several potential adversaries along an extensive frontier. Of all the NATO allies, Turkey maintains the largest standing army; but much of its equipment is in bad shape and outdated. Increased standing assistance to Turkey to correct this deficiency is critical for the successful defense of Europe. In this regard, the Joint Chiefs support the Administration's "On-Budget" proposal in that it improves affordability of security assistance programs to our security partners.

The International Military Education and Training (IMET) program deserves the whole-hearted support of the Congress. Training military personnel from allied and friendly nations is a very effective way of establishing and maintaining long-term cooperative security relationships with nations whose interests are closely linked to those of the United States. The program has a side benefit by giving a first-hand look at American life and democracy to future leaders from many different countries. Over the years, such training here has paid real dividends for the United States. Thousands of foreign leaders have undergone training at senior U.S. military schools during their military careers. For example, fully one-third of the foreign graduates of the U.S. Army Command and General Staff School have attained general or flag officer rank. During one recently surveyed five-year period, 160 foreign graduates of U.S. senior service schools had become cabinet ministers, legislators, or ambassadors, and over 1,800 foreign graduates had attained general or flag officer rank.

The extension of U.S. influence also has a multiplier effect since U.S.-trained foreigners train still others. We need to make wider use of training as a security assistance tool. One initiative the Joint Chiefs support would permit exchanges of training for individuals or units on a reciprocal, no-cost basis. Many countries cannot afford U.S. costs and the IMET budget can go only so far. This keeps both sides from benefiting from reciprocal training, and we need to correct that.

The Joint Chiefs also support changing the law so that there is a single, standardized cost for Foreign Military Sales (FMS) training of foreign personnel in U.S. military facilities. A single FMS price would reduce confusion on the part of our allies, reduce fiscal impediments to formal U.S. military training, and remove inequities in the current FMS pricing structure.

In the past, urgent requests from our friends necessitated a drawdown of U.S. equipment and munition inventories to supply their time-sensitive needs in a crisis. Some of these actions had an adverse impact on U.S. force readiness in that a large quantity of the material supplied was from inventory. Time was required to recover from these transfers. The Special Defense Acquisition Fund (SDAF) provides a limited buffer and will enable faster recovery for items already on order. The Joint Chiefs are confident the SDAF can be a useful tool when funded to the levels requested in the budget. We encourage raining the obligation authority and increasing the capitalization rate so the SDAF can be more effective.

A number of other initiatives have been submitted to the Congress over the last two years, all of which the Joint Chiefs continue to support. I understand many received favorable action in the committee reports last year. We would appreciate your efforts to complete an Authorization Bill this year.

Regional Considerations

The United States is now helping vulnerable Central America countries achieve self-determination and economic and social development. Progress is hampered by the lack of necessary funds to develop adequate defense capabilities to meet threats to the security of the region, particularly in El Salvador and Honduras. Nicaragua continues to threaten Honduras and other countries with the largest military force in the region and insurgency continues in El Salvador. Only through a comprehensive four-part approach, which includes development of economic, political, and social reforms as well as development of the indigenous military capability, will lasting stability be achieved. Grant assistance is most appropriate to achieve force development without further burdening the fragile institutions of the countries in the region.

About one-fourth of the funds from Central America are for Honduras, and about half for El Salvador. In El Salvador, we clearly need to provide economic assistance and the impetus for social reform. However, it would be fundamentally unsound not to provide also the means for that country to provide for its own security. Without a security shield, the Salvadoran government will be unable to prevent Marxists from destroying any economic or social progress made. As the National Bipartisan Commission on Central America pointed out, U.S. military assistance programs require "greater continuity and predictability." The operational commanders and our advisors in the field report that, because of the sudden starts and stops of U.S. military assistance there, Salvadoran forces must constrain their operations and thereby cede advantages to the guerillas. The Joint Chiefs urge the Congress to provide more timely, predictable and adequate support to the Salvadoran forces.

In Grenada we saw how important cooperation among states in the region could be. We also saw that the self-defense forces of many countries are only small police forces which have only limited paramilitary capabilities. These police forces are not prepared to assume duties in low-intensity conflict. If current restrictions on the training of police forces are modified or lifted, the ability of the self-defense forces of Caribbean Basin nations and Costa Rica to maintain their nations' security could be enhanced.

In the case of Lebanon, public attention has been riveted on the role of the multinational force (MNF), of which our forces are a part. As we all know, the situation there is extremely volatile. Nevertheless, we should not be diverted from the larger issue of helping the Government of Lebanon restore Lebanese sovereignty throughout the country. One major portion of that effort is the development of strong Lebanese Armed Forces (LAF) to give breathing room to the political process. This nation, in cooperation with the British, French and Italians, has been assisting the LAF. We are making progress in helping the LAF to forge a more effective force capable of assuming larger, more comprehensive control of its territory as foreign forces withdraw. As the national government of Lebanon reconstitutes itself, we will be prepared to continue to provide assistance in the hopes that our objectives can be eventually achieved.

Conclusion

The Administration has put forward a number of carefully thought-out proposals for funding the security assistance programs for the remainder of this fiscal year and for FY 85. The Administration has also put forward important proposals to increase the flexibility and effectiveness of those programs.

I want you to know that the Joint Chiefs fully support the legislation placed before you. The legislative initiatives contained in this program and the funds and other resources sought are essential to support what the Joint Chiefs believe are necessary and sensible needs from friendly and allied governments. They look to us for assistance in a dangerous world. They also look to us for steadfastness of purpose. I urge your support for these programs.

**Remarks at the SOCIETY OF
THE SONS OF THE REVOLUTION
At the Annual Banquet in Honor of the
Birthday of George Washington
Richmond, VA
22 February 1984**

Thanks very much. It is nice to be here with the Society to celebrate the 253rd birthday of George Washington—Father of our Nation and the first head of the Army. And, it is a special pleasure to be in this great city of Richmond. It is the city with the distinction of celebrating Washington's Birthday as a holiday for the first time. In 1782, 202 years ago today, the local newspaper said that, "Tuesday last being the birthday of his Excellency, General George Washington, our illustrious Commander in Chief, the same was celebrated here with utmost demonstrations of joy." And I feel that we are doing that very well here tonight.

I can see that Richmond has lost none of its pride in Virginia's most famous son. It is a great tradition that you have here, to gather every year to celebrate the heritage of George Washington. He was a great man, certainly; but he was a man—and he was a patriot like you people gathered here tonight. He had an abiding faith in America. And he had a great faith in God. His wisdom and understanding of human frailties is summed up in what he often told his soldiers. He said, "Tis not in mortals to command success."

Over the span of many generations, we tend to forget the greatness of George Washington. Up in the northern part of Virginia where we ought to remember him particularly, we in Washington, D.C., seem to treat his birthday as simply just another holiday.

Two hundred years ago today we would have found George Washington at his home in Mount Vernon—having just disbanded his Army in late November of 1783 at Newburgh, New York. He hadn't yet received the call to become the first President. He was settling down to run the farm, to tend the business, to handle the bills. And, as I came down here tonight in the helicopter, I could see other things that reminded me of George Washington. I guess maybe those things are the only things the two of us have in common. We both have our houses pointed toward the water; we both love to fish; and we both became military officers.

George Washington was not only a fisherman and a gentleman, but he knew well the horrors of war. He was in fact a man of peace. He knew from hard experience that the Good Lord didn't promise us a perfect world. He knew that peace could only be maintained through the military strength necessary to deter our enemies from attacking us. We call that "deterrence" in Washington and that means that if anyone tries to pick a fight with us, we'll kick the tar out of them. He said that "If we desire to avoid insult, we must be able to repel it. If we desire to secure peace, it must be known that we are at all times ready for war."

That principle is the cornerstone of our national security policy today. The necessity for maintaining adequate defenses hasn't changed. Each of these speakers here tonight has said of his own Service that we have good forces. You can be justly proud of those men and women in uniform today. As in Washington's day, it is the individual soldier, sailor, airman, Marine and Coast Guardsman in our forces—both Active and Reserve—who is the guarantor of our freedom. I can tell you from my observations that our people in uniform today fully measure up to their heritage as descendents of the Continental Army and Navy which won our liberty.

As I flew up here tonight, I looked out and was able to see Mount Vernon. Along the banks of the Potomac, I could see Bolling Air Force Base and Anacostia Naval Air Station; I flew on past Fort Belvoir, past the Coast Guard Radio Station; down past Quantico, and further on down I could imagine Fort

A.P. Hill, Fort Lee, Fort Eustis, Fort Monroe, Langley Air Force Base and Norfolk Naval Air Station. I couldn't help but think that George Washington would certainly be proud today as much of the Armed Forces have been stationed on the land on which he grew up.

But, the world is much different today that it was in the late 1770s. It is more complex. There are many more nation-states out there; the pressures from political, religious and ethnic factions seem even greater than they did in George Washington's time. The economic changes have brought about a greater interdependence between our nation and the other nations of the world.

In Washington's time, he could take comfort in what he called the great "Atlantic Barrier." Today, that barrier can be bridged in hours by jet aircraft and in minutes by nuclear missiles. In Washington's time, he could rightly advise the Congress to "avoid foreign entanglements." Today, we see that our economy and security are inextricably intertwined with the rest of the world. In Washington's era, the area covered by his whole Army at Yorktown could have been defended by one Infantry battalion today. In Washington's time, after the Revolution, there were no communists around in this part of the world to foment disorder and pervert legitimate revolution, such as we saw in Nicaragua, into rigid totalitarianism. This is a new system of repression which now threatens its neighbors in Central America.

Added to this is the relentless buildup of Soviet military power, both nuclear and conventional—recognizing their increasing willingness to use that power as demonstrated over the past three years in Afghanistan, Africa, Southeast Asia, Europe and here, right in the territory of our own free people. And we can see it is a dangerous world. If this Nation of ours is going to steer a safe course through these troubled waters, we must show that we can meet the military threats posed by potential enemies. We don't want to invite a war; we want to preserve peace. I just want to tell you in the most simple, direct terms that we don't want a war. We don't want any kind of war—we particularly don't want a nuclear war. But at the same time, it seems very important to all of us that we don't want to be paralyzed by the fear of war as we go about our business in this world of nation-states.

We need to pursue sensible policies that will secure the security of our own people—the liberty of our people—and reduce the probability of war. Our goal is to preserve the peace through strength. Our hope is that if we persevere, the Soviets and their allies may finally conclude that it is in their best interests to sit down with us to reduce the level of nuclear arms in a verifiable way that will ensure a safer world. I am sure if George Washington was here tonight, he would warn us against being diverted away from the security of our nation with any of these emotionally appealing, miraculous solutions to the problems of peace and security.

Yesterday, I was testifying with the Secretary of Defense before the House Budget Committee. I listened to attack after attack on the defense budget by members of that committee. The public media was there to inform the American people. One of the curious things that I observed was that every time one of these guys critical of defense would talk, the cameraman would perk up and point their cameras at him. Late in the afternoon, finally, a Congressman from Texas named Phil Gramm got up and made a very sensible remark about the need for defense; and he asked some very sensible questions. I said to myself, "I hope these television guys get him on the news." Then I looked over at them. Two of them were dead asleep and the rest of them were sitting down with their cameras pointed at the ceiling.

That reminds me of a time in our early history. One of the delegates to the Continental Congress made the motion to limit the active Army to no more than 5,000. George Washington, himself a delegate, turned to the fellow next to him and whispered in a loud voice, "That's a good idea. And we'll pass another motion which limits the attackers to no more than 3,000."

George Washington knew the price of freedom. He circulated among the States in 1783 what he called the "Four Pillars of Freedom." The first Pillar was "An indissoluble Union of the States under one Federal Government." The second was "A sacred regard for public justice." Thirdly, "The adoption of a proper peace establishment"—and I think he had the right name for the Armed Forces. And, fourthly, he said the "The prevalence of that pacific and friendly disposition among the people of the United States, which will induce them to forget their local prejudices and policies, to make those mutual concessions which are requisites to the general prosperity and, in some instances, to sacrifice their individual advantages to the interest of the community."

I will tell you that wrapped up in that last Pillar of George Washington is the concept of service to the Nation, which is what made this country great. It is based on the recognition that life has little meaning if we as individuals are not part of something greater than just ourselves. The Nation was founded on a mutual commitment among its citizens to the highest ideals of human dignity for ourselves and all mankind. There is nothing in which we should take greater pride as citizens of this nation and as human beings in the world of ours.

The very essence of service to country was exemplified by the life of George Washington. Men and women from his day and through the days to the present have sacrificed their lives and their fortunes to preserve their sacred honor and to preserve this great country of ours. I believe that it is our duty as citizens of this country to do exactly the same, not only for us but also for our prosperity—to preserve the liberty that we so greatly desire and want for this great country of ours.

The cost of vigilance is sometimes high. It is never as high as the price of war. We pay taxes in dollars today. The President is asking $305 billion for the defense of this country today. But, it is not nearly as much as it will cost if we have to go to war and then we would not only pay in dollars but in a coin far more precious. And that would be in the blood of our citizens.I am reminded of the extraordinary foresight of George Washington when he was to accept the British surrender at Yorktown. He said to his troops:

"My brave fellows ... let no shouting or cheers increase the shame of the fallen enemy. It is sufficient for us that we witness their humiliation." And then he said, "*Posterity* will cheer for us."

We have important work to do. You have important work to do here in Richmond. I and my fellow colleagues on the Joint Chiefs of Staff have important work to do. Whatever we do in this great country, we've got work to do to keep this country strong and free. I would hope and pray to the good Lord that we do our work and we do it well. These are trying times. Nevertheless, we can't forget our responsibilities for those who will follow us. I, like Washington, say that I hope that *posterity* will cheer for us. I pray that they will.

Remarks before the
ASSOCIATION OF THE UNITED STATES ARMY
Fort Hood, TX
15 March 1984

The great advantage that the United States has over the Russians is our professional non-commissioned officer corps. We have about ten times the number of professionals, as a percentage, in our Armed Forces than the Russians do. Their tanks are commanded by-and-large by two-year draftees. We've got *experts* on ours. That is what is going to make the difference if we ever go to war. And as long as the Russians recognize that, they won't want to fight us. That is the most important job we have: that is, to prepare those people for tomorrow. That is the job not only for you people in the military, but it is part of the responsibility of you people in the civilian community to help the Armed Forces get and keep good people and equipment. That is the heart of our defense.

A Letter to the
Army Aviation Association of America
29 March 1984

Army Aviation faces some important challenges. The first challenge is to make certain that its activation as a branch by itself doesn't move it away from the other combat branches; rather it must move even closer if we are to get the most out of the capabilities of the new hardware and the top-notch Aviation officers and soldiers we now have in the force. There will be a tendency for some to say that the Armed Forces now has four air forces instead of three. The members of the Army Aviation Branch must make it clear that Army Aviation is a ground combat branch that uses the medium of the air to provide extraordinary mobility for ground combat operations. Army Aviation uses air to provide roads where there are no roads and hills where there are no hills. Yet, at the same time, it uses the existing terrain for cover and concealment just as do the Infantry and the Armor.

We must make certain that we use the extraordinary capabilities we have built into the Army in the best possible way. The new helicopters, the new tanks, the Infantry Fighting Vehicles, MLRS and other modernized artillery, new sensors, new intelligence-fusion techniques, distributed information systems, and, above all, very good soldiers to give us the opportunity to make combat teams on the battlefield more effective than any that have ever been before. The key to all that is the teamwork of the Infantry, Armor, Artillery, and Aviation units. All have to understand each other's capabilities and limitations. I firmly believe that we will find that smaller, integrated teams will be far more useful than in the past. The Aviation Branch is the new player in this exercise and as such will carry an extraordinary burden for ensuring that teamwork exists.

Address to the
**ANNUAL CONVENTION OF THE
SOCIETY OF MILITARY ENGINEERS**
St. Paul, MN
26 April 1984

It was pointed out that I started my military career in the State of Minnesota. It's a state that doesn't noticeably show much of the active military services. I had breakfast with the Governor this morning and he reminded me of that fact. But, it is a state that has a long, distinguished military tradition. I suspect that this Color Guard is made up of men from the State of Minnesota.

Minnesota provided more soldiers per capita into the Union Army—even though it had been a state only a couple of years before the war—than any other state in Union. Its outfits were among the first to fight in World War I. I was with the outfit to fire the first American artillery round against the Germans in World War II. It was a Minnesota National Guard outfit. So, you're in a place that has a great military tradition although it may not be evident in the number of active military posts here.

Flying out here, one can be reminded of what American military engineers have done for this country. We came out on a great day yesterday. We flew over Pittsburgh; we could look down and see the beginning of the Ohio

River and later the great waters of the Mississippi. I couldn't help but think of what American military engineering has done from the days of the beginning of the country, from George Washington as a surveyor to what has been done today—not just to support our military operations but to support the development of this country.

Among other things that Harry Griffith always talks about is that he was an aide to General Kelly Volpe, who was Division Commander during the last years of World War II. General Volpe always used to say when he was an instructor at the Infantry School at Fort Benning that a slide rule in the hands of an Infantryman was a dangerous tool. It only belonged to the Engineers. As I told General Volpe, it was many years later when I was an instructor at the Artillery School Gunnery Department and taught a slide rule course there. I told those guys, "Don't expect me to teach you how to use this because you're not smart enough. I'll just teach you how to keep from getting your fingers caught. It really belongs to the Engineers."

But all military people are Engineers in one sense or another. I am often reminded of one of Bill Mauldin's great cartoons in World War II. It shows two Engineer soldiers out there with that great, modern engineering tool, the Number Two D-handled shovel, trying to drain away the water from a hole that's hub-deep in mud and there's a jeep with a star on the front of it. One soldier says to the other, "O.K., O.K., so he's a general. What do you want me to do? Pass in review?"

Admiral Bull Halsey at Guadalcanal said that during World War II, every time he saw a bulldozer, he wanted to kiss it and the operator because they typified what military engineers are to the combat operations, no matter where, no matter what Service—the Army, the Navy, the Air Force or the Marine Corps.

In December, I was back in Italy for the fortieth anniversary of the battle of Mignano-Monte Lungo. It was the first battle in which the Italians fought on our side. And it was just up from where we had crossed the Volturno River three times. I recall watching four successive Engineer-soldier bulldozer operators get the Silver Star within the space of about an hour while they were trying to create bridge approaches, because a bridge was desperately needed to get ammunition to the other side of that river.

I am happy to greet all of you on behalf of my colleagues on the Joint Chiefs of Staff and to be with this organization. Seeing the uniforms of all the Services represented here reminds me that the Society of American Military Engineers represents the principle Eisenhower enunciated in 1958 when he sponsored the last great reorganization of the Joint Chiefs of Staff. He said there will be no more single-Service fights or single-Service wars. He said the Services simply had to work together in the future in order to be able to defend this nation jointly, together.

The extent to which you enhance communications among the Services and among the various engineering branches will help us all to do our jobs better.

Your program says I am the keynote speaker. The definition for "keynote," as I understand it is to lay out the unifying theme. I looked at your program and I am not sure that I'm capable of laying out the unifying theme. But what I would like to do is talk a little bit about national strategy and how military installation planning fits into national strategy and then have some plain talk—planner to Engineers—and talk about some of the problems that we face.

Every budget cycle that we go through in Washington starts with some fundamental questions. The same questions are asked from two different directions. Some people say, "What can we do with the money that we get?" And others say, "What should be done and how much will it cost to do it to do it to protect the interests of the United States?"

Now, there may be some similarities in those two ways to answer those questions but I would submit that there is a fundamental difference. My own personal bias is for asking, "What should be done?" because that leads us to better planning and to getting down to what is really needed to protect the United States.

In asking the questions in that direction, we make some reasonable assumptions about the future. Now, if there is anything that the past has taught us, it is that the world is certain to change in a fashion that we cannot predict. Indeed, we will certainly not anticipate all the changes that will come to the world in the days ahead. We won't bat a thousand in the assumptions that we make in developing our war plans or any other types of planning. But, at the same time, we must look to the future and make the best possible estimates that we can because our problems won't go away just because we've assumed them away.

I tend to be a little conservative when I examine what to do with our Armed Forces. I usually stick with evolutionary changes rather than revolutionary changes. But I want to tell you that I also recognize that, as surely as we fail to anticipate the future, we will be forced to make some hurried or wasteful changes and additions when the future arrives.

As Screwtape told his nephew, Wormwood, in C.S. Lewis' wonderful book, humans fail to remember the future is approaching us at a constant rate of 60 minutes per hour. We forget that sometimes; however, in the world we face today, the *rate* of change that we see is not often constant within those 60 minutes. Certainly, when we look at recent changes in society—technology, military forces—the clock seems to be rolling around much faster than 60 seconds in every minute and 60 minutes in every hour. So, whatever the future brings, we'll be somewhat surprised. We need to plan for the future and we need to anticipate what is likely to come, but we also need to be able to adjust to the future that will come no matter what it is. Recognizing those two dichotomies in our planning will help us to make better plans.

Whatever the future brings, we will need to continue to do what needs to be done to protect our nation and the peace and our way of life. Our strategy for the last 40 years has been fairly constant. It is a strategy of deterrence. We are only trying to maintain the peace by maintaining forces self-evidently capable of guaranteeing that anyone who attacks the United States would not achieve his objectives, either by war or by the threat of war. Our strategy has counted on certain fundamental elements. One is alliances. We have ties with the rest of the world. It seems to me that as we go through time, we will see that our society and our economy become even more inextricably intertwined with the rest of the world. So the alliances continue to have their importance and, if anything, their military importance will increase.

Consistent with this business of alliances is the fact that we will have overseas bases and forward-deployed forces. They are important to the alliances because they lend political cohesion to the alliances by letting people know that the United States is committed to the common defense of certain parts of the world. They also lend military strength to the alliances by having our Armed Forces there. We also count on the strong central reserve of land, air, naval and amphibious forces, both Active and Reserve Component forces, based here in the United States—forces that can go to reinforce those alliances or go elsewhere in the world where our interests are threatened.

How do people in your positions relate to that particular strategy? There is an old Corps of Engineers manual dated 1919 and it defined "forts" as "tactics applied to the earth." I believe that our bases, posts, facilities, harbors, airstrips, and MX silos today are our national strategy converted to reinforced steel rods, concrete, and asphalt. They are a manifestation of what our strategy was and what our strategy is—what it will be and what it can be. At least, that is the linkage to what our strategy can do.

By looking at what our Engineers have done in the past, we can see what our strategy once was. You look at old forts on the beaches of Hawaii, Corregidor, and the Philippines and you will see what the strategy was. Certainly, one can do that with a history book as well. Ed Luttwak wrote a book, *The Grand Strategy of the Roman Empire*. He took a look at a few of the ruins of Rome. Merely by walking through several centuries of Roman ruins— looking at their engineering works, their frontier roads, barracks, fortifications and so forth—Dr. Luttwak was able to deduce Roman strategy throughout the history of the Roman empire.

Our problems are a little more difficult. We don't want to look back into the past to see what the strategy has been. What we want to do is look into the future and see what the strategy should be and what we should do today to carry out that strategy.

There are a number of very practical demands that challenge us in carrying out the management of installations and facilities to support our national strategy. You know what they are but it is probably worth our going through them: The first is to ensure that we have healthy forces in being, including those in our Reserves. We have to take care of those forces. Secondly, we have to be able to support those forces in time of war. And that means rapid mobilization, along with the necessary reception stations, barracks, and training areas.

Those two components are made all the more challenging by the strategy that I outlined earlier—that is, this business of forward-deployed forces. Those forward-deployed forces are our frontline forces today. Their efficiency, their morale and their health are visible signs of the United States' commitment to those alliances and to that strategy—and of our commitment to defend well-forward. If those installations are shoddy, if the overseas barracks are run-down and over-crowded, if the training areas are inadequate, if all those things that make up our installations overseas don't contribute to the perception by both allies and potential foes alike that those installations belong to top-notch fighting forces of the strongest, freest nation in the world, then the credibility of United States power and our commitment to those alliances is on the wane; and the danger of war simply goes up.

Secondly, we have to be able to reinforce those forces whenever needed and we have to be able to go to other places in the world that we may not now really anticipate. I know that last year this conference heard from General Bob Kingston, the Commander in Chief of Central Command, and I am sure that he spent a lot of time emphasizing the facilities problems in carrying out any sort of strategy for securing the peace and our interests in the Middle East and Southwest Asia. Overflight rights, facilities, and bases are key. If you don't have overflight rights and facilities and bases in the area, you don't have any strategy—if you don't have access, you don't have a strategy.

There are a number of realities that we have to wrestle with:

There is the reality of domestic and foreign political considerations. Certainly, we have to operate within our political system. We wouldn't want it any other way. That is what we are here to do. We have to operate within the constraints of our own government's relationships with other countries.

One important point that is often forgotten is that military construction and real property maintenance in the United States has immediate political implications. Every military installation in our own country is in somebody's Congressional district. At the same time, almost 40 percent of our forces overseas have no immediate representatives in the Congress of the United States. Their principal constituency is the men and women in uniform, and those of you here today. And I know that you understand the importance of good facilities for our men and women overseas, and their families. However, it is a genuine difficulty with the Congress. When you look at what happens to the military construction budget, you see what I mean.

I recall traveling from Fort Carson, Colorado, were there were absolutely magnificent new barracks and then going over to Korea to see soldiers in 25-year old Quonset huts—all leaking, no insulation, space heaters, and 25 consecutive years with that kind of winter, all because of a lack of adequate resources and the difficulties in getting Congress to help us. We need to put our minds to work on finding ways to solve those problems.

The problems besetting management of the overseas basing and facilities have other obstacles. Just as our ability to employ forces is preceded by our ability to provide forward bases and access rights and transit authority, getting the bases and access rights and transit authority is preceded by the requisite agreements among the nations involved. Often those negotiations must be done quietly to be effective and sometimes, in this open society of ours, that just isn't very easy to do.

Further, as a part of our coalition strategy, we give needed assistance to our friends and allies so that they can act in their own defense. Sometimes this security assistance is in the terms of sales and loans or grants involving military equipment but many times it is in terms of help with facilities—facilities that can be used by both that nation and our own nation.

I had the good fortune to command the Army troops in Thailand during the last two years of the road building in Thailand. And I remember Congressmen marching out to us and saying, "Why in the world are they building these roads out there? What value can they possibly have for the United States?" What those roads have done for the United States is that the dominos have stopped falling at the Thai border. Prime Minister Prern was here to see our President last week. He and I talked about those roads in northeastern Thailand. He talked about the old northeast district which used to be a hotbed of communism. That used to be where the Thai communist party was so successful. He said there are no longer any communists there, and the people are now tied to the rest of Thailand. He said, ""We have regular commerce. The people up on the long border need fish from the Gulf of Thailand. Now, they send their own groups back down to Bangkok by the road that the United States Army Engineers built." So, our assistance there has been a great contribution to peace and stability in that part of the world.

We are trying to do the same thing in Central America today. So, it is important that this is understood by the people of the United States. We have a very modest construction program underway to help some friends of ours in Central America so that they can defend themselves. They really won't need forces from the United States to do that for them. However, that construction program is criticized inaccurately and widely. No one focuses on the fact that over in Nicaragua the Russians and the Cubans are putting in military construction programs that are many, many times the modest size of the United States construction program in Honduras. But those are the considerations with which we must deal if we look at facilities management and at our strategy.

There is another reality: This is a practical one and it is that the facilities, by their very nature, last a long time. We often hear today that the B-52's that we have are older than their crews, and that the aircraft carrier MIDWAY has been around since the middle of World War II. That is true of many weapons systems. In the case of facilities and facilities planning and how that affects what can be done in the future, the problems are much magnified. For example, the Commanding Officer of Fort Sill, Oklahoma, lives in a house that soldiers built for General Sherman. And that is not unique. The same sort of thing is true throughout the West and the South.

We have to think through this business of what construction will fit the future and what won't fit the future and how we manage that business. We have a great tendency to build buildings, marvelous buildings, that will last forever; and sometimes they shouldn't last forever. Maybe, we shouldn't build them that way because, if they're designed for today's installations and facilities, they won't fit our needs in the future. We might well be better off starting from the ground up. Wonderful barracks that were built 50 years ago are now headquarters buildings—not very efficient headquarters buildings, but they're better than no headquarters buildings at all. Hospitals are a particular planning problem. Almost every single new hospital, no matter how old it is, has got medical equipment sitting around in hallways because the medical equipment designers go faster than the hospital building designers and builders can possibly go. The power department for hospitals—almost every single hospital—is underpowered for today's modern equipment.

We have good, smart people thinking through these problems. I saw one hospital recently that has some smart planning. It has been built so that the add-on capability is ready: the pipes, the electricity, the hydraulics, and so forth go right up to the top floor. The inside building walls are such that they can be adjusted quickly and easily as medical equipment sizes change. All that needs to be added to that hospital is the heating plant and the air conditioning plant and it will be ready for an expanded hospital.

We look around and we see plywood partitions in old German barracks. We've got latrines that are shared in fairly new buildings. There are little signs on the outside that flip over and say "Men" and "Women" because ten years ago we didn't really believe that we'd have both men and women in the same barracks.

Unforeseen organizational changes will upset today's best-designed facilities—changes designed by some soldier, sailor, airman or Marine in green eye-shades in the basement of the Pentagon. He'll ruin the design of the facility that was designed to fit perfectly and efficiently the organization that's on the ground today. So, how we deal with those particular anomalies in the facilities planning that seems to make the just-designed or just-built installations no longer efficient is something that goes beyond your communications between you and the planner. And that's one thing that I want to emphasize to you today.

Certainly, opportunities exist for all sorts of new ideas. On your agenda, I see you asking what can be done. We've got all sorts of generalized pound-foolish operations and I don't have to tell this crowd that. Maintenance seems to be the popular bill-payer. When I was Vice Chief of Staff of the Army, as many of you know, I established the "John W. Vessey Memorial Program" and I would not touch the programs which go below a predetermined line of "irreducible minimums." Service barracks that were built in World War II to last five years lasted over 40 years and were being held together by tape in many places.

When I was Commander of U.N. forces in Korea, Congress was seized with the temporary nature of our forces in Korea and said that we should build only "relocatable barracks." Now, we took that to heart. We took that to heart and we let out a contract for something called "relocatable barracks"—a great design had come along with sandwich walls, aluminum and corrugated paperboard between the aluminum sheets, and put together with glue that didn't hold. The barracks weren't "soldier-proof." One kick by a disgruntled soldier put a hole through the wall. The net result has been that in nine short years we have redone those barracks about three times; and when I was in Korea last November, I witnessed the third modernization of those barracks.

I say these things not to be critical of Engineers because it is not the Engineer's fault; but I say this to illustrate my point: that between ourselves and our civilian masters, we can do some pretty wasteful things. We must strike the right balance for the future, between what the future looks like it is going to be and hedging for the fact the future probably won't be what we expect it to be. Certainly, we have some examples of absolutely outstanding work. One of those is the Pentagon. I marvel at the Pentagon every time I spend a day there. It is a design wonder—probably the most efficient office building in the world, one that can be adjusted to meet tomorrow's conditions. The designers certainly have to get great marks. (I guess maybe they didn't have to put up with inquiries on the environmental impact statement!)

However, in those cases where we were not successful in thinking through the problems, there is waste, at great expense to the citizens of the country. What is worse yet is that we don't have the installations that we need to support the strategy and maintain the peace. So, in the long haul, it is the planning, and it is the strategic planners—the Engineers, the facilities planners, and the constructors—getting together and wrestling through what the future will be like, what is the probability that our view of the future is wrong and how do we make the necessary adjustments today to hedge against that. That's what will save taxpayers' money and will give us the installations to support our strategy in the future. It won't be done by publicity in the newspapers. It can be done only by thorough study and hard work—something I know the Nation can trust you Engineers to do well. Thank you.

Interview with
Sea Power **Magazine**
May 1984

Question: Are you happy with what has been done to give you more sealift?
Answer: I'm happy that we have done what we have done but I want to see more. If there is anything that has happened to change the strategic equation for the United States it is the decline of the American Merchant Marine. It is a sad thing, and it is probably not well understood by the American people. But it has happened. On the other hand, for contingencies short of general war, there are all kinds of ships out there. And someone with a bag of money can hire ships and we can get to places. That's not the sound way for us to be able to do it; but the fact of the matter is that the Defense Department has spent more on sealift recently than it has in all the rest of the time from World War II

to date. But we have to continue to think through how to use modern sealift to get us where we are going.

Extract, Remarks on the 40th ANNIVERSARY
OF THE LIBERATION OF ROME
Rome, Italy
2 June 1984

On behalf of the men and women of the Armed Forces of the United States, I would like to thank President Pertini, Prime Minister Craxi, the people of Italy, especially Mayor Vetere, and the citizens of Rome for your hospitality and for permitting us to celebrate the 40th Anniversary of the Liberation of Rome.

I also want to thank the veterans of the First Special Service Force who worked hard to help sponsor this celebration. Today we pay special tribute to those Canadian and United States soldiers who first reached Rome. That action was made possible by the fighting and support of many thousands of soldiers, airmen and sailors from many countries of the great alliance. Today, we also pay tribute to all members of the alliance—the British, the New Zealanders, the Indians, the French, the Moroccans, the Algerians, the Poles, the Brazilians, the other Canadian and United States Forces. We pay a very special tribute to those Italian patriots who fought for the liberation of their homeland, whether in the partisan forces or the brave men of the reconstructed Italian Army which started with a few battalions from Alpini and Bersaglieri in the bloody fighting at Mignano-Monte Lungo. My own division fought from Salerno to Lago di Como, and I tell you that in the tough fighting south of Bologna we were particularly pleased to have the Legnano Grupe on our flank. And, forty years later, I cannot help but pay tribute to the German soldiers who fought and died—valiantly, but for the wrong cause.

For those of us who had participated in the battles of the autumn of 1943 and the spring of 1944, June 4, 1944, was a very important day. We were helping liberate Rome, the Queen City of Western civilization, the first major capitol to be liberated in World War II. We knew that there would be a lot more difficult fighting ahead, but seeing this beautiful city, beautiful even during the war, and experiencing the warm gratitude of the Italian people was exhilarating—the flowers, the smiles, even a few kisses and an occasional glass of vino were added to the wonder of the day. I must explain that we were not permitted to stop. We were sent directly through the city to attack toward Civitavecchia.

Today, the 4th of June, 1944, looks far more important than it did then. Europe has had 39 years without war. This year we celebrate the 35th anniversary of the North Atlantic Treaty. The world continues to be haunted by the fear of war and aggression, but the free nations of NATO have banded together in a strong alliance to serve the cause of peace. The Federal Republic of Germany is a member of that alliance.

The great NATO alliance threatens no one, but it tells the world that free people will remain strong to defend their freedom. The Soviet Union needs to heed and understand those facts.

I also want to pay a special tribute to all the veterans of the Italian Campaign and their families who have come to this celebration. Many famous names are represented. From my own country—General Clark's son, General Frederick's daughter, Bill Mauldin, the soldier-cartoonist who did much to make the war bearable for those who fought it and understandable for those who didn't—just to name a few.

Special thanks to General Bartolucci and the men and women of the Italian Armed Forces, our staunch allies from Mignano—Monte Lungo to today. It is my fervent prayer that Rome has seen its last war and that the peace you have enjoyed for the last 40 years will be with you forever. Thank you.

**Remarks to the ST. LOUIS REGIONAL
COMMERCE AND GROWTH ASSOCIATION/
AIR FORCE ASSOCIATION LUNCHEON
AND MID-AMERICA BALL
St. Louis, MO
15 June 1984**

Two weeks ago I was in Rome. I was there to help commemorate the Fortieth Anniversary of the Liberation of that queen city of Western civilization. Forty years earlier I had been a minor "bit part" player in that play. At that time, 40 years ago, our outfit had taken some objectives in the Alban Hills. When Rome was liberated, we were sent through Rome. We were told, "Don't stop. Keep moving. Go up Highway One to the north. Your objective is to reach Civitavecchia." So we went through the city very quickly. But we collected a few of the handshakes, a lot of the smiles, a couple of kisses, and a few glasses of wine from the grateful population. And I would say that when I went back there the same girl was there who kissed me when I came through earlier. She said she wished she'd asked for my grandson to return instead of me.

The next day we were all buoyed by the news of the invasion at Normandy. Our outfit had been in combat since November 1942, and we really didn't see any end to the fighting at that particular time. It didn't seem to be in sight. But, in fact, we had really reached the denouement of World War II.

At that time, I hardly realized that what had begun then was the beginning of that great alliance, NATO, which restored the peace a year later and which has kept the peace with liberty and preserved freedom in the West for more years than Europe has known for any other period in modern times. As I stood there for the ceremonies two weeks ago, it occurred to me again that a lot of good had come out of those very difficult battles: a Western security system and a concept which embraces NATO and the free nations of the West was born.

A great transformation was set in motion. It turned comrades-in-arms into partners in peace, and made friends and allies even out of past foes. That strength still exists today and it still preserves the peace. But I become troubled when I sense some slackening of our will to do that, and some views that our common partnership should be dissolved. Now, what I say to you is that the real question is, "Will this nation let that happen? Will we allow ourselves to lose what has kept the peace for so long?"

Some of you will say that an awful lot has changed since I was foxhole-deep in that European real estate 40 years ago. And that is true. The world has changed dramatically. The world has grown smaller, certainly in time, and it has become more inextricably intertwined in its economies. In 1944 there were barely 60 independent nations. Today there are over 170, and we've developed close cultural, religious, moral and political ties with many nations of the world that didn't exist in 1944.

Further, we have become dependent on foreign markets, on overseas resources, and on global lines of communication to keep our own economy going. In 1939, the year that I first enlisted, the United States was a net exporter of oil—not much by today's standards, about 20,000 barrels a day. But 44 years later, we import 3.3 million barrels of oil a day. And if you look at metals, it's an even more complicated story.

As the world has become more complex and intertwined, it appears to have become more dangerous and troubled, too. Since World War II, by some measures, there have been 150 wars with the loss of 25 million lives. If you count a war as something in which regular armed forces are engaged, there are 23 wars going on in the world today. When one looks around the Middle East, at East Asia, at Central America, the world seems to boil.

Other things have changed. Japan and Germany, our former foes, are now our friends and allies. The Soviet Union, an ally in World War II now seems to be an uncompromising adversary with a value system that seems to be the antithesis of our own and of all free people. Yet, we know that it is composed of human beings just like you and me and that there must be some bond that we can find to do away with that adversarial relationship.

We are having a hard time finding it. The Soviets have armed themselves to the teeth, and at a level that is unprecedented in peacetime. The result is a truly one-dimensional great power—a military power. The agriculture of the Soviet Union is less efficient now than it was in time of the Tsars. It is the only principal nation in the world with a life expectancy that is going down. Yet, at the same time, it is a great power; and particularly in the military field, it is a power that we absolutely must recognize.

So, the military picture has changed. In 1941, except for the few valiant forces that were under attack on the 7th of December, the rest of our forces were not engaged and it took us nearly a year to get sizeable combat forces into action. If war starts today with the Soviets, nearly 40 percent of our peacetime forces will be in action immediately if the war is a conventional war. If the war is a nuclear war, it could be minutes before the entire populations of both countries are involved.

Despite all these differences, I believe that there are some fundamental similarities between now and 1944. When you remember the world steering towards war in the 1930s, you can't help but think of the 1938 episode in Munich that sealed the fate of Czechoslovakia. At that time, the British Prime Minister, Mr. Chamberlain, said, "How horribly fantastic and incredible it is that we should be digging trenches or trying on gas masks here because of a quarrel in a faraway country between people of whom we know nothing!" He was speaking of Czechoslovakia. And he said, "I myself am a man of peace to the depths of my soul." He undoubtedly was a man of peace, but Britain got war anyway! Munich was for Britain the culmination of a process, the erosion of national will.

In the 1930s, while our adversaries armed, Britain and America slept. Many in both countries, like many of our own people today, had the idea that defense appropriations were far too high. Now, these weren't stupid or disloyal people but they were wrong—dead wrong. They hadn't learned from H.L. Mencken when he said that, "There is no record in history of a nation that ever gained anything valuable by being unprepared to defend itself." Or what Churchill said to his own people a couple of years earlier that "We can afford what we need for defense. What we cannot afford is to say, 'We can only afford what is easy to provide.'"

Are there parallels today, with the Soviets marching into Afghanistan, with the North Koreans rattling their swords on the Korean Peninsula, with the Cubans, Vietnamese and their other Soviet friends involved on a global scale in a mass of Third World countries? I believe there are.

The people who believe that war can be prevented through unilateral disarmament or wishing away the Soviet nuclear armament are not disloyal or stupid but they are wrong. They are dead wrong.

I want to make it very clear that I don't think we should charge around looking for war. Like Chamberlain, I'm a man of peace and I suspect that every person in here is a person of peace. But, I think the first message for America today is the message that came from our first President, George Washington, when he said, "If we desire to secure peace, it must be known that we are at all times ready for war." That's the first lesson for man today. We've got a great country—with all its warts, it's the freest and greatest and potentially the strongest nation on earth. And it will be so long as its citizens are willing to serve it and protect it. That's our first lesson.

That's our strategy today—preserve the peace. Preserve peace and liberty for ourselves and not just for ourselves but for those who follow us—for our posterity—as those who passed before us preserved it for us.

The second lesson from that war is closely aligned with the first: Effective deterrence means good armed forces. And that requires the support of our nation to provide adequate armed forces. It means good equipment—good equipment to give our people in uniform the edge in battle. And, good armed forces also mean good people. People are the heart of our defenses. It was so in Normandy; it was so in Rome; it was so in Korea; it was so in Vietnam; and it was so in Grenada. I have heard it said that armed forces are like fresh bread. If you want fresh bread, you've got to make it every day. Otherwise you get stale bread. The same is true for the Armed Forces. If you want good military forces, you have to pay attention to them continually.

The members of the Joint Chiefs of Staff understand that point; and, I want to assure you that we work very hard to ensure that our budgets make sense and that the budgets can provide for ready forces today and provide for ready forces in the future.

Speaking of those four colleagues of mine on the Joint Chiefs of Staff, I often read that we engage in a lot of "bickering"; and I want to report to you that we want to keep that myth alive so we schedule bickering on the training schedule. Every weekend we try to assemble on the golf course and we bicker. We usually bicker about who should give putts to whom within the leather. I want to report to these Air Force Association people here that Charlie Gabriel always wants me to give him putts within the leather. But he can't putt that well, so I won't do it.

I would say to you also from my own personal observation that you are fortunate in having four good Service Chiefs; good, loyal, hard-working and intelligent people. It's a great pleasure for me to work with them.

One thing the Joint Chiefs do agree on completely and that is that our strategy starts from a single point. Our nation shares with all free peoples of the world a hope for liberty and justice and a responsibility to prevent war—not just nuclear war, but all war. At the same time, we want to preserve our liberty and make sure that totalitarianism doesn't move on. The United States has a defensive strategy. We want to go about our business in this world of nation-states and conduct that business peacefully. We don't want to be coerced by Soviet power and we don't want our allies or friends coerced by Soviet power. We don't want a war. We don't want a nuclear war or *any* kind of war.

But at the same time we want to be able to pursue our legitimate political, economic, social and cultural objectives in this world and "We the people" don't want to be paralyzed by the fear of war as we go about our business. As I said earlier, we have to make it very clear to the Soviets and any other potential adversaries that we are sufficiently strong so that they can't obtain their objectives by starting a war.

Russ Dougherty sitting down here had a marvelous editorial in the June 1984 issue of Air Force Magazine and I suggest that you read it. Russ said that deterrence is the product of capability, that is the people and the equipment, times the will of the Nation. If we have the will to deter and not the capability, it won't work. The same thing applies the other way around. If we have the people and the equipment but we don't have the will, deterrence won't work either.

All of that is pretty much indicated in the Nation in a day-to-day way by its defense budget. And I'd like to talk for just a minute about the budget and I'd like to talk about one part of it, the strategic nuclear deterrence part of the budget. Strategic nuclear weapons are a subject that has the whole world aboil. I'd like to make a couple of points:

Last year the President's Bipartisan Commission, the so-called Scowcroft Commission, made some very sensible recommendations to the President and to the American people. The President and the Congress and the JCS fully concurred with those recommendations.

The Commission said that we must modernize our strategic nuclear forces to counter the growing power of the Soviets' strategic nuclear forces. At the same time, the Commission said we have to engage in negotiations with the Soviets to try to control nuclear arms and to seek a more stable world and, if possible, to reduce the number of nuclear arms in the world. The modernization of our strategic forces—the PEACEKEEPER missile, the TRIDENT submarine, the B-1 bomber, cruise missiles, and the necessary command and control—is essential, the Commission said. And it is essential now.

Our negotiation strategy with the Soviet Union is tied very closely to the modernization of our forces. Everyone knows these negotiations are at "top dead center" right now. We didn't walk out. The Soviets walked out of those negotiations. However, every once in a while I hear Americans—politicians, news analysts, public figures—talking in a fashion that suggests that they believe that *we* are the ones who walked out of the negotiations. That is not the case.

Why did the Soviets walk out? I don't think we know. We may find out someday. We will probably read some memoirs that come out of the Kremlin some years from now. And, I suspect if we do, we will read that 1983 and 1984 were years in which the Soviet strategy was a 'full court press" to separate the United States from its principal allies in the rest of the world. Those were the negotiating tactics. It was almost like a charade.

It was focused around the modernization of the intermediate-range nuclear missiles in Europe. We have to remember it was the Soviets who upset the balance by deploying some 1200 warheads with their new intermediate-range nuclear forces, the SS-20's. They tried to prevent the Western allies from deploying any to restore that balance. But the alliance held together.

We also have to remember that the Soviets have added about 3500 new, modern intercontinental ballistic missile warheads to their forces since SALT II was signed. We haven't added any. Yesterday, the Senate *by one vote* agreed to produce 21 missiles with the 1985 budget instead of the 40 the Administration asked for. The House earlier agreed to produce 15 with some restrictions on the production. So, the balance will be somewhere between 15 and 21, somewhere between 150 warheads and 210 warheads, in contrast to 3500.

Now, what I want to tell you is that, if the Soviets see us faltering with the PEACEKEEPER or deciding not to build the B-1 or the TRIDENT, they're not going to have any particular reason to come back to the table. We need to keep a steady hand and march ahead with the strategic arms modernization. If they do come back to the table after we have limited our own arms, they will come back with a handful of aces while we are sitting there with deuces and treys. We need to remember that their objective is to control our arms and ours is to control theirs.

We ought to recognize that we will not prevent war by strategic arms negotiations alone. Salvador da Madariaga, the great Spanish philosopher and historian who served for many, many years on the old League of Nations Disarmament Commission, said that the world has the issue of war and peace and disarmament upside down. He said, "Nations don't distrust each other because they are armed, they arm because they distrust each other." The Soviets distrust us and we distrust them. We need to work on that distrust.

But, in the meantime, our business is the business of preventing war. It is like that television ad I see every once in a while about the house burning down. The announcer comes on and says, "When is the worst time to find out that you had the wrong insurance coverage on your house?" Well, the same is true for defense. The worst time to find out your defenses are not any good is after the war starts.

In early 1950, I remember having our cooks in Army mess halls cut fat from the meat so that we could render it into lard and then make soap. We were tearing up newspapers for the troops to use as toilet paper. We were really skimping on defense. And General Bradley, the first officer to hold the job that I now hold, made a speech early in that year about the importance of having enough defenses to prevent war. We *didn't* spend enough and we *didn't* prevent war.

In June of 1950, the Korean War broke out and the defense budget went up by a factor of four; but, worse than that, it went up in a different coin. It went up in blood and we paid for it with the blood of our citizens. And if that's what we want to avoid, we need to do what needs to be done.

So, I say to you, that's our job. We have to make sure our people and our posterity can remain free and secure. If we don't need armed forces or we don't need defense, we shouldn't spend a dime on them. But we do need armed forces and we do need to be prepared for war so that we can preserve the peace. If we do that, I am sure that we will do just exactly that—continue to preserve the peace. Thank you very much.

**Remarks to JOINT STAFF ACTION
OFFICER ORIENTATION PROGRAM
In the Pentagon
Washington, DC
20 June 1984**

Let me just spend a few minutes with you and give you the view from my foxhole. Part of our duty as members of the defense establishment of the United States is to provide security for the United States today and tomorrow—and by "tomorrow" I mean a long way from now: when I'm in my rocking chair and when you are in your rocking chairs. The decisions we make today will have a lot to do about what kind of security the Nation has in those days.

The principal guy under the President in developing the security of the United States is the Secretary of Defense. The more you look at it, the more sweeping those duties of the Secretary seem. He provides the civilian control of the Armed Forces of the United States. He is the President's agent for doing that. He has two staffs. He has a civilian staff that serves him in matters of overall policy on how to deal with the rest of the Federal Government, how to deal with the Legislative Branch of the Government, and how to get help from the industrial and scientific community.

Then he has a military staff. And his military staff is a staff of five. It is composed of the Chairman of the Joint Chiefs of Staff, the Chief of Staff of the Army, the Chief of Naval Operations, the Chief of Staff of the Air Force and the Commandant of the Marine Corps—commonly called the "Joint Chiefs of Staff." The Secretary is forbidden by law from having any other military staff. The law also says that the duties of those five are to be the principal military advisers to the President, the Secretary of Defense and the National Security Council.

Now, that group of five has a staff of its own. It is called the "Joint Staff," and its duties are laid out for them in the law. The Joint Staff is to serve the Joint Chiefs of Staff and through them the Secretary of Defense in developing strategic plans and providing strategic direction for the Armed Forces of the United States, logistics plans to support those strategic plans and the assignment of logistic responsibilities to the Services. With the help of the Joint Staff, the Joint Chiefs review the personnel and material requirements for the Armed Forces, they establish joint training and education systems for the Armed Forces, and they provide representation at the UN Military Committee.

They also provide for the establishment of the strategic commands and for strategic direction to the Armed Forces of the United States through another group of guys, the CINCs of the unified and specified commands. That is the system that provides the strategic direction of the Armed Forces of the United States.

Now, what about the Services? There are duties for the Services, too—the Army, the Navy, the Air Force and the Marine Corps. Those outfits organize, train, equip and support the Armed Forces that are to be fought by the unified and specified commanders.

The Services respond to the Secretary of Defense, too; and they build forces in response to the requirements laid out in the strategic direction that is set out by the Joint Chiefs of Staff and endorsed by the Secretary of Defense. Sometimes that relationship gets cluttered or is not understood. Part of the reason is that there is an understandable, direct and good connection between the Joint Chiefs of Staff and the Services; the members of the Joint Chiefs of Staff also happen to be the uniformed heads of their respective Services, with the exception of the Chairman.

The Joint Chiefs of Staff have two different sets of duties, one as heads of their Services to organize, train, equip and support forces to be fought by the unified and specified commands and the other to come back in from the other side of the house, hang their hats on the peg, put on a different hat, and go in the Tank with the other Chiefs.

You see that there has been a great debate in the newspapers in the last few years about whether or not this body which heads the Services, coupled together with the Chairman, can also do these other tasks as members of the Joint Chiefs of Staff. Some would suggest that because they are so wed to building an Army or a Navy or an Air Force or a Marine Corps that they can't be objective enough to do the other tasks. On the other hand, I would suggest to you it is a very good arrangement. With the Chiefs being in those other chairs, who knows more about the Army, the Navy, the Air Force or the Marine Corps than the uniformed heads of the Services? So, it is my firm belief that they are the right people to be the strategic advisers to the President and the Secretary of Defense.

Now, the Chairman's role in this is a unique role. He has some duties specified in the law. They are fairly simple duties like the duties of the JCS. But by and large, I can summarize all his duties by saying the Chairman is a *servant*. He serves three bodies. He serves the President and the Secretary of Defense, that sort of mythical body called the "National Command Authority"—and, sometimes, the Secretary of Defense delegates duties to the Deputy Secretary of Defense. But his duties as part of the National Command Authority are only delegated when the Secretary is not present.

Then, the Chairman serves another body. He is a servant of the body of which he is a member, the Joint Chiefs of Staff. His service to those two bodies is as a channel of communication principally because the Chairman is the guy who sits with the President and the Secretary of Defense at National Security Council meetings and National Security Planning Group meetings or small security meetings with the President and the Secretary of Defense. He is also the guy who sits in the meetings with the Joint Chiefs of Staff. So, I am a "messenger boy." I carry messages beck and forth and it is important that I carry those messages clearly. It is important that I serve both of those bodies in my relationship with the other body.

The Chairman is also the servant of the third group and that is the Commanders in Chief of the unified and specified commands. He brings their points of view to the JCS. He also takes those views to the Secretary of Defense and the President and into the other fora through which the Secretary of

Defense does his job. For example, the Defense Resources Board is an important forum where decisions are made on allocating resources to build the forces—the Army, the Navy, the Air Force and the Marine Corps. The Chairman's duty is to help make sure that the forces that those CINCs want *get built* by the force builders in the Services.

Those are the duties that I have. You who are members of the Joint Staff or those agencies which serve the Joint Chiefs of Staff—your job is to help me and the other four members of the Joint Chiefs of Staff do their jobs. You who are members of Service staffs are to help the members of the Joint Chiefs of Staff do their other job—that is, build, organize, train, equip and support the forces that are fought by the unified and specified commands. Sometimes, you may help make the strategy for the forces but that is not your primary task. That is the job of the Joint Staff. Are there any questions on that?

Two years ago when I took over this job I made out a "menu" for the JCS and for the CINCs of the unified and specified commands and they endorsed that menu. We have pursued those items with some vigor. I have a fancy chart of that menu here. And I'll go through it with you because it is important that you understand what the JCS are trying to do.

The thing we said that was the number one item on the menu is *war plans* because they drive force requirements. War plans are the one area that we as the Joint Chiefs of Staff and the CINCs are solely responsible for. Nobody else makes the war plans. We can complain about the suppliers of weaponry because weapons are not built to standards. We can squawk about the recruits because the secondary education system doesn't work as well as it ought to. We can grumble about the Congress because Congress doesn't provide enough money. But, if the war plans are wrong, we can point only to ourselves. So, war plans call for particular attention.

What we have done is start out with a unique exercise; we brought the Commanders in Chief of the unified and specified commands in here and I told them they could bring one staff officer. If they had to have slides, they could bring one staff officer to flip the slides for them. But their duty was to explain to the JCS the concept of the operation for their most demanding war plan and we didn't want any staff officer explanations. We wanted the explanations of *the commanders.* Then, we started from there with the idea of doing some things like giving top-down guidance on the way the war plans should work. It is my theory that they should not grow like moss up from the basement but should start with guidance from the top.

The second thing we put on the menu is to provide planning support for the CINCs. The idea behind this is to give "Modern Aids to Planning" to those CINCs of the unified and specified commands. Every Service has an analytical agency; every war college has a war gaming facility; but, there are a lot of CINCs with only yellow foolscap and number two pencils, hand-held calculators and slide rules. Our objective is to harness all this computer horsepower and give it to the warfighters out there making plans.

Some of these other menu items are sort of old hat—such as tying military strategy to the national strategy. That is the duty of the Chiefs.

Another is reviewing the NATO strategy and addressing the changes that take place. Some changes are taking place right this afternoon with the Congress voting on whether or not to mandate a withdrawal of U.S. forces from NATO because some of the NATO nations have very little percent growth in defense budgets.

Another is increasing the influence of the CINCs of the unified and specified commands in the POM and the budgets. We have come a long way with that. In two weeks, the CINCs will be in again to meet with the Secretary of Defense and with all of his advisers on the Defense Resources Board. The Chiefs and the CINCs have made considerable progress in making our views known there. We have examined the cross-Service issues, the things that make the unified and specified commands work. Those issues are primarily command and control and communications, intelligence and mobility plus logistics support. Then there were some of the other things that we agreed should be on the menu: Arms control, JCS organization (which is still an issue which gets some attention), the Unified Command Plan "seams," joint doctrine, and how to handle joint manpower.

We will update that menu here in a few days and have it ready for the CINCs the next time they come in here. We will reaffirm the general direction for the next two years.

Now, what is your job? How do I view your job? Well, you're like me—you are a servant of the two groups, with a similar relationship to the third group. The first group is the Joint Chiefs of Staff, and you help them do those jobs that they are to do. Their principal job, again, is providing military advice to the Secretary of Defense and the President.

When this group of stalwarts of mine assembled two years ago, we talked about military advice. When was military advice good and timely? Through the years the men who were the JCS oscillated between giving advice that was unsolicited or waiting until the Secretary of Defense and the President asked for it. We came to the conclusion that if we were to do our job correctly then we had to give them timely advice. We set a rule for ourselves for timely advice: that was, "Give them advice before they know they need it." And if they get advice before they know they need it, they've gotten timely advice. If they have to ask us for advice on what to do, it is probably already too late and we haven't done our job. So, that's our goal. As staff members of the Joint Staff, your objective is to help us do that. Help us see the world and anticipate what is to happen and give that advice to the Secretary of Defense and the President before they know they need it.

The spread of duties you may have is as wide as the spread of duties on the Staff itself. But what I want to tell you is that whatever you are doing it is important. Some of you may be down there counting money for the exercise budget. You may have done that out in a subordinate command at a far lower level and what you're doing here doesn't seem to be much different except that you're aggregating bigger numbers. What I want to tell you is that *there are no unimportant duties here.*

You are dealing with issues that have risen to the *highest level of military authority in the country.* Some of the issues perhaps could have been solved below, somewhere else. But, the fact of the matter is they're here now and *the fact that they are here makes them important.* Somebody thought they were important enough to get here. They're here. They're ours to solve and *none of them are unimportant.* None of you will perform duties that are any more or less important than the others. The sum total of our effectiveness is what we do as a whole. The more I travel around in a uniform the more I recognize that there is nothing that requires teamwork more than military operations. No other place in which you are requires teamwork more than here.

So, it means understanding the programming and budgeting system. It means understanding the joint planning system. It means understanding who knows what around the Staff and how to get that information and use it for yourself for the problem that you have to solve; and it means how to get along with the other members of the Staff.

There are some qualities that I believe are important, particularly while you are here. You will be dealing with issues that affect the security of the country now and which will affect the security of the country in the future. They are issues that should be dealt with within the fora that are assigned for solving those problems. We don't need to write out our problems on the front page of the *Washington Post* or the *New York Times.* In other words, if you have by proclivity a tendency to chatter to newspaper reporters or in cocktail bars or wherever it happens to be, please see me or the Personnel officer after this formation and we can part friends now. But, I'll tell you that if that is your proclivity and you do it *later,* we will part but we will not part friends.

The second part of that is that you come here wearing Army green, Navy white or blue, Air Force blue, Marine olive drab or civilian clothes and you bring here the expertise that is needed because *you're an expert in your own particular Service.* Oftentimes we hear the issue of, "Well, we need the guys that aren't experts in their Services but experts in joint planning," or something like that. Well, joint planning requires experts from the Army, the Navy, the Air Force and the Marine Corps. Those are the only people who can do the jobs here correctly. And it requires them to work together toward the common goal. This means that you come here as an Army officer, as a Naval officer, or whatever it is; but, you're not working for the Army or the Navy. You're working for the JCS to produce plans that provide for the security of the United States.

You need to put a little "purple" in your green or your white or your olive drab or whatever it happens to be in your addressal of problems. When you operate, you are expected to be an expert in all and you must learn that while you are here.

Not only is there no unimportant work, there is also more than enough work for everybody to do and we are not inhibited by a lack of room for improvement. We have plenty of room for improvement in whatever we do, so there is a great opportunity for you guys to make a great contribution to the country today and in the future. I kiddingly tell the guys up in my office "We'll work half days on Sunday—about 6 to 6. The rest of the time you will put in a full day." But, I say that to *you* for a purpose because you will have those kinds of days as well. We had a session over the weekend when I know one fellow had to miss the surprise birthday party he had planned for his wife. He had no choice because he was the expert in this particular field. The President needed an answer.

On the other hand, there are times when there may be some slack time in your particular field and I don't want you sitting around here or standing around waiting for somebody to issue orders because somebody three levels up is still sitting there playing golf on the carpet in his office. Go home because tomorrow you may not have the opportunity.

Once again, welcome to the staff. It's the highest military staff in the land. So, do good work. Thank you.

Remarks to the Combined 1984
Graduating Classes of the Naval War College
US Naval War College Campus
Newport, RI
21 June 1984

A Concept of Service

You finish the War College here in its Centennial Year. It's an exciting time. It's an exciting time at the War College and it's an exciting time in the world. In fact, some might say it's a scary time in the world—war in the Persian Gulf with the danger of that war spreading to interrupt the flow of oil to the Western economies, war in Afghanistan, war in Kampuchea, trouble on the China-Vietnam border, and wars and rumors of wars in this hemisphere almost next door in Central America. The Soviets have left the arms control talks. The Middle East peace efforts seem to be stalled at "top dead center."

For those of you in the Armed Forces of the United States, you leave here at an exciting time from the perspective of your profession. There is more going on in the development of tactical concepts, in equipment modernization, in innovative training, and in genuine cooperation among our Armed Forces than I've seen in the 45 years I've been in uniform. We see cooperation among the four Services on a scale not seen before. You've read of the recent Army-Air Force announcements about battlefield collaboration and the work between the Navy and the Air Force on collateral maritime missions. For you, what makes it even more exciting is the fact that we, as a nation and as Armed Forces, are absolutely uninhibited by lack of room for improvement. There is a lot of good and very important work for you to do out there.

Now, you've had a long course here. You culminated it with a look at strategy. You've gone through tactics and techniques and doctrine and things of that nature; and I realize that my job title is one that calls for me to lead that body which is responsible for providing the strategic direction for the Armed Forces of the United States. But I'm not going to talk to you about strategy today or about tactics or techniques or doctrine or anything else. I want to talk to you about *you* and about the institutions you serve, the Armed Forces of the United States. Now, I realize that I'm talking to officers from other nations and I think you'll see that what I have to say perhaps fits the concepts of your nations. I realize I'm talking to some civilian graduates of the College and I think that you'll see that perhaps these same general concepts apply to you—if not exactly, then at least generally.

You military people have chosen to serve the Nation through service in the Armed Forces. The key word is "service." You serve *in* the Army, Navy, Air Force, Marine Corps, or Coast Guard. You don't work for them.

The reason for your service is because "We the People" agreed to provide for our common defense. You serve the people, and you do it best by helping preserve the peace by preparing for war. The people of this Nation need to have confidence that you do not promote war. You don't advocate war, but war is in fact your *business* and *you are ready for it.*

In April I was in Greece. When I was in Athens, I went to the Acropolis; and while there I couldn't help but think of that marvelous dialogue that Plato relates in the "Second Book" of the *Republic* wherein he has Glaucon and Socrates talking about the attributes of the armed forces of the day, which Plato called the "Guardians"—the Guardians of the city. At one point in the dialogue, Plato has Socrates saying, "Nothing can be more important than that the work of the Guardians should be well done." He said, "If shoemakers become inferior and claim to be what they are not, the state is not in peril; but if the Guardians of our city only appear to be Guardians and are *not* Guardians, you surely see that they utterly destroy the city."

Socrates and Glaucon go on to describe desirable attributes for the Guardians. They said they should be "quick to see, swift to overtake the enemy, and strong." Socrates adds that they should be "brave" and that their strength is spiritual as well as physical. Then they go on to decide that "...one man cannot practice many arts, and that war is an art and must be studied and practiced. And Socrates adds that "The higher the duties of the Guardian, the more time and skill and art and application will be needed by him."

Socrates and Glaucon conclude their description of the Guardians by recognizing, "They ought to be dangerous to their enemies but gentle to their friends," and by "their friends," they mean the citizens of the Republic. Then, they go on to wonder if it's possible to find these conflicting natures in a single person.

Through the years, most civilized countries have wrestled with the same questions about their armed forces: How to have warriors with the necessary skill and ferocity in times of war and not have them be a menace to the society in times of peace. Our Forefathers in this great Nation were very concerned about those issues. The product of their concern is the relationship that exists today between our society and its warriors. That relationship was founded in the *Declaration of Independence* and in the *Constitution.*

The Nation has always been skeptical of military power—witness Ben Franklin's brilliant but unsuccessful pamphlet, "Plain Talk," asking his fellow colonists in 1747 to do more in their own self defense, and Thomas Jefferson's initial opposition to a Navy. And, in 1784, the Continental Congress declared that standing armies in peace were inconsistent with the principles of the Republic. The Congress reduced the Continental Army to about a hundred officers and men and then they stationed them as far away from civilization as they possibly could. As some of you know, we still do that today.

Later, at the Constitutional Convention, one delegate proposed that the *Constitution* prohibit the Army from ever being larger than five thousand men. Now, George Washington was also a delegate to the Convention and it's reported that he said, "That's fine—as long as we have another provision in the *Constitution* that no enemy will be permitted to attack the Nation with more than three thousand men."

That skepticism was later developed in the *Federalist Papers*, and it all relates to why our military, springing from the society it serves and is sworn to defend, embodies the principles that govern the society. We, the military, are a part of "We the *people.*" That is why our military forces have never produced a "man on horseback"; why the military forces have not been involved in the political affairs of the Nation; and why they've not strayed from the narrow path of defending the *Constitution* as it was originally intended—that is, protecting the society and not policing the society.

You, the officers, the men and women of the Armed Forces of today, are the Nation's Guardians, Guardians of today. You're the warrior class of the United States in the 1980s and 1990s. You have chosen to give up some of the benefits of your own personal liberty so that the citizens of the Nation may enjoy those benefits in full. You have chosen to serve the Nation; but, it's also important that you recognize that the Nation has chosen you to serve. That's a unique relationship. As with Socrates' Guardians, your higher duties will require more of your time, skill, art and application. And that's the reason for your attendance here at the Naval War College. As with the Guardians of Plato's *Republic, nothing* is more important than that your work be well done.

As you go on to your assignments, your skill and your concept of service and your values and your loyalties to the Nation and to your Service will carry you through the years ahead. The skills you learned here, the issues that were exposed, are all important; and you need to develop them and hone them through the years ahead. But you also need to continue to hone the concept of service. The concept of selfless service is essential for the Armed Forces as an institution; it is essential for you as members of the Guardian class; and it is essential for the security of the Nation.

You don't choose the wars you fight or the places you serve, whether it's fighting a war or preserving the peace. You don't go home until the job's done. And, in doing the job, you may well have to put life and limb at risk. Sir John Hackett called it the military's "unlimited liability contract." That's a good name for it. Many years ago a great sailor, Lord Nelson, said, "Duty is the great business of a sea-officer; all private considerations must give way to it, however painful it may be." Petty considerations just don't apply.

The ultimate test for the Armed Forces is the survival of the Nation; but the service of every sailor, soldier, airman, Marine or Coast Guardsman is tested in less awesome ways every day. It is the sum of the performance of all its members that defines the success of the Armed Forces. Each member of our military forces is accountable for his or her compliance with orders under law; but for the Guardian, compliance with orders alone is not enough. The security of the Nation requires that you comply with orders and laws and regulations but it also requires that you comply with the unique sense of service to your fellow Guardians, the fellow members of your class. Matt Dillon used to say on *Gunsmoke*, "it's a chancy job and a little lonely."

There are no degrees of importance in the service you perform. Some of you will go from here to command ships and squadrons; others will be working in logistic outfits supplying weapons and equipment or doing research and development. Some of you will be buried in the anonymity of staff work. Some of you will go to faraway places that your mother-in-law won't be able to find on the map.

One thing that I want to emphasize to you is that whatever the duty, it is important. Under the code of the Guardians, there is no unimportant duty. Under that code, the sailor who died in insignificant sorties against pirates some place was as important as the crewmen who saved the remnants of the ill-fated Greeley expedition on the Arctic ice a hundred years ago today, or as important as those Rangers who scaled Pointe du Hoc at Normandy 40 years ago, a couple of weeks past, or as important as the naval officers who directed the gunfire to support that operation.

There is no service that is more important than the other in our scheme of Armed Services and there is no duty that's more important than the other under the code of the Guardian. Once in a while we aviators like to think that when we're up in the air—free—that we have mastery over all. How many times have you sat on the ramp, waiting for a maintenance man to show up when the airplane was broken? You were absolutely unable to move until that maintenance man showed up.

We, the fighters, sometimes think it all belongs to us. But, when we're wounded and picked up by some obscure medic to ease our pain, then we realize that we are no more important than he is.

The fighter pilots often think that recce guys don't do anything important. Yet, when you read the history of the battle of the Coral Sea, you will see that the Japanese lost the battle because a recce pilot didn't do his duty correctly and they probably lost the war because of that. The fighter pilot who was picked up out of the jungle or out of the water by an old helicopter pilot knows that his duty is not more important than the other fellow's duty.

Some three weeks ago, I was in Italy for the 40th Anniversary of the Liberations of Rome—visiting some of the battlefields of my youth. At the ceremonies, I think I was the last of the World War II veterans on active duty; but I want to tell you I was only a drummer boy. A young television reporter cornered me and asked me if I wasn't disappointed about what had happened 40 years ago when Rome was liberated and then overshadowed by the D-Day events in Normandy a couple of days later. He asked me if I wasn't disappointed to have participated in great battles which some historians later had characterized as unimportant? And I told him that if he wasn't a member of the warrior class, if he wasn't a Guardian, he wouldn't understand the answer so there was no point in my telling him.

On the previous Monday, on Memorial Day, my present squad, the Joint Chiefs of Staff, fell in; and marched in step the six miles from the Capital to the Tomb of the Unknown Soldier for the burial of the Vietnam Unknown. We did that as sort of a sign to all present and future members of the Guardians, a confirmation of our belief in the code. That is that there are no unimportant duties, that whoever has fallen serving his country, wherever he is, even if he is unknown, has died performing important duty.

Now speaking of those JCS, sometimes you may hear about JCS "bickering." I want you to know that we do bicker. We have it on the training schedule—it's a myth that has gone on for years so we schedule them. We bicker on the golf course every weekend and we bicker about whether or not we should give putts within the leather. And the Chief of Naval Operations can't putt that well so we won't give him those putts.

But I want to emphasize to you that whatever the tasks assigned, they are all important. None can be left undone without peril to the Nation. Twenty years or so from now, one of you, by the Grace of God and through the confidence of your fellow members of the Guardian Class, may be serving as Chief of Naval Operations or as Chairman of the Joint Chiefs of Staff. For whomever that is, I want to tell you today it's important for you to recognize your service is no more important than that of your classmates here who will not have risen to such rank.

Inseparable from the concept of service is the concept of integrity. The citizens of this great nation place great trust in their military services. They will continue to judge us by stricter rules that they apply to themselves. And they *should* do that because, ultimately, their security rests with us and the way we perform our duties. The people of this Nation have entrusted their Armed Forces with the most awesome weapons the world has ever seen, but they have also placed the lives of their sons and daughters who serve and the safety of their own families for now and in the future in the hands of the Armed Forces.

Don't confuse integrity with infallibility. There's a great tendency to do that. As Gary Cooper said in *High Noon*, you should "aim to be high-regarded"; but you should remember that you are human and fallible. Those who serve with you and under you are also human and fallible. Those who will lead you are also human and fallible. The code of the Guardian has room for fallibility. Certainly, the higher up the flagpole you go, the more of your fallible backside will show. There is room for that; but, there is *no room* for a lack of integrity or for those who place self before duty or self before comrades or self before country. Careerism is the *one great sin*, and it has no place among you.

Now, you may sit there and say, "Well, that's pretty well for you to say that when you're high on the lofty perch as Chairman of the Joint Chiefs of Staff but we all want to get ahead." And I know you want to get ahead. I understand that. I applaud it. But if you get there over the bodies of careers and your comrades, you have served your nation poorly and you have violated the code of the Guardian.

There won't be any tribunal to judge your actions at the height of battle; there are only the hopes of the citizenry who are relying upon your integrity and skill. They may well criticize you later amid the relative calm of victory or defeat. But, there is a crucial moment in crisis or battle when those you lead and the citizens of the Nation can only trust that you are doing what is right. And you develop that concept through integrity.

There is a marvelous passage in the last pages of Field Marshal Montgomery's book. He said, "But there are times in war when men must do hazardous jobs, and when success and the Nation's fate depend upon the courage, determination and tenacity of officers and men. When those who set duty before self give of themselves to see the task committed to them through to its completion, they win the day and the highest honor that mortal man can give."

To the international students here today, let me say, "Thank you for attending." I hope that your attendance here was as valuable for you as it was for us. I'm sure that the United States students and the staff and faculty have enjoyed your company and profited from your presence. It is my firm belief that nurturing contacts among the military forces of the nations of the world will help reduce the risk of war.

I'd like to say just a word to the families here. Your husbands or wives, as the case may be, have reached a point in their careers that is very important to them and it's important to you obviously. It is also important to the institutions they serve and important to the Nation. They needed your support as they went through this school and they need your support now as they go on to new duties. I realize that lecture is not necessary for you families because if you hadn't supported them, they probably wouldn't be here in the first place.

But I just want to tell you that I acknowledge that the family serves as surely as does the member of the family who wears the uniform, and I acknowledge your great importance to the military community. So, as you leave here tomorrow, know that you have my thanks and the thanks of the Joint Chiefs of Staff and best wishes for the exciting days ahead.

In the liturgy for morning prayer in the *Lutheran Book of Worship*, there is a prayer which is a good prayer for the Guardians and their families. It goes like this:

"Lord God, You have called Your servants to ventures of which we cannot see the ending, by paths as yet untrodden, through perils unknown. Give us faith to go out with good courage, not knowing where we go , but only that Your hand is leading us and Your love is supporting us."

I want you to know that that's my prayer for you and I give you my congratulations. Best wishes to all of you. It's been a pleasure to be here.

Interview in EURONET
By Harry Ellis, USIA
Washington, DC
27 June 1984

I want to say that I'm a member of the largest peace-marching group in the world and that's the NATO military forces—5 million strong, all in uniform, marching for peace. I think that we in the West need to understand that's what we're doing—we're preventing war and keeping the peace.

Remarks at the
SYMPOSIUM OF THE AMERICAN
ACADEMY OF ACHIEVEMENT
Minneapolis, MN
7 July 1984

Thank you, Spence. President and Mrs. Carter, friends, and guests. It is a delight to be here again with the Academy. This is a talented group of young people and I want to congratulate Bryan and Wayne for conducting this symposium in Minnesota this year. Some people think I am Chairman of the Joint Chiefs of Staff. I'm actually a secret agent for the Minnesota Tourist Bureau. I have just bottled up about five cases of mason jars full of this Minnesota air and weather and I am going to take it back to Washington and sell it.

You have come here as a talented, gifted group of young people and I want to leave you with one message: that you are certainly talented—some would say privileged—but I say you're also *obligated.* In this marvelous city of Minneapolis, just a couple of blocks away, is the City Auditorium. It is a marvelous old building and if you go over there and look up on the corner of the building, you will see a sign. It says, "Participation in the rights of citizenship assumes participation in the duties of citizenship." That's your obligation.

Mr. Pickens told you today, "Preserve the system that allows this country to be great, that allows people to do what they want to do." Dr. DeBakery at noon told us, "Strive for excellence in education." It is important that all Americans, all people in a democracy, have an opportunity for a good education. Certainly, those are some of the duties of citizenship.

I want to leave you with a couple of thoughts. First, 45 years in the uniform of the United States has taught me that there is no unimportant work. Last month we celebrated the fortieth anniversary of the landing at Normandy. General Bernard Rogers represented me at the celebrations there. I went instead to Rome to the commemoration of the battle that I participated in 40 years ago at the liberation of Rome. And I couldn't help but recall the sacrifices that had been made by many, very talented young people *just like you* in order to take on those particular tasks. Through the years the fact that there is no unimportant work comes home to me more and more. We aviators think we're great when we're flying and soaring through the air; but, if the mechanic hasn't done his work, the airplane won't work and we won't get off the ground. So, his work is just as important as ours. The general may think he has made a wonderful battle plan but if those Rangers who scaled the cliffs at Pointe du Hoc at Normandy had not succeeded, the battle plan would have been for nothing.

So, there is no unimportant work. In whatever you do, to strive for excellence in that work is absolutely key.

I'd like to leave with you a thought about this great country of ours. I read something the other day you might be interested in because it says that "Our youth love luxury. They have bad manners and contempt for authority. They show disrespect for their elders and they love to chatter. They contradict their parents and gobble up their food and tyrannize their parents...." Socrates wrote that, over two thousand years ago! And I suspect that someone in every age has written something like that and we can probably read it in tonight's newspapers if we look.

This country is a country whose pronoun is "we" not "they." Too often I hear the ubiquitous saying that "They did it"; "They are responsible for the tyranny of the people"; "They are responsible for government debts"; "They are responsible for the arms race"; "They are responsible for the danger of war." But for this country, the pronoun is "we." "We the People of the United States in order to form a more perfect Union." "We hold these truths to be self-evident that all men are created equal." "We pledge our lives, our fortunes and our sacred honor" so "we" can do whatever "we" want to do. Whatever is done in or by this country, "we" will have charge—not *"they,"* but *"we."* So, it is important that each of us accept our responsibilities and our obligations, not only to ourselves and our families but to our community, our country and the world at large.

Now, I have to put in one last plug and that is for an opportunity to *serve*. George Washington said that "If we want peace, let it be at all times be known that we are ready for war." The Armed Forces of the United States help protect the Nation. They are only a small part of the protection but they're an important part. And for those of you who would like to serve the Nation in whatever capacity, the Armed Forces are a great place to serve. If you want to be a rich man, I would tell you that if you rise to the top and get my job—the top of the Armed Forces of the United States—and live a thousand years—after all that salary for a thousand years, you won't make as much money as many stockbrokers do on one stock deal.

Or, if you don't want to live that long, if you live 120 years, you can make as much money as he did on the tender of stock. But if you want to have some fun and want to serve your country, it's a good place to serve. But, as in the stock market, it's not the place for everybody; but give it an opportunity.

Congratulations on your selection. I wish you all the best from the Armed Forces of the United States and from our State of Minnesota.

**Remarks to the 8th ANNUAL
PLANNERS CONFERENCE
At the Armed Forces Staff College
Norfolk, VA
12 July 1984**

Thank you, it's nice to be here. I thought I would be a little early, but I was called down to the Omni Hotel by the manager. He wanted to know if I could do something to change the theme for the conference; he thought it was "Bop 'til you drop."

It's good to be here with you; and on behalf of the Joint Chiefs of Staff, I want to thank you for your hard work. I haven't come down here to tell you how to solve the problems. If I knew how to solve the problems, we wouldn't have this conference. We'd get them solved and get on with it. What I want to do is tell you how important your work is in getting on with the problems that you have to solve.

The Joint Chiefs of Staff is a unique body. I constantly read in the newspapers that we engage in inter-Service "bickering;" and I want you to know that, in a certain sense, we probably do. In fact, we're so convinced that that myth needs to be maintained that we schedule inter-Service bickering on the training schedule. The way we do it is we meet every weekend for a game of golf and we bicker about who should give putts to whom. It usually winds up that the Chief of Naval Operations and the Chief of Staff of thc Air Force think I should give them "putts within the leather;" but, neither of them can putt that well and I won't do it. So, we bicker.

After two years as Chairman of the Joint Chiefs of Staff, I've come to the conclusion that it's not inter-Service bickering; it's just understanding how to explain things. There's one thing on which the Joint Chiefs of Staff agreed unanimously, and that is that the duties laid out in the law under Section 141 of Title 10 of the U.S. Code for the Joint Chiefs are the right duties. And some of those duties tie in very closely to what you're doing. So, I'd like to just read four of them:

—The first is to prepare strategic plans and provide the strategic direction for the Armed Forces of the United States.

—Then, to prepare joint logistics plans and assign logistics responsibilities to the Services in accordance with those plans.

—To establish unified commands in strategic areas.

—And then to review the material and personnel requirements of the Armed Forces in accordance with those strategic and logistics plans.

Now, there are a few other duties laid out for the Joint Chiefs, but those are the major ones. You can see that the key to the Joint Chiefs carrying out their duties is war planning. Some of you probably heard me say that what's wrong with the war planning system is that too many of the plans grow like moss in the basement of headquarters. They're kept in the dark and they're not exposed to the light of day.

I want to tell you that, when I took this job, the Chiefs and the CINCs and I sat down and said, "What are our priorities? What is the menu of things that we need to do?" And we concluded among us, with no differences of opinion, that the first priority is the war planning—making good war plans. We recognized that we could blame the parents, perhaps, if the young people coming into the Armed Forces lacked discipline; we could blame the educators if the young people coming into the Armed Forces couldn't add and subtract and use the English language; we could blame defense contractors if the material didn't work well, and we could blame the Congress if the budgets weren't quite as good as they ought to be. But, the fact of the matter is that if the war plans were wrong, there is only one place the finger pointed, and that was at us. So, we concluded that we needed to put in every effort that we could to have sensible war plans and to have all those knots tied together that make effective war plans in support of the strategy of the Nation.

Our strategy is a deterrent strategy, one that calls for preventing war. That is why when people look at what we do in peacetime sometimes they say, "Well, it's not exactly the way we would want to fight." That's right; it isn't. Yet, at the same time the essence of deterrence is the clear understanding by your potential enemies that if they start fighting with you they're going to get their clock cleaned.

Our global strategy is a coalition strategy, one that calls for the integration of our efforts with those of our allies. There will be no "U.S.-only" global war anywhere. It will involve a wide range of alliances.

To buttress our coalition strategy we have forces forward-deployed in a number of places, but principally in East Asia and in Europe. We keep this basis of forward-deployed forces for two reasons: One is to provide peacetime military strength to our alliances so that our potential enemies can look at those forces and see that our alliances are militarily healthy; and the other is to uphold the political health of the alliances. Both of these are important; and *neither is more or less important than the other.* You can see that in what's happened in the last couple years with the negotiations with the Soviet Union on nuclear weapons. The Soviet Union has spent its time trying to separate us from our allies. Its goal has not been to defeat us militarily; its goal has been to defeat us *politically* in the arena of world opinion and doing so by separating us from our allies.

Now, our system of global command is understood by you, I'm sure. We have a global system of unified command under the CINCs that the law lays out for the command of United States forces. But overlaid on top of that is the system of allied command. And in many cases, our own unified commanders also double as allied commanders. I hate words that end in "ize", but this one is used so often that I have to use it: "rationalize" our own national military plans with the alliance plans is a very important function for us and for our CINCs.

Each of those CINCs out there is unique. Each has a unique set of allies, a unique chunk of geography for the geographic CINCs, a unique facet of the potential threat that faces us, unique command and control problems, and, by and large, unique command arrangements in the range of how many hats he wears. So, it is important as we look at our planning system that we understand that uniqueness.

The dual-hatted command relationships for our major war-fighting commands calls for discipline and efficiency in our armed forces; but, principally, discipline and efficiency in our planning system. The CINCs' missions that have been given them call for them to have an understanding of the concept of the operation under which they themselves will fight and under which the Nation will fight as a nation.

There are some challenges that each CINC faces:

The first challenge is ensuring that the Services are integrated properly, that he gets the most out of the forces provided him; that he has sustainment and lift capabilities to carry out his war plans; that he recognizes our strategy calls for rather small forces for the size of the commitments we have; and that we will not be able to do everything at one time.

The key elements of our strategy are, first, extraordinarily good intelligence. We sit around and squawk about the intelligence being poor, but the fact of the matter is we have intelligence capabilities far beyond anything anybody ever dreamed of a few years ago. Distributed information systems permit us to make small unit commanders wiser than larger unit commanders were a few years ago. That first element is coupled with a central reserve, a strong central reserve of reasonably ready forces. I use the words "reasonably ready" because it is important that we understand that they will never be more than reasonably ready. We will have to bust their tails to make them reasonably ready, and it doesn't make sense to have them any more than reasonably ready because *the readiness that we buy for today that can't be carried over to tomorrow is the cost of peace for today.* So, when the clock strikes midnight tonight, if there is no war today, we want to be able to carry over as much of that readiness as we possibly can until tomorrow.

We plan for the "big wars." We spend most of our time planning for the big wars. We sort of operate under the philosophy that the "small wars" are lesser-included conflicts of the big wars; and if we can take care of the big wars, we can handle the small wars. Now, what I would tell you is that in one sense that's wise; and, in another sense, it is risky. Not counting the Vietnam War, the United States since the end of World War II has committed its military forces in over 215 different instances short of major war. And most of them have been in deterrent efforts; and, some have been in shooting situations. So, that means that our planning system has to be able to adjust to that.

Flexibility is the key note. Many of you know there's a very fine line between flexibility and weakness; and we certainly don't want to build a planning system that's so flexible that it's absolutely "limp" and unable to do anything. On the other hand, it is unwise to build a planning system so rigid that it cannot adjust to the tomorrow which comes over the horizon. If there's anything which history tells us it is that the assumptions we put into our plans will not be exactly right. They simply will not fit the tomorrow that comes over the horizon. Our job is to have a planning system that recognizes that fact and that uses modern technology and the wisdom we have to adapt to the tomorrow which does come over the horizon and adjust to the tomorrow which does come over the horizon and adjust our war plans quickly to fit whatever situation occurs.

This brings us to the heart of what you people will face as you develop Joint Operations Planning and Execution System (JOPES) or the follow-on planning system: *How much rigidity, how much flexibility, and how much refinement?* It has been my firm belief, through the years, that we have spent entirely too much time adjusting the war plans for precision inside the "probable error" of the plans themselves. And it has driven all sorts of strange things. We have seen changes in the force structure being driven by changes in the war plans.

If you want to see the effect of the war plans, march out to some of the Combat Service Support units in the Reserves of any of the Services—but look more particularly at the Reserves of the Army because of the broader nature of their responsibilities. You will find officers who have changed branches of service four or five times in the space of 25 years because somebody has changed the war plan. That change has driven the change in the force structure that has driven the unit to change its designation from Quartermaster to Engineer, or whatever it happens to be. The fact of the matter is that the change in the war plan was probably miniscule but the changes that it drove were broad changes in the case of those particular units—sort of like the guy with his hand on the whip, you know: you make a little shift at the handle of the whip and there's a change out there on the tip of the whip that is accelerated thousands of times.

So, it is an issue with which we must grapple: How often to change the war plan? How much good is brought about by changing the war plan for refinement?

Some changes are absolutely inevitable; they must be made. We're modernizing the force. It doesn't make sense to have war plans for yesterday's force. At the same time, it probably doesn't make a lot of sense to have war plans for tomorrow's force that will never be reached. So, the degree of precision in our planning is something with which we must grapple.

A bad plan is one that can't be altered—one that can't be altered to fit the situation. The purpose of our armed forces is to be ready to fight and having *good plans* will ensure that we are ready to fight or be able to execute good plans. As Clausewitz said, "Everything in war is simple but the simplest thing is difficult." And the difficulties accumulate and, in the end, produce that "friction" of war. This notion of "friction" certainly comes to us in the words of that great American philosopher, Murphy, who said, "If anything can be screwed up, it will be screwed up." That's what can happen in the case of our war plans.

The issue of discipline in the planning system—flexibility in the planning system—and the issue of how much effort goes into the process of planning are the issues with which we have to deal. This is particularly true in making refinements now with automated planning and information systems JOPS, JDS, and then into JOPES and WIS and how we get from one to the other, and in the process keep plans that are effective and permit us to make those changes and at the same time build toward the goals that we want. Effective planning rests on the understanding that we know what we're trying to do in the first place.

Planning to do what? When the Joint Chiefs undertook this task of improving the planning system, the first thing we did was ask each of the CINCs to come in and brief his concept of operation to the Joint Chiefs. And we said, "We don't want any staff officers. You may bring a staff officer to change the slides if you want to, but you can have no staff officer in the room. And you must explain *your* concept of the operation to the Joint Chiefs so they can understand it." And then we could go on to ask ourselves what made sense about the plan and what did not.

Now, that may sound like a simple thing to you. But I want to tell you that it is the *first* time that that's happened. And it was perhaps the most useful exercise that the JCS have gone through in the time that I have been Chairman. It made us realize that we have a number of very, very good plans. Yet, we have some clear disconnects in the plans that we have. We set about fixing those disconnects.

It is reminiscent of when Churchill was in Parliament, back sometime before World War I. The Parliament received word that the telegraph cable to South Africa was laid. There was a great cheering in the Parliament and shouting and clapping and so forth and finally when all this had stopped, Churchill rose and said, "Now what shall we *say* to the Africans?"

This is really the essence of what it is we're trying to do in refining our planning system. We need to use modern technology to help us. We have begun a program we call "Modern Aids to Planning." It is a recognition that while each of the Services and each of the War Colleges and many of the Staff Colleges have absolutely remarkable, computer-driven wargaming simulation capabilities, many of the CINCs are out there with yellow foolscap, pencils, and hand-held calculators trying to make their war plans. The object of the exercise is to find a way to harness the planning potential of the entire Armed Services and make it available to the people who are going to make the *real* war plans, the CINCs of the unified and specified commands, and who are also the people who are going to execute whatever war plan is adjusted to meet the tomorrow that comes over the horizon—those same CINCs of the unified and specified commands.

From a Letter to the Veterans of the
Second Polish Corps on the
Fortieth Anniversary of the Victory at
Monte Cassino, Italy
July, 1984

On the occasion of the Fortieth Anniversary of the victory at Monte Cassino, I am happy to join with my fellow veterans of the Italian Campaign to reflect on what was achieved and to commemorate the heroism and the memory of our comrades in arms.

I wish to extend my special greetings to the brave veterans of the Second Polish Corps. It was a proud outfit whose reputation is best summed up by then Fifth Army Commander, General Mark Clark. He hailed the Corps as the "... splendid fighting outfit ... which achieved what the rest of us had failed to do, to take Cassino."

But, it was a victory for us all, shared in by every nation and by every Service which contributed to the final victory. It is both a source of pride and a tribute to what the free peoples of the world can do together in pursuit of peace and freedom.

We live in a world of heightened tensions that pose great threats to world peace. Whatever demands we face in the future, the achievements during those tough days in World War II will continue to serve as an example to the men and women in our armed forces today as they go about their dangerous tasks of deterring war and safeguarding the peace.

Remarks at a Dinner in Honor of General El Orabi
Chief of Staff of the Armed Forces of the Arab Republic of Egypt
Quarters 6, the Chairman's House
Fort Myer, Virginia
9 August 1984

General El Orabi,

As the American military people here tonight know, I have only three speeches: one is on tank maintenance, one is on helicopter maintenance, and the third is on re-enlistment. Yet, I won't give any of those tonight.

We are very pleased to have you here in the Chairman's House. This house has an interesting history. The first three Chairmen of the Joint Chiefs of Staff lived in the respective houses of the Service Chiefs. But when General Lemnitzer became the Chairman of the Joint Chiefs of Staff, a former military man was President of our country, President Eisenhower. He himself had moved into the house just down the street from here when he was the Chief of Staff of our Army.

So, when General Lemnitzer reported in as the Chairman, the President called him to the White House and said, "What house are you living in?" He said, "Sir, I am living in my old quarters on Fort Myer, Quarters One." And the President said, "You can't live there. That house belongs to the Chief of Staff of the Army." And, so, Gen Lemnitzer didn't know what to say. He said, "But..."; and the President said, "You have one week to choose the new house for the Chairman of the Joint Chiefs of Staff. You are to engage no staff officers and you are not to talk to the Secretary of Defense. In one week you will choose the house and come back here and tell me which house it is."

So, Lemnitzer told me he didn't know what to do. He walked down the street from his quarters as Chief of Staff, and stood in front of this house. He looked out and saw the best view of Washington from the front porch and said, "This is the house." So, he went to President Eisenhower. He said, "I have chosen the house." He and the President then drew the plans to make this house—which at the time was a house in which the families of two officers lived—into the Chairman's House. And so it is today.

It is not the Vessey house—it is not our house—but it is the Chairman's House; and we are very pleased to have you here. For the rest of you here, welcome to Quarters Six. We welcome you to this dinner to honor General and Mrs. El Orabi. They have been in the country here now for a week, having visited Air Force installations at Nellis Air Force Base, Fort Sill, Fort Knox, and here in Washington.

I think it is significant that General El Orabi is here at a time when our Armed Forces are again cooperating in ventures to help preserve peace in the world. For example, we are helping in a very modest way the Armed Forces of Egypt as they deal with the problems of mines in the Red Sea. Our help, I hope, will be useful to Egypt; yet, it is to be noted that the Armed Forces of Egypt are quite capable and are the primary dealers with the challenge. That cooperation, nevertheless, demonstrates what we have been able to demonstrate several times in recent years: that our Armed Forces can cooperate very well on projects that help preserve peace in the world.

Indeed, our debts to Egypt are characterized by the fact that this year is the 100th anniversary of the completion of the Washington Monument—which General Lemnitzer so generously allowed us to see from the front porch of this house. Now, you know that we "borrowed" the Washington Monument from Egypt—modeled after the ancient Egyptian obelisks. I think it symbolizes the fact that we, the younger of the nations of the world, owe the older nations of the world, as is Egypt, a great debt for our civilization—science, mathematics, astronomical sciences, military prowess. So, it is a great pleasure for us to welcome you here.

For those of you who don't know the name "El Orabi" and what it means to Egypt, it means that he is a military leader from a long line of important Egyptian leaders and military leaders and who, himself, is a renowned military leader of proven great qualities, having led armored formations up through every echelon to Field Army and to Chief of Staff of the Egyptian Armed Forces.

He was honored today by the President of the United States with the Degree of Commander, the Legion of Merit, the highest award we give to foreign officers. So, we are very pleased to have you here and we hope that this will be but one in a series of many visits to our country.

Now, please, to all of you, join me in a toast to General and Mrs El Orabi and to the Armed Forces of Egypt, and the friendship of those Armed Forces with our own.

**Address to the SOCIETY
OF LOGISTICS ENGINEERS
Minneapolis, MN
21 August 1984**

Over fifty years ago, when General Douglas MacArthur left his post as Chief of Staff of the Army, he reminded the Congress that free, peace-loving nations such as ours might not want war but it might come anyway. He said that "Hasty improvisation of an efficient fighting force is totally impossible without extensive, reasonable preparation constantly carried forward as a regular feature of national policy. It is not only necessary to assure avoidance of the bitterest consequences of war, but it is also a wise investment in the maintenance of peace."

Later, when we were not successful in deterring World War II, General George Marshall, Chief of Staff of the Army some six years after MacArthur, said "We used to have all the time in the world but no money. Now we have all the money, but no time."

These two quotes from our history characterize both some of our problems and some of our attitudes today. Today, we certainly don't have all the money that we need; but, we seem to have all the time in the world. However, the fact of the matter is that when the need arises, we would have very little time. We live in a dangerous and complicated world and I am personally convinced that it is the moral, political, economic and military power of the United States and its friends and allies that keep the enemies of our way of life and of our freedom at bay.

Weakness is provocative. It is lack of preparation that will tempt our enemies and lead to the very war we seek to avoid. This nation has no other responsible option than to make realistic preparations to deter those who would threaten war. A couple of years ago I was listening to a radio interview with Bobby Knight, our great Olympics basketball coach. He was asked about the will to win. And he said, "That's not the problem. Everyone has the will to win. But, not everyone has the will *to prepare* to win." And I say to you that we won't have time to recover from the lack of preparation as we did in World War II. If we don't have the will to prepare for war, we will not deter war and we will surely not win the war should war occur.

There are two trends in recent years to remember. First, the industrial world has grown more interdependent and our own economy has grown more dependent on foreign raw materials and energy sources than ever before. When I joined the National Guard in 1939, the United States was a net oil exporter—not much by today's standards, but about 20,000 barrels a day. In 1984, we now import 3.4 million barrels a day. Those energy resources by chance and geography are far away from us but many of them are very close to the Soviet Union.

The second trend to remember is that the Soviets' military capability to threaten our interests and those economic resources that are important to the economies of the entire Free World has increased dramatically. This is especially reflected in the Soviet ability and willingness to move military power far beyond its borders to meddle in places like the south of Africa, Central America, and Southeast Asia. Their buildup in all areas of military power can be described with two words: "relentless" and "massive." They outspent us by some $500 billion in the decade of the seventies and, that was an investment primarily in hardware whereas most of our expenditures were personnel costs.

Our defense strategy to counter the threats to our interests is a global strategy which relies on alliances. We have allied ourselves with other free nations of the world, all pursuing the idea that by putting up a unified front, we can make the world a safer place. We have overseas bases and forces deployed in connection with those alliances. Those forces lend important

157

political cohesion to the alliances because they underwrite the United States commitment to those alliances—the commitment to the common defense—and they also lend military strength to the alliances.

There are other important aspects to our national strategy. We count on a strong central reserve of forces based here in the United States—land, air, naval and amphibious forces, both Active and Reserve Component forces—forces that can reinforce those alliances or go anywhere else in the world where our interests are threatened.

To make those forces effective, we rely on several other components of strategy which are uniquely American. First, good intelligence—extraordinarily good intelligence that lets us know what is going on in the world, warns us of dangers to come and informs us of what has happened. Good command and control. We don't have large forces. We have small forces and if we're going to make them effective, we have to be able to make the most of them with good command and control. Finally, we must have superior mobility to get our power wherever we may need to use it. That means that, in addition to superior air and sealift, we need freedom of the seas and the ability to control the air; and we need the free use of space. Overarching all of this are our nuclear deterrent forces.

Now, how do logistics and logisticians play in this strategy? An important part of the answer is that logisticians and those who are operators and strategic planners need to communicate with each other; and, that communication needs to improve. Some of the people who think they are strategists and operators tend to forget how important logisticians are. One of the great "explainers" of military history was Winston Churchill. He said that, "Supply and transport stand or fall together and history and success in battle depend on both." Or as Admiral King said during World War II, "I don't know what the hell this word 'logistics' is that General Marshall is always talking about; but, whatever it is I want some of it."

Logistics defined by Churchill as simply supply and transport is inadequate. It is the totality of national preparedness to support our defenses. This military business of providing for the common defense is also public business. If General Motors, General Electric, US Steel and AT&T, (before "Ma Bell" broke up) were combined, their gross revenue would total less than half that of the defense budget and the number of employees less than a third. So, national defense is public business, not just for those people in uniform but for all Americans.

Logistics is both a science and an art and it must start even before we buy equipment and end only after we send the weapons to the junk heap. We must be concerned about research and development, about acquisition, about life-cycle performance and the totality of the supporting system throughout the service life of whatever it is we buy. We must build our forces and equipment so that they can be supported in the first place. These are complex tasks and we need the help of the best minds in the country to make them work.

One thing that has colored attitudes towards logistics in recent years is the issue of nuclear weapons. There have been those who believe that a major

158

war will inevitably go nuclear—particularly if there is war between the Soviet Union and the United States—and, consequently, a "short" war. That point of view defies common sense. First, it is not inevitable that a major war would go nuclear. Second, if we prepare only for a short war, we may well guarantee we have the nuclear war we're trying to prevent. So, we as a nation cannot be found lacking in the sustaining power for our conventional forces. Our conventional forces simply cannot be short of breath if we're going to prevent war or, God forbid, if we have to fight one.

Another view that has influenced attitudes toward logistics is that we can somehow do again what was done in 1941 and 1942—that is, mobilize our economy with what seems to be astounding speed. However, our strategy has changed since World War II. Today, not only are our vital interests threatened but we also have forward-deployed forces if there is a war; and that is far different from the situation we faced in 1941. It will be a "come as you are, and stay until it's over" war. So, we need to be able to fight immediately and to mobilize rapidly; but, that task is growing more difficult. We simply have to recognize that it is growing more difficult and take steps to accommodate that.

Many things have changed to make it more difficult for the United States to mobilize rapidly. Today, the increasing sophistication of technology means that we probably can't inject an untrained labor force into defense production immediately and expect success. The lead times for production have increased and certain critical parts are made from raw materials that we obtain from foreign sources. Supplier networks in some cases are shrinking at an alarming rate. The high costs of capital and of technological expertise are impediments to new companies entering important defense areas. Additionally, we see years and years of what I characterize as tax and accounting policies in which we were eating our capital plant through taxes and profits; and all that has affected our industrial base.

The military, the Congress, the departments of government and private citizens in industry need to pay attention and work hard—and I say again, work hard—to prepare this country to be able to mobilize and to support our forward-defense posture. Logisticians and planners and businessmen alike can help by working this problem and by bringing it to the forefront of national attention and by seeking ways to solve some of these very difficult problems.

Certainly, the economy has changed dramatically. When I went to the Industrial College of the Armed Forces in Washington in the 1960s, we were told that whatever else happened in the world, the American machine tool industry was the unshakable bedrock of our industrial power. A couple of years ago when I was Vice Chief of Staff of the Army, we wanted to modernize our large cannon plant. We went out for bids for machine tools and we didn't get a *single bid* from American machine tool manufacturers!

Another example is our transportation system. We no longer have the Merchant Marine ships that we built or that we mustered into service during World War II. As a matter of fact, we have only a tenth of the American flagged ships that we had during the Vietnam War. You may say, "Well, that's all right. We'll just do what we did in World War II, just build the ships again." The fact of the matter is we no longer have the shipyards either!

Look at our entire transportation and economic systems—and I don't pass any value judgment on the economy which we now have. The simple reality is we have what we have and what we don't have we do not have. We can't change that overnight and we can't wish that away. The economy has changed and has grown more interdependent with those of other nations. Our economy is tied to the rest of the world and we need to be able to call on that *as a strength, not as a liability*, and to work with our allies so that we can pull together and be able to mobilize the Free World to defend itself.

Good logistics is made all the more challenging by the strategy that I outlined earlier—that is, the fact that we have forces forward-deployed today. Those forces are really on the front lines of freedom. Their health is a visible sign of the commitment of the United States to those alliances and those forces must not only *be good* in order to serve our strategy but they must also *look* good. If their installations are shoddy, or run-down and over-crowded, if their logistics are inadequate—if all those things don't contribute to the perception of both allies and friends as well as our potential enemies that those are top-notch fighting forces from the *strongest, freest nation in the world*, then the credibility of the United States and its strategy comes into question and the danger of war simply goes up.

Secondly, we have to be able to reinforce those forces and we have to be able to go rapidly to other places in the world that we may not now anticipate. We don't have all the money in the world so that we can pre-position equipment and forces in every corner of the world where we might expect trouble. So, that means we have to think of innovative ways to use transportation and information systems to support the forces that we have so we can go wherever we may need to go. Certainly, we need to be able to muster our civilian and well as our military airlift and sealift and to draw on help from our friends as well. If we can't—if we don't have overflight rights, base rights and support from other nations—our strategy will be empty.

There are a number of logistical challenges that we have to wrestle to the ground:

There's the reality of domestic and foreign political considerations. This precious democratic system of ours is a major factor in what happens to our defense systems. We have to operate within our political system and we have to operate within the constraints of our own government's relationships with other countries. We wouldn't want it any other way, but that is a constraint nevertheless.

One important point often forgotten is that every military installation in the United States is in *somebody's* Congressional district and we don't seem to have much trouble getting support for those. At the same time, with almost 40 percent of our operating forces overseas have no immediate "representative" in the Congress, although there are some very capable Congressmen who recognize the problems. When the time comes to put in priority either supporting forces overseas or supporting those in the United States, we don't seem to have as much difficulty getting support for the installations in the United States.

Logistics planning has other obstacles. Getting the bases that we need as well as the access rights, transit authority and other agreements is preceded by the requisite agreements among the nations involved. Those negotiations must be done quietly to be effective; but, in this open society of ours, that isn't easy. Almost every morning in Washington I can read about the Top Secret conference I attended the day before.

Nevertheless, our ability to cooperate with our allies is a real success story. Our cooperation with NATO allies and with our allies in East Asia—Japan and Korea—is an astounding success story about the ability of nations to get together and provide logistics support for the common defense. So, we need to continue to work at it. We need to recognize that it needs to be a two-way street or we're not going to get good cooperation from those nations.

There's another reality of the Eighties. Facilities and weapons, by their nature, last a long time. We say we'd like to replace our physical plant once every 50 years; but, the Commanding Officer at Fort Sill, Oklahoma, lives in a house built by soldiers for General Sherman. That's not unique. Our B-52's are older than their crews—every one of them. The aircraft carrier MIDWAY is in operation off the coast of Korea today and she has been in service since World War II.

These facts imply a real challenge in planning for sensible designs which can be altered to accept improvements as they come along. We shouldn't do what the Russians do—that is, keep everything, never throw anything away. Nevertheless, our weapons need to have logistics systems that look to the long haul, that recognize they have to support and maintain equipment for 20 or 30 years and still be effective.

This is a difficult task. Over the long haul, unforeseen requirements will upset today's best logistical plans. It isn't the tomorrow we expect to see that is the difficult problem for planners. It is the tomorrow that will come over the horizon that is *completely different* from the one we expected that will give us the problems. And that goes double for the logisticians because even a minor change in an operational and strategic plan is like the handle on a whip for the logistician. A small change at the handle of an organizational chart or an operations plan leaves logisticians of the tip of the whip making changes which are orders of magnitude larger.

New information systems and capabilities to manipulate and transmit information should help us conduct planning more effectively and more flexibly. We need to use the new systems in a sensible way to relieve the burden but not to choke the decision makers. Information systems and communications channels are like bridges across the Potomac in Washington. If you don't have discipline in the system, you can cover the Potomac River with bridges from Alexandria in the south to Cabin John Bridge in northwest Washington and still have a traffic jam in the morning. The same is true with information systems and communications systems. If you don't have discipline in them, information and data choke up decision making and thoroughly frustrate problem-solving. We have a marvelous capability if we just take it on ourselves to use it effectively.

New technology is a major claimant for resources. Some would allege that we have become technology-dependent, others that our hardware is not sustainment-oriented—that we are too enamored with the idea that we should have new, fancy gadgets and that we don't think about supporting them. There may be some truth in that; but, if we are to enhance the combat capability of our soldiers, sailors, airmen and Marines, it is *technology* that will provide the leverage. Technology will help us put more punch into our fighting forces. We can fight with far fewer forces and far more effectively if we use technology well. But we must guard against Parkinson's Law that the "Shrinkage in the combat forces results in exactly proportionate increases in headquarters personnel."

The challenge is to improve our productivity and to reduce our logistics tail by the smart use of technology. There are some great examples. The ring laser gyroscope is now predicting between 15,000 and 40,000 man-hours mean-time-between-failure. The Army's new BLACKHAWK helicopter's T-7000 engine breaks down so infrequently that its mechanics have trouble maintaining proficiency.

But, technology will not substitute for the support required to sustain ourselves in battle. Van Creveld in his book, *Supplying War*, showed how logistics can be like a self-licking ice cream cone. He said the Frederick the Great's horses in a supply train consumed 20 pounds of fodder a day. If the supply wagon carried nothing else but fodder, leaving out ammunition and the other combat essentials, the horses could consume the whole load in 120 miles. Van Creveld also demonstrated that Patton's five-ton truck carrying nothing but fuel to the front lines some 200 years later made only about 300 miles. It was logistics *not the enemy* that stopped Patton's forces. So, we need to use technology to reduce demands on the logistics system and to improve the efficiency of the logistics system itself.

As we field forces today, sustainability must be there. It must be on the ground to support our forces. If it is not, the forces can't fight. At the same time, we must look far into the future for the opportunities that technology provides. As we do, we must also plan for logistics support so that we may realize the foxhole effectiveness of new systems as they are fielded. We must do "double duty' by providing for today's forces and by supporting the forces of the future. Because, as surely as prevent war today, tomorrow will come and we will need to prevent war tomorrow as well.

We must strike the right balance for the future—between what the future looks like while hedging against the fact that the future probably won't look like the future we expect it to be. Logistics is the mucilage of strategy. So, planners must get with the logisticians and wrestle through what the future will be like and the possibility that our view of the future may well be wrong. That's what will prevent war while employing each and every taxpayer's dollars to buy the best defense possible for least cost.

Remarks to the
INDIAN NATIONAL DEFENSE
COLLEGE VISITING STUDENTS
In the Pentagon
Washington, DC
21 September 1984

I am pleased to welcome you here. Welcome to our country and to the opportunity to see our armed forces. While you are here, you will see one of our two largest naval bases and you will see an installation at which we have an airborne division and some other forces. While you are there you will have the opportunity, perhaps to deduce a few things about our national defense strategy; but I want to tell you a couple things before you go.

The strategy of the United States is a defensive strategy. We have no intention of starting a war with anyone. Our strategy revolves around a few fundamental ingredients. The first is that we are allied with a number of other nations in the world whose security and political interests are similar to ours. Those nations are in three large blocs: in Europe and the western part of Asia, in East Asia and the Pacific, and in this hemisphere, as in Central America. As you go around our country this week, those of you who have been here before will recognize that. Additionally, over here at Fort McNair where our National Defense University is, you will see the Inter-American Defense College in which officers from all the nations of this hemisphere study together.

We have a saying about the two great oceans in the world. We say we live *on* the Atlantic and we have ties across the Atlantic; but about the other great ocean, the Pacific, we say we don't live *on* the Pacific, we live *in* the Pacific. One of our states is almost 3,000 miles from the west coast of North America, out in the Pacific, and one of our other states runs just below the Arctic Circle, all the way from North America to the eastern tip of Asia and the Soviet Union. So, we have different relationships between the two oceans.

Our strategy is tied very closely to our alliances. We have forces stationed overseas in conjunction with those alliances. The forces have two purposes. One is to help give self-evident strength to our military alliances and the other is to provide political cohesion to the alliances—that is, to let our allies know that if there is an attack, we will be there. If our friends are attacked, we will be attacked as well, and they know they can count on us.

That strategy calls for certain other facets of our armed forces and you'll see some of this when you visit our forces. It calls for a strong central reserve. In our central reserve we have both active forces—people who serve every day— and Reserve Component forces—that is, civilians who are called to active duty as we mobilize. Our Reserves spend more time in training than those of most countries. A Reserve soldier, sailor, airman or Marine spends about 48 days a year in training. He trains one weekend a month and during the summer he trains for a two-week period.

To make our concept work, our strategy needs several other ingredients: one is extraordinarily good mobility. You will see a little bit of that, perhaps, at Fort Bragg in our airborne units. But our strategy also calls for mobility on the seas and for a navy that can control the seas and provide essential mobility. You'll see that when you go to Norfolk.

We believe that the Soviet Union is the principal threat to our security interests in the world and we believe that we and our allies would be outnumbered if we were to be attacked by the Soviet Union or the Warsaw Pact. Consequently, another ingredient of our strategy is to use technology to make smaller forces more effective on the battlefield. I use the word "battlefield" because I am a soldier but I mean the battle in the air and the battle on the sea and the battle under the sea. We think that those battlefield ingredients are somewhat the same as the strategic ingredients—good intelligence, good command and control and communications, and extraordinarily good mobility on the battlefield. It means that by combining those, we can take smaller forces and make them effective against larger forces.

Our armed forces today are healthy. We are modernizing our equipment. We have good people. Our soldiers, sailors, airmen and Marines are like those in every other army, navy or air force in the world. They are human beings; some make mistakes but we think we have the leadership to take care of that.

All of this strategic concept operates under a security umbrella of our strategic nuclear force. We have been attempting to engage with the Soviet Union in arms control negotiations to help make the world a safer place. We want to deal with the danger of nuclear war. We haven't had much success. I am sure that when the Soviets look at the lack of success, they probably blame us. When we look at it, we blame them. The fault probably lies somewhere in between; but we are convinced that there are sensible limitations on nuclear arms and that we must keep a modern nuclear force to guarantee our own security. We are not looking for nuclear superiority or to build more weapons or any such thing as that. We simply want a force that makes it self-evident to our potential enemies that they cannot employ their force against us and our allies with any hope of success.

Again, I would say to you I'm very pleased to have you here. It was members of the Indian Armed Forces who hosted our National Defense University in April 1983. I thank you for that. And 40 years ago in 1944, the Indian Armed Forces were a great help to me personally. In the spring of '44, I was fighting in the battle of Monte Cassino in Italy. In fact, we were relieved from our offensive positions there by some of the first troops from India to fight in Europe during World War II. They were from the famous 4th Indian Division and when we were attacked by the Germans, I recall very affectionately the 10 days or so I spent in a foxhole with an Indian soldier from the 4th Division at Monte Cassino.

Once again, welcome and thanks for coming.

Extract from Remarks on the
126th Birthday of Theodore Roosevelt
National Defense University
Washington, DC
26 October 1984

President Roosevelt chose to establish the War College and he chose to lay the cornerstone himself. As he did so, he gave a speech and I would like to quote from that speech. He said, "As a people, whether we like it or not, we have reached the stage where we must play a great part in this world. It is not open to us to decide whether or not we shall play it. All we have to decide is whether we shall play it well or ill .... This nation by the mere trend of events has been forced into a position of world power. It cannot bear these responsibilities aright unless its voice is potent for peace and justice, as its voice can be potent for peace and justice only on condition ... that we ask peace not in the spirit of the weakling and the craven but with the assured self-confidence of the just man armed."

I would say to you that those words are timely. They apply to us today even more than to the situation which faced those who heard those words spoken here in 1903.

Tomorrow, the United States will launch a new aircraft carrier in Norfolk, Virginia. I think it is very fitting that we have such an aircraft carrier, a very modern one, the *Theodore Roosevelt*, named for the great man. The power of that aircraft carrier, and of all of our Armed Forces, fits the last part of his speech—that is, the United States must be like a "just man armed."

Theodore Roosevelt recognized in his speech that we must use our power wisely—not only our military power but also our economic strength, our political strength, our diplomatic strength and, above all, our spiritual strength. It was, I think, Theodore Roosevelt's recognition of these other components of national power—not just military power—which inspired him to establish the War College: to improve the leadership of our Armed Forces by establishing what was the basis for this great National Defense University today. And I say to you, we pray that the sailors and Marines manning that aircraft carrier will manage and employ her with great skill and that those of us who are the leaders will use it and all our forces wisely to further the great cause of peace and justice.

Article for
THE 106ᵗʰ GENERAL CONFERENCE
Journal of the National Guard Association
October 1984

On behalf of my colleagues, the Joint Chiefs of Staff, I send you the warm greetings of all soldiers, sailors, airmen and Marines in the active force on this occasion of your 106ᵗʰ General Conference of the National Guard Association.

As members of our National Guard—volunteers all—you are the inheritors of America's great militia heritage. The citizen-at-arms is a concept fundamental to the health of our Republic and to the security of this great nation. Personally, I am proud to number myself as a former Guardsman. I joined the Guard in 1939 and I can remember the camaraderie and the personal satisfaction of service to country among my fellow citizen-soldiers.

Today, I am happy to see the revitalization of the Guard and the Reserves as full partners with the active force in the defense of freedom. It's a Total Force now. For example, the Air Force has increased its use of the National Guard and Reserves to the point that over 40 percent of strategic airlift and tanker crews, over 50 percent of tactical reconnaissance assets and over 65 percent of CONUS strategic interceptors are from the Guard and Reserve. The Army National Guard provides 46 percent of the Army's total combat units and 37 percent of the combat support capability.

Our nation needs to continue to find ways to employ all its strengths to keep the peace in a troubled world. We know our defense commitments cannot be lessened, nor can we somehow turn our backs on an increasingly interdependent world. We must find ways to make our strategy more effective, not to change it. That is why the Guard is so important.

Our strategy is one of deterrence. Through the self-evident effectiveness of our forces, we hope to make it unavoidably clear to any aggressor that he cannot achieve his objectives by force or by the threat of force. To do that we maintain forward-deployed forces in key areas, especially where we have long-standing allies. This forward-deployed stance is backed up by a reserve of quick-reaction forces here in the United States. These forces, always ready, must be prepared to reinforce our forward-deployed forces or to go wherever our interests are threatened.

The *sine qua non* of our armed forces is their preparedness to fight and win. It will be a "come as you are, stay until it's over fight." And, I believe that if our forward-deployed forces and those in the United States are ready and that if the enemy knows they're ready, we won't have to fight in the first place. He will know that he can't achieve his objectives by force and he won't pick a fight with the United States and its allies.

So, our National Guard of today figures even more prominently in our strategy. That is why I am enheartened to see the great improvements in our forces begun at the end of the last decade. They're the best I've seen in peacetime in my 45 years in the uniform of our country. The Guard is at last getting good equipment. F-16 fighters are already in one Air Guard outfit, with others scheduled, and the F-15 is scheduled to arrive soon. Army Guard units are getting new helicopters and the very best main battle tank in the world, the ABRAMS.

But, equipment alone is not enough. The challenge is before us all to find new ways to train better and to gain maximum preparedness from every tax dollar spent. New training techniques will help us. Moreover, we must take care of our people. People aren't just in the National Guard, they *are* the Guard. They're our most precious asset and they lie at the heart of the improvements we're seeing today. So, I say to you: Take care of our people in uniform. The freedom and security of this great nation depend on them.

Remarks to the
ANNUAL BANQUET OF ALUMNI OF
SUPREME HEADQUARTERS, ALLIED
POWERS, EUROPE (SHAPE)
Washington, DC
2 November 1984

Thanks, General Lemnitzer. I'm very happy to be here with this distinguished group of SHAPE Alumni and friends of the North Atlantic Treaty Organization. We hear a lot about peace movements in the world today and, certainly, the greatest and the most important peace movement in the world has been NATO. I look at the audience tonight and along the head table and I see distinguished military officers and civil servants from a number of nations—people who have served the cause of peace with dedicated service and great talent, helping to keep NATO strong. I am particularly honored to be here with people like General Lemnitzer, General Goodpaster, General Schulze, Ed Rowney, and General Wood. At the same time I must confess that standing up here in front of old bosses is a little bit frightening.

Now, I did learn something. I thought this was to be a great gathering with old warriors having some drinks and telling lies about past battles. I thought that was very nice but then the chief musician got up and said he was happy to be in front of this SHAPE "political-military" gathering. I had often heard that compound adjective, "political-military," and I didn't know what it meant. But now I understand that the political part is the lies and the military part is the drinking.

I just returned from the last of two trips to NATO meetings in 40 days. The last trip was to the Nuclear Planning Group meeting in Stresa, which is on the shores of Lago de Maggiore, and that just happens to be the place where my old outfit ended up in World war II. Speaking of that war, we've had a little conclave here—a small set of old war stories here: we have my outfit that was at Cassino and General Goodpaster's outfit which was behind us, supporting us and shooting to keep us up there, and we have General Schulze whose outfit was shooting in the other direction .... As General Lemnitzer said, "It didn't move very fast." The reason is because these two guys were shooting at us from both directions!

At any rate, being there in Stresa brought the same thoughts that came to my mind when I went back to the fortieth anniversary of the liberation of Rome last year: that is, out of those great battles of the Second World War grew something none of us realized would grow at that particular time. It is that concept of Western security we now have today—a concept which embraces NATO and all the free countries of the world; a great transformation which turned comrades in arms of those days into partners in peace, which made friends out of foes and which has stood as a bulwark against some very great threats to Western security and Western civilization.

NATO hasn't been content to stand still since its founding. Five years after its founding—and 30 years ago today—Britain's Lord Ismay, who was the first Secretary General of NATO, published a report called *NATO, the First Five Years*. The report could justifiably be proud of the incorporation of the Federal Republic of Germany into the Alliance 30 years ago on the 22nd of October, 1954. In his brief introduction to that report, Lord Ismay had much to say that is of use to us today. The words are so wise and so timely and contain such important guidance that I would like to read them to you now.

He said, "The signature of the North Atlantic Treaty in April 1949 marked the beginning of a revolutionary and constructive experiment in international relations. In signing the treaty, twelve independent sovereign states—later to be joined by others—undertook pledges which called for immediate and continuous collective action, not only in the military, but also in the political, economic and social fields."

Then he went on to say, "Many difficulties, however, still remain, and others will surely arise as time goes by. Our community of free nations, with interests extending to many parts of the world, is bound to be constantly faced with new problems requiring new solutions. Indeed, we in NATO will need, for years to come, a great deal of imagination and energy in order to develop by collective action the defensive power of our alliance and to tighten in all the fields the bonds between member states on both sides of the Atlantic Ocean."

I would submit to you that that could have been written by the Secretary General today and be as applicable as it was 30 years ago.

Change has certainly been the dominant feature of the decades since Lord Ismay wrote those words. Change challenges us today as we seek new solutions for the problems that face the North Atlantic Treaty Alliance today. The world has grown stronger and more inextricably intertwined. The interdependence among nations of the world has grown. Nations have proliferated. When Lord Ismay wrote that report, there were barely 60 independent nations in the world; today, there are over 170. And we have important ties with many nations today that didn't even exist at the time that report was written.

Even as the world has become more complex and intertwined, it has become more troublesome and dangerous. Since World War II there have been 150 wars with the loss of over 25 million lives. And if you say that war is something in which regular military forces engage and shoot at each other, there are some 23 wars going on in the world today. When you look at Southeast Asia, Central America, the Middle East, the world seems to boil.

There have been many other changes. Japan and Germany, once our foes, are now our friends. The Soviet Union is now an uncompromising adversary with a value system that seems to be the very antithesis of our own and of all free people. The Soviets have armed themselves to the teeth and at a level unprecedented in peacetime history. And the result is a great power but it's a one-dimensional power—a military power. As I often say, it's the one nation, the only nation in the world, that's surrounded by hostile communist neighbors. But it is a power which we have to recognize. It challenges NATO and the entire Free World. Not only NATO in the Central Front but NATO on the flanks—Norway, Denmark and Iceland in the north; Italy, Greece and Turkey in the south. The growing nuclear might and technological expertise of the Soviets have added to its long-standing numerical advantages.

The Soviets challenge us, particularly the United States, in a global sense. I have a picture outside my office on the wall. It is a picture of Avis and me when I was CINC, UN Forces, Korea. We were in costumes of Yi Dynasty royalty and underneath it a friend of mine had lettered a sign that says, "We're for NATO, too." I keep it there as a sign to officers on the Joint Staff to help remind them that the security of NATO depends as much upon the Russians understanding that they don't have a secure flank in East Asia as it does on our contribution to NATO.

The military picture has changed. It remains for the nations of the West to continue work with our friends and allies *not only* in the North Atlantic Treaty Alliance but also with all the free nations of the world to guarantee the peace that we now have.

There have been plenty of critics of this great Alliance. There are probably more today than there ever have been because criticism seems to be a way of life; and one can probably make a little extra change by criticizing something that already exists and seems good. Many of those critics have had good advice which is contributing to responsible changes in the Alliance. However, many of the critics go through sort of a ritual fire dance every year as if the demise of NATO were guaranteed in advance. Those critics don't have any responsibility to provide reasonable solutions for the great problems that the Alliance faces.

A couple of weeks ago the Joint Chiefs of Staff met with Lord Carrington, the new Secretary General of NATO, and I want to tell you that we were impressed with the new Secretary General. He steps into a field of giants who have held that post before and I think he will hold his own. He gave us an outline of his particular plan for how he intends to work with the NATO nations to contribute to the strengthening of the Alliance and to help us understand each other as we go through the political problems in each of our countries.

169

One of the things he told us is that other NATO nations contribute great things to the defense of NATO that don't seem apparent to those of us in the United States. And he talked about the Federal Republic and the great contribution that they make by having the forces of the other nations of the Alliance on their soil. I thought about that as I visited Germany a couple of weeks ago. It sort of comes home to you that if you take a state about the size of Oregon and you multiply the population by 30 and then you stuff into it all of the active duty Army and Air Forces that we have in the United States and then a couple of times a year double that with forces from the outside for maneuvers, then you get some measure of what the people of the Federal Republic endure in order to provide their fair contribution to the defense of the West.

In the past few weeks, I have had the opportunity to visit armed forces of five allied nations, including our own. And I want to tell you that the Alliance today is healthy. I spent five days with the German Armed Forces two weeks ago. I visited with the Army in Munster, the Air Force at Oldendorf, and the Navy at Wilhelmshaven; but, more importantly for you Americans, I visited the Heimatschutz Brigada 51, the Home Defense Forces brigade, which is a combination outfit of active and reserve forces. It was really heartening to see that combination of active duty and reserve forces providing a very strong contribution to the Alliance.

I want to tell you that the forces I saw in all those nations were well-equipped, well-trained, and well-led. More importantly, I didn't find a sullen soldier, sailor, airman or Marine in the armed forces of any of those five nations. Now, people say, "Well, you're a four-star general. You know they're going to lead you around to the good guys." I want to tell you that I have been in uniform 45 years and I spent five years as an enlisted man before I became an officer and if something is wrong, I can *smell* it. Those people I saw were absolutely top-notch; and they had good morale and they knew what they were doing and they were doing it very well.

I want to tell you Americans a little bit of the story about what I saw because it has to do with what you need to do in order to keep this country on course. I went to Grafenwohr where many of you men have served. I looked at the fielding of the M-1 tank and the M-2 BRADLEY Fighting Vehicle. I want to tell you a little bit of what I saw because about five years earlier I went over to Congress to defend the M-1 tank in its most critical hearing, a hearing in which the GAO was there to say that the tank was no good, that they had investigated the testing and that it wasn't worth a hoot. I had just come back from Korea so I went down to Fort Knox to look at the follow-on testing of the tank. I decided I needed to drive it and shoot it myself and I did that. I was to testify the next day and I really didn't know what I was going to say. Suddenly, it occurred to me that the sergeants there knew more about that tank than anybody else in the world. So, I asked two of them if they had a good, pressed uniform. And they said they did. I said, "Come along with me. You're going to Washington." And I took them into that Congressional hearing and they absolutely destroyed the GAO's witness and the testimony he was giving. And we got that tank by just a couple of votes in the Congress.

Now, let me tell you what has happened. There are 1300 M-1 tanks in Europe today. In the past year, the operational readiness rate for the M-1 tank has been 95 percent. There was a great debate about whether or not the turbine engine would work in the tank. But the 5 percent of the time that those tanks have been down, the engine had contributed only 4 percent of 5 percent. There was a great question about whether or not the gunfire control mechanism would work. On the tank gunnery range which is now absolutely mechanized, all computer-driven, there is no guesswork about whether you hit or miss. The first round hits for the M-1 are 50 percent higher than for the M-60A3. That's a fabulous increase in the combat capability.

I saw the same sort of thing in the German armed forces with the new equipment that they have. Also, I saw the new fast sea-lift ship—the new Roll-on, Roll-off ship which can carry 271 tracked vehicles and 652 wheeled vehicles and which took them to the NATO exercises this fall. Those ships are being made ready to reinforce NATO very quickly.

I visited the INF units, those with the new GLCM and the P-II. The cooperation between Italy, Germany, the United Kingdom and the United States in fielding those systems has been superb; and the Soviets have to know it. The Soviets spent the last couple of years trying to divide NATO over that particular issue. They were unsuccessful in doing it.

But, still there are some muddle-headed people, both here and in Europe, who think that we're in great trouble because the Soviets are responding to our viewpoint. They have forgotten the fact that we're deploying those missiles in response to the 1100 warheads that the *Soviets* deployed on their SS-20's. It is very important for us to remember that.

Both here and in Europe we have some people who think that they'd like to wish nuclear weapons away. We won't wish them away. God will not let us "uninvent" nuclear weapons. They're here. It's sort of like golf. God doesn't give any mulligans. The ball is where it lies. We have those nuclear weapons out there today and we have to learn to live with them and we have to have a strategy that deals with the Soviet Union with that understanding. And we can do that.

Lord Ismay concluded his report 30 years ago and he said, "Complacency and weariness are among the evils we must guard against. The longer a man carries a load, the heavier it becomes; and all the member countries have been carrying a heavy load of defense expenditure for a long time."—That was 30 years ago.—"Nevertheless, the threat from the Soviet Union remains and it would be a mockery of all the exertions and sacrifices that have been made if the members of the North Atlantic Alliance were, under whatever pretext, to allow their unity to be disrupted."

"The North Atlantic Treaty remains a basic element in our foreign policies. Let us keep these words uppermost in our minds. Our fate is in our own hands. If we remain united, true to ourselves, true to each other, we will avoid the unspeakable horrors of another war and be able to devote to the tasks of peace an ever-increasing measure of our energy and resources."

I would say to you that if you look at the better condition of the peoples of our nations and the prosperity that has existed in the intervening years, then you will agree those words are exactly true; and if we look to the future, those words will bear us through the years ahead.

**Remarks at the WORLD
PEACE LUNCHEON,
NATIONAL VETERANS DAY
Birmingham, AL
12 November 1984**

Thanks to all of you for that welcome. It is an honor for me to be introduced by a great patriot and supporter of national defense like Congressman Bill Nichols. Governor, Mayor, Senators, Congressman, fellow veterans, friends of veterans, you distinguished Gold Star Mothers, the families of POWs and MIAs, and all you admirals and generals. Now, I ask the rest of you folks, "Did you ever see so many Admirals and Generals in all your life?" I just wonder if this much brass ever got into the same mess hall before at one time.

I am very glad to be here at this World Peace Luncheon and to help in this the oldest Veterans Day ceremony in America. I bring you the greetings of my fellow members of the Joint Chiefs of Staff and on behalf of all the men and women in the Armed Forces of the United States, I thank you for your support. I also bring you the personal greetings of my boss, Secretary Weinberger. He was your guest here last year and he wanted me to thank you again for your hospitality and to give special thanks to Raymond Weeks for all that he has done and continues to do for veterans.

As an Army aviator, I had the opportunity to serve at Fort Rucker. I didn't see an awful lot of Alabama. I thought Dothan was simply a navigational checkpoint for pilots and had no people there. But I found out later that it was a very nice town. I learned to have a great affection for the State, and so, when Mr. Weeks asked me to come here, I was delighted to accept. Besides, I know that Alabama State Law, Title 13A, Section 11-53, protects public speakers from harm. It makes "possession of brass knuckles and slingshots in the audience punishable by a fine of not less than $50." So I feel safe up here.

I don't know very many generals who are good public speakers. We've had a few—MacArthur and some others. Most of us are lousy. So, I concluded that I was really invited because I was a veteran. But, even veterans don't necessarily have good reputations for public speaking. They tell the story about "Stonewall" Jackson presiding at a courts martial; and one of the defense counsels said, "General, you should go easy on the old veteran. He has been through many campaigns." And old Jackson said, "Yeah, that may be so. But look at that mule over yonder. He's been through many campaigns, too, but he's still a jackass."

Birmingham can be justifiably proud of the great part it has played in promoting Veterans Day. Veterans Day is certainly the logical outgrowth of what was originally the celebration of the Armistice after World War I. Sixty-six years ago, when those guns were silenced, a young private tried to put into words how he felt when peace was declared in a poem entitled "November 11" and he wrote:

> "We stood up and didn't say a word. It felt
> Just like when you have dropped your pack
> After a hike, and straightened out your back,
> And seemed just twice as light as any bird ...
> But all we did was stand and stare and stare,
> Just stare and stand and never say a word."

What for tired troops of that American Expeditionary Force of World War I on Armistice Day was an instinctive response is now for us a national expression of gratitude to those who have fought for the nation's freedoms in all our wars. Veterans Day is a time when those of us who returned home safe from the nation's wars stop to remember our friends who never had a chance to find out what it was like when they "dropped their pack." It is also a time for us to look at lessons of the past.

The nation that forgets the sacrifices of its heroes and those who served risks everything that was won for that nation. I believe that one of the most encouraging signs of our renewed spirit as a free people is the recognition we have at last extended to those who fought and died in Vietnam. Two years ago, thousands of Americans gathered to witness the dedication of the Vietnam Veterans Memorial in Washington. This past weekend there was another ceremony at the Memorial to unveil a magnificent statue that completes the monument. And the President accepted the monument as a national monument. This morning, Senator Denton and other leaders of Alabama from national and state levels, and from county and town governments, gathered to honor Alabama's families with members still missing in Vietnam.

There is work yet to be done. We can't forget the nearly 2,500 Americans still missing from that war. Accounting for those Americans is a task we must complete. Neither can we forget the veterans of every other war—those who have returned home to help rebuild our lives and theirs. As a nation we have committed ourselves to give them the help they need and deserve.

Nor should we forget the single great lesson of *all* the wars of this century—that all of us in our nation share with all our allies and the free peoples of the world a common responsibility to prevent war—not just nuclear war but all war, and to do so in a fashion that preserves freedom and liberty.

We have to confront *both* those issues if we want to stay on the path toward peace and liberty for ourselves and, more importantly, for our posterity.

We can't shrink from our obligations to preserve peace and liberty in the face of the challenges of the Soviet system. While we try to negotiate with them and to work with them to reduce the risk of war, we have to insure the adequacy of our own defense. There is some great guidance for us in the last words of the 20th Psalm where David said, "The Lord will give strength unto His people; and the Lord will bless His people with peace." I believe for us in this age and time that strength and peace are bound together. In this world of nation-states in which we live, only a free nation which is also strong can deter the enemies of peace and justice.

Those words imply two parallel ideas that contribute to peace. The first is that we must be sufficiently strong to deter war or the threat of war. We don't want war—nuclear war or any kind of war—but at the same time we don't want to be paralyzed by the fear of war as we go about our business in this world. So, our strategy of deterrence is one to preserve peace and freedom and to protect our vital interests by making it self-evidently clear to any potential enemies that they can't achieve their aims through war or the threat of war. "Deterrence" is a fancy Washington word; but, where I come from, Crow Wing County, Minnesota—and I suspect here in Alabama—it really means that "If you pick a fight with us, you're in great danger of getting the tar kicked out of you."

Second, we should seek by every reasonable means to reduce the risks of war. Certainly, arms control negotiations are one of the means that we need to pursue. But, we need to recognize that arms control alone will not prevent war. Salvador de Madariaga, the great Spanish philosopher and historian who worked for many, many years on the old League of Nations Disarmament Commission, said in his memoirs, "Nations don't distrust each other because they are armed." He said, "They arm because they distrust each other." And that's a very important point for us to remember.

Our objectives in this country have been relatively constant over the years. But the world itself has changed and the threats to our security have changed and grown. In the 1950s and the early 1960s, we had clear nuclear superiority; and, our conventional forces, although outnumbered by those of our potential enemies, were technologically far superior. Since that time there has been a shift of power. The Soviets have armed themselves to the teeth. Certainly, they are not ten feet tall. They have problems of their own. We don't see people trying to escape to the Soviet Union. We don't see them clamoring to buy Soviet automobiles or Soviet computers or even Soviet blue jeans. Their economy is in serious trouble by their own admission and their ideology is laid bare even to their friends as being militant and aggressive. Russia is the only country in the world that is surrounded by hostile communist neighbors.

But, still their vast military power is something with which we have to reckon. They have added over 3,000 new, modern, Intercontinental Ballistic Missile warheads over the last few years while we have been arguing about whether or not we should modernize our force at all. They have added about

174

1,400 modern, intermediate-range nuclear warheads aimed at our allies in NATO. Then they tried to convince NATO and the people of the United States that it is immoral for us to respond even though we do so with less than half that number. They continue to meddle all the way around the globe—in Southeast Asia, Afghanistan, Africa and in Central America, as the activities of the last few days should have brought home to us.

Because peace and the preservation of liberty remain our unending objectives, it is essential that we see to the health of our military forces. Our willingness to rebuild our strategic forces and to strengthen our conventional forces can send important signs to all those who would threaten peace.

I am heartened today to see more consensus in this nation toward that end. Last year we saw a favorable vote in the Congress to support the recommendations of the Bipartisan Scowcroft Commission for the modernization of our strategic nuclear forces—the MX, the B-1, the sea-based forces and the command and control. But, there is a hesitancy in the Congress to continue that and there are still many, many important votes to come while that issue continues to hang in the balance. We need steadiness in the pursuit of strength and we need steadiness in the pursuit of arms control.

As the senior military officer of the United States, let me just take a moment to report to you stockholders in America's security that the condition of your Armed Forces is good. I have visited our Armed Forces all over the world. I report to you that they are doing well: the tougher the job is, the higher their spirits are; and that's a good sign for the United States. You can be proud of what your Armed Forces are doing—both the active forces and the Reserve Components. They are on the land, on the sea, under the sea, in the skies, doing remarkable things and doing them remarkably well wherever you have asked them to do those tasks.

Our people in the Armed Forces are dedicated and they serve unselfishly. The people in the active forces and in the Reserves and the National Guard do more than just work for the Armed Forces; they *serve* in the Armed Forces. And that is a completely different concept from just being part of a work force. People in the Armed Forces, whether in the active force or the Reserves and the Guard, are going to go where you, the citizens of this country, want them to go; and they are going to do whatever you, the citizens of this country want them to do, whatever the risk.

Just as our Armed Forces have a duty to you and a duty to the Nation, I believe that the Nation has a duty to our people in uniform—to those who have served in the past, to those who serve now, and to those who will serve in the future. We're not at war today. There are many, many reasons why we are not at war today. But one of those, one of the very important reasons, is that we have 2.1 million very good men and women in the active force and we have another million plus in the National Guard and Reserves. And they are serving to let our potential enemies know that this nation will remain strong.

Very much a part of the willingness and the readiness of the people in the Armed Forces to defend this nation is the knowledge that the people of the country, during peacetime and war, will take care of the people in uniform and take care of the veterans. While they are in the Service, we expect to give them good equipment, good training, and adequate pay and compensation; we will take care of their families if they have to march off to war; we will pick up our wounded and give them decent medical care; we will pick up our dead and provide reverent treatment; we will do what's necessary to get back prisoners or those missing; and we will provide sensible help and care for all who served.

The people in our Armed Services deserve good equipment, top-notch equipment, equipment that works and gives our people the edge in battle. Our strategy calls for the use of American technology, one of America's strong points. We do that because we value human life more than we value things. I frequently hear misguided people say, "Why don't we just buy cheaper weapons? That way we can buy more equipment and then we won't feel so badly if we lose it to the enemy." Now the problem with all that is that when the equipment gets destroyed, so do the people who are operating it. I don't want your sons or daughters or any young American out there in battle with cheap, bargain-basement, ineffective weapons and equipment trying to protect our freedom.

I am also happy to see the great cooperation between the active forces, the National Guard and the Reserves. And that certainly exists right here in the State of Alabama as well as anywhere else. It is essential that we keep our Reserve forces strong because they figure more prominently in our strategy than they ever have before. They are truly Minutemen. We expect them to have a state of readiness beyond anything that we have ever expected before, and we expect them to be able to march off in a hurry. I have seen the National Guard and the Reserves of all four Services on maneuvers all over the world—in Europe, East Asia, the Middle East—certainly a demonstration of the readiness of this country. But they need special help from you in the civilian community. They particularly need help from the employers and I call for your support to the Employers Support for the Guard and Reserve.

At the same time, it is also important for us in uniform to remember that the taxpayer deserves a very fair shake in all this, too. He deserves to have us buy good equipment—equipment that is worth the price and equipment that is effective but not "gold-plated." By the same token, the Armed Forces and the taxpayer deserve a fair shake from American industry and labor by having them produce quality equipment and by seeing that a fair price is asked for it.

All these factors lie at the heart of our military health—good people, good equipment, good training, and dedicated leadership. And I am buoyed by the progress I have seen. Yet, I am concerned about our willingness to continue to provide for our security. We have heard it mentioned here many times today that we owe our security to those patriots who served before us—to our Forefathers who secured our liberty and freedom. They at their time in history did what was necessary. Now, it is time for us to pay our part of the price if we are to reap the benefits and to have our posterity reap the benefits of liberty. The price we have to pay is high but it is money; it is not blood. If we don't pay it in money, we will pay it in blood eventually.

I recall what President Reagan said to me when I took this job two and a half years ago. He said, as he announced my appointment, "Keep us strong, keep us ready, so that we may keep the peace." The essence of our strategy is keeping the peace by keeping strong and ready. The United States is not charging around looking for war. No one who has ever experienced war could ever want another one. I am reminded of that great cartoon by Bill Mauldin from World War II. It shows "Willie and Joe" all dirty and scruffy and tired, sitting on the bombed-out steps of what was once a house. A clean, confident-looking soldier swaggers by and Willie turns to Joe and says, "That can't be no real combat soldier, Joe. He's actually out *lookin'* fer a fight."

We face a difficult and uncertain world. But, we can face that world with confidence. We have just finished a national election, an important demonstration that the pronoun for the United States is "We." Sometimes, when I listen to people talk, I believe they think that it's "they": "They did it." "They are responsible"—that ubiquitous "they" without any antecedent to the pronoun. But, in fact, America's pronoun is "we." "We hold these truths to be self-evident that all men are created equal." "We, the People of the United States, in order to form a more perfect Union, establish justice, insure domestic Tranquility, provide for the common defence." "We pledge our lives, our fortunes and our sacred honor"—Whatever this country does or fails to do, "we" will do it, "we" the people. "We" are responsible for it.

There aren't any cheap, easy gimmicks as we seek world peace and national security. Strength, steadiness, hewing to the cause of freedom and justice, helping friends and willing allies, a willingness to serve—all are great contributors. Military strength alone will not guarantee world peace or even our own security. We need our political health, economic and social health and certainly, above all, we need moral and spiritual health in order to sustain our freedoms.

Every coin we have has written on it "In God We Trust." As we march off into this uncertain future seeking to secure our liberty and freedom, there is a good prayer in the Lutheran *Book of Worship* in the Order of Matins and it goes, "Lord God, You have called Your servants to ventures of which we cannot see the ending, by paths as yet untrodden, through perils unknown. Give us faith to go out with good courage, not knowing where we go, but only that Your hand is leading us and Your love is supporting us."

I thank you for having me here today. My colleagues, the Joint Chiefs of Staff, know that we have a special duty to work very hard to help protect this nation and I want you to know that we are going to do it. With the help of God, with the loyal and selfless service of our armed forces, with the help of patriots like you, and the support of the President and the Congress, and the people of the other states, we will preserve peace and liberty, not only for ourselves but for those who follow. Thank you.

**Memorandum for the
Deputy Secretary of Defense
Subject: Enhanced CINC
Participation in the PPBS
19 November 1984**

[A natural tension exists between the civilian staff of the Secretary of Defense and his military staff, the JCS. Here is an example, wherein the DEPSECDEF essentially told the CJCS not to carry out his Title X responsibilities. This dialogue was handled without staffs so as to keep the dispute out of the Press. The DepSecDef memorandum was quietly withdrawn as a result of this correspondence.]

Your memorandum, subject as above, dated 14 November 1984, has been received, reviewed and implemented. The steps you have taken to enhance the role of the CINCs are both welcome and appreciated.

In light of your personal memorandum to me and the last section of the broadly distributed memorandum, it appears appropriate to review briefly the background of this issue in order to keep it in perspective.

a. The Joint Chiefs of Staff examined the CINCs role in the POM and program review process in response to your request and in a search for "useful adjustments to enhance and improve the CINCs role."

b. The Joint Chiefs of Staff unanimously approved rather modest changes to the procedures they have followed for the past few years and advised the Secretary of Defense of our proposed internal course of action on 9 October.

c. The action taken by the Joint Chiefs of Staff was believed to be well within the responsibilities imposed upon us by the Secretary of Defense and Congress—and in accord with what we perceived to be your policies.

The question is one of responsibility.

a. As the SecDef's immediate military staff, it is the duty of the Joint Chiefs to:

(1) Coordinate all communications in matters of joint interest to the CINCs.

(2) Review major armed forces requirements in relation to strategic and logistics plans.

(3) Review CINC plans and programs to determine their adequacy, feasibility, and suitability.

b. Subject to the authority of SecDef, the CJCS acts as the CINCs spokesman on operational requirements. [10 USC Section 124 C (2)]

This change in the US Code was only recently passed and has not as yet been formally implemented. It is, I believe, self-executing.

The actions taken by the Joint Chiefs of Staff were designed to be within the scope of their responsibilities and to expand and improve the dialogue among the key uniformed participants. The Joint Chiefs of Staff want to play a helpful role in the process. We wish to enhance our ability to provide competent, professional advice; but our role and how our advice is used depend on the entire DOD organization—not just upon us. The Joint Chiefs of Staff have only taken those necessary first steps to prepare ourselves to discharge our obligation—not to change the PPBS process or to direct how others participate in the process. If any thing the Joint Chiefs of Staff or I have said is subject to a contrary influence, it is regretted. It seems to me that the differences in your 14 November memorandum and my 6 November are more apparent than real.

The information and guidance the Joint Chiefs of Staff intend to furnish the CINCs is attached at Enclosure 2.

I would be remiss if I failed to make one essential point. The Joint Chiefs of Staff and I have always conducted our affairs not only to serve the Nation's security interests but also to try to ease the burdens of the President and the Secretary of Defense, and you. Our focus has been and remains on improving SecDef's effectiveness by doing our job as well as we can as committed members of a team under clear civilian control. I do not believe there is any issue here, but if there is concern about these essential elements, I hope we can discuss them without delay.

Article for *DEFENSE* 84
"ON THE FRONT LINES OF DETERRENCE"
November-December 1984 Edition

Our nation has a defensive strategy. We exclude the possibility we will initiate a war or launch a preemptive strike. We rely on the maintenance of strong, always-ready nuclear and conventional forces supported by superb intelligence, good mobility, and superior command and control to make it self-evidently clear to any adversary that the cost of aggression would be too high to justify an attack.

Our global strategy and policy place great emphasis on a collective defense posture. Our strategy is a coalition strategy, and we are fortunate to have reliable allies. To buttress our coalition strategy and to assure its effectiveness, we maintain a balanced mix of forward-deployed forces and a flexible force structure of rapid-reacting forces in our central reserve.

Our unified or joint system of command, in keeping with our strategy and our global perspective, is unique. Unified command calls for a single operational commander responsible to the National Command Authorities and exercising command over all the units of his assigned forces, regardless of

Service. This system of command has worked well since President Eisenhower on April 3, 1958, set out the guidelines for a system of "operational commands that are truly unified, each assigned a mission in full accord with our objectives." Further, his concept was that the Joint Chiefs of Staff would serve "as staff in assisting the Secretary of Defense in his exercise of direction over the unified commands."

In this arrangement, information flows up and down a ladder. Command guidance, coordinated intelligence, policy, and strategy flow down to the field commanders. Operational reports, requests, and raw information flow back up; and these communications must flow laterally, too. They may skip a rung or two descending or ascending. Nevertheless, our system is disciplined by the principle that decisions are made at the lowest possible level so that flexibility is given, along with the resources, authority, initiative, and responsibility, to those who can use it to best advantage—the commanders on the scene, that is the Commanders in Chief of our nine unified and specified commands, the CINCs.

We give our CINCs the necessary information and resources, and then we give them the rattle-room to exploit the situation or to resolve problems under a system in which orders are given as broad descriptions of the intended outcome—not as detailed descriptions of what precisely is to be done. The missions of the Commanders in Chief under this concept are demanding and require excellent support to accomplish the tasks. Let me address some general aspects of the challenges that I see.

First, our Commanders in Chief exist to be ready to fight and to fight successfully. Should deterrence fail, they are the ones who will carry out our war plans. Under those plans, each unified and specified command has a unique mission, a unique slice of geography, and a unique set of allies. Accordingly, the views of the CINCs must be fully considered as we build and maintain our forces in peacetime. Also, the Commanders in Chief need good planning support to develop their war plans. We need to harness modern computer technology so the CINCs can use it to develop better war plans.

Second, we must ensure that the forces from each of the Services are integrated properly so we get the most out of them. The Commanders in Chief and the forces provided by the Services to the Commanders in Chief must be as effective as we can make them. Our nation has small forces in relation to the myriad requirements for those forces. We must realize the full potential of our military might by ensuring these forces can work together. Through sensible equipment, joint doctrine, and exercises, we ensure interoperability and we get a payoff that's greater than the sum of the individual parts.

That ties into my third point of ensuring we have the capability to work with allies. We have fought three major wars in the last 40 years, all of which required close cooperation with our friends. Should we have to fight again, we'll do it in cooperation with our allies.

We share with a number of nations common goals and objectives so that they're willing to join us in the defense of the freedom that we cherish. Some nations have different military heritages—some of them compatible with ours

and some not as compatible. Our languages and cultures may be different.
The task for us is to maintain forces and to exercise and train them in
combined exercises so that our Commanders in Chief can operate effectively
within a coalition framework.

Everything we do must stand that one test, "Have we improved the
warfighting capabilities of the Commanders in Chief and that of the forces
assigned to the operating forces under the Commanders in Chief?" Our nation
cannot lose sight of this objective as we build, exercise, and maintain our
forces in peacetime. The effectiveness of our Commanders in Chief is the basis
upon which our deterrent strategy is built and through which peace is
maintained and liberty preserved in a troubled world.

1985

Selected Works

**Remarks to the PEOPLE'S LIBERATION
ARMY MILITARY ACADEMY
Beijing, People's Republic of China
14 January 1985**

Thank you for the warm welcome. I am honored to be here. Some of my colleagues in the United States asked me, "Why are you going to China in winter? Beijing is cold in winter." First, I say in response that I am from the coldest region of my own country, Minnesota, and I enjoy the winter.

Second, I remember something I read about the art of Chinese painting. It said, "If you want to learn to paint a tree, do so in winter when leaves no longer block the view of its true form and character." Similarly, I believe that if military leaders from our two nations understand the true form and character of each other, we can advance the cause of peace.

I am here to become acquainted with your military leaders and your armed forces, and to understand your strategy, your military doctrine and tactics, and the form and character of your armed forces—all to improve my own understanding of the ways in which the military forces of our two countries, our two independent nations, might help each other.

The defense requirements of our two nations are different, and your defense requirements are in many ways more complex than ours. I look to the north of my own country and I see Canada and the longest peaceful, undefended border in the world. Then, I look to the north of China and I see the Soviets poised on your border with around sixty divisions, as well as Soviet-supported aggression in countries to the south and west of China.

Your armed forces are different from those of the United States; but, we have many common problems. We both face the same threat, the heavily mechanized, modern forces of the Soviet Union. We both have friends who face aggression from Soviet surrogates. We share a common desire for the well-being of our peoples.

I believe that we as soldiers can help work for peace if we understand one another. To help you understand the United States military forces, let me take the time allotted me to trace quickly from the fundamental elements of our military strategy through the structure of our military forces, the weapons we provide our forces, and the training and support of those forces. Then, I hope I can answer your questions.

Our forces, our doctrine and weapons are developed to support our strategy. Our society, our heritage, and the character of our people have a great influence on our strategy and the building of our armed forces. Our strategy is defensive. Our fundamental objective is to defend our people, our institutions and our way of life, and to help other independent nations maintain a peaceful world in which we can all pursue the legitimate economic, political and social goals of our people. We have no intention of starting a war with anyone. We believe we can best prevent war by being self-evidently prepared to defend ourselves and our friends. We want to discourage war. A word we often use is "deterrence." We have absolutely no ambitions for territorial gain. We have fought in two World Wars in this century and the only territory we sought was burial grounds for our dead in the countries we were helping defend.

Our strategy is shaped by our economic and cultural ties to many parts of the world. We share common goals with many nations. We have ties across both the Atlantic and the Pacific, but we are uniquely tied to the nations of the Pacific. One of our states, Hawaii, is completely surrounded by the Pacific. Another, Alaska, extends just below the Arctic Circle to the eastern tip of Asia and the Soviet Union. And, we have more trade with countries in the Pacific than with any other region of the world. We also have great trade and cultural ties to Europe, Africa and the other nations in the Western Hemisphere.

In keeping with our global outlook, our strategy revolves around a few fundamental ingredients. The first is that we are allied with a number of other nations in the world whose security and political interests are similar to ours. Those nations are in three large blocs: in Europe and the western part of Asia, in East Asia and the Pacific, and in the Western Hemisphere.

We have forces stationed overseas and afloat in conjunction with those alliances and at the invitation of the nations where stationed. These forces have two purposes: one is to give self-evident military strength to the alliances and the other is to help provide cohesion for the alliances—that is, to let our friends know that if they are attacked, we will consider ourselves attacked as well. Our forces are designed so that they can operate far from home bases and in cooperation with the forces of many other nations.

Historically, the American people have been opposed to large standing military forces and opposed to stationing forces overseas. Before World War II we had very small regular forces and very few forces overseas. In both World War I and World War II we were forced into hasty, expensive mobilizations after we or our friends were attacked. Today, our forces are larger; and more of them are overseas than we would want. The combination of modern warfare and the world political situation seems to dictate both. Our people accept the need to do what we are doing, but the policies are questioned and reviewed every year.

Our strategy calls for a strong, responsive central reserve of forces which can reinforce our deployed forces or go other places where needed. In our central reserve we have regular full-time forces and Reserve forces—that is, those forces composed of civilians who are called to active duty as we mobilize. Our Reserve forces spend more time in training than those of many countries. A Reserve soldier, sailor, airman or Marine spends about 38 days a year training in his combat tasks. He trains two days and nights each month and for one full two-week period each year.

Perhaps I can give an example of that. On my way here I had airplane trouble in Alaska. My airplane had to stop until I picked up a Reserve airplane crew, some civilians who were on active duty for two days. And it was a surprise to them that they had to fly me the rest of the way to Japan.

Considering the size of our country and our global ties, our forces are not large in number. Our population is close in size to that of the Soviets. We have 238 million people; they have 278 million people. We have 2.1 million men and women in our active forces in contrast to the Soviets 4.8 million. We have organized Reserve forces of 1 million in contrast to the Soviets' 10 million. We also have a trained reserve manpower pool of 400,000 which can be mobilized.

From the fundamental ingredients of our strategy—that is, defensive and deterrent, relatively small forces, cooperation with allies, deployed forces and a central reserve—flow other ingredients we believe necessary to make the strategy a success. Those ingredients are, first, very good intelligence, good command and control, then good mobility—that is, both strategic mobility and tactical battlefield mobility—the ability to control the air over the battle area, and to operate on our lines of communication without undue influence from enemy air forces; the ability to control and use the seas at places of our choosing; and the ability to use space for legitimate missions without interference.

The last element of our strategy is the maintenance of nuclear forces which are strong, flexible and modern. The purpose of the nuclear forces is to make it very clear to any potential enemy that they cannot achieve their war aims by attacking us or our allies with nuclear forces and also to help discourage attacks with non-nuclear forces.

First, concerning intelligence. We want good, timely intelligence to warn us of attack and to help us decide on our course of action. We devote a lot of effort to assuring that all our leaders, from the head of the government down to platoon and squad leaders, are well-informed about the situations they face. By coupling modern sensors, computers and communications with traditional battlefield intelligence techniques, we want to give our commanders at every echelon more knowledge about the battlefield situation than the enemy commanders they face. We want our company commanders to know more than the enemy regimental commanders.

With good intelligence, our commanders can then use good command and control and extraordinarily good mobility to get the necessary forces to the point of decision. We believe these principles apply to the global strategic

185

situation as well as to the tactical battlefield situation. I use the word "battlefield" in the broadest context, meaning in addition to the land battlefield the battle areas in the air, on the sea and under the sea.

You can see that with the combination of our very long coast-line—12,130 miles long—having an island state among our fifty states, our extensive world trade, our commitments to allies, and our deployed forces dictates that we have strong naval forces; and we do have those. We have a 540-ship Navy and we plan to increase it to 600 ships. At the heart of our naval forces are our aircraft carrier battle groups—13 of them, with a goal of 15 groups of ships built around aircraft carriers, each with over 100 modern aircraft. The naval forces are designed to control the seas at places of our choosing and to take the battle to the enemy's naval forces and their land bases. Four Marine amphibious divisions and supporting air wings are ready to support the naval campaign.

Control of the air over the battle area and our lines of communication is provided by 140 Air Force modern fighter and attack squadrons, by 110 Navy and Marine Corps fighter and attack squadrons, and by surface-to-air missiles and guns on our ships and by a force of mobile surface-to-air missiles and anti-aircraft guns with our land forces.

Our Army has 27 divisions and 30 independent brigades. About half are armored or mechanized forces. The others are a variety of so-called light forces, including a parachute division and a helicopter-borne, air-assault division. Our divisions are large—between 15,000 and 18,500 personnel.

I mentioned the freedom to use space for legitimate missions. We use satellites for communications, for weather reconnaissance, and for warning of attack by land- and sea-based ballistic missiles. We use technology to protect our satellites from electronic attack and we are developing a limited anti-satellite weapon to deter physical attacks on our satellites by being able to threaten attacks on enemy satellites. As you may know, the Soviets have already built and tested an anti-satellite weapon.

Our nuclear forces are designed to deter attack and are not designed for a first strike. About 80 percent of our strategic weapons are in the bomber and submarine forces and only 20 percent in intercontinental ballistic missiles. In contrast, the Soviets have 70 percent of their warheads in their intercontinental ballistic missile force, the force most useable for a first strike. We keep all three elements—bombers, submarine missiles and intercontinental ballistic missiles—in our force because we believe each provides special strengths which will help ensure against tactical or technical surprise.

We are now modernizing all parts of the force. We have consistently sought greater accuracy and greater reliability for our weapons systems. Consequently, we have been able to reduce the yields and the number of warheads required for our objectives. Our weapons are designed to retaliate against the key elements of Soviet military power and not against cities and people. As important as the weapons systems themselves is having reliable space-based and land-based warning systems and a good modern, survivable communications and control system. We believe it important to keep all facets modern, reliable and ready in order to help keep the peace.

In Geneva last week, our Secretary of State Shultz and Soviet Foreign Minister Gromyko agreed to resume negotiations to try to reduce offensive nuclear arms and to discuss space and defensive weapons. The United States will enter those negotiations in good faith and with the sincere hope that we can find a way to reduce the level of nuclear arms on both sides.

We believe that our scientific and technological strength should be used to strengthen our Armed Forces. We place great value on each man and woman in uniform and we go to great lengths to provide them good, reliable, effective tools for battle. We spend a lot of time and effort training for success in modern battle. As is the case for all nations whose strategies are defensive, we are continually modernizing our forces to meet defense challenges of the future while recognizing that we help keep the peace in the present by having ready, effective forces today.

People are the heart of our Armed Forces. All the best equipment in the world is useless without good people—good people who are well-led, well-disciplined, physically fit, and who are well-trained in good, combined arms doctrine. All members of our Armed Forces are volunteers. About half of them we call "careerists." We expect them to serve between 20 and 30 years. The other half are on their first enlistment and have less than four years of service. Thirteen percent of the forces are officers or warrant officers. The officers are university graduates and 33 percent of them have graduate degrees. Ninety-three percent of the enlisted force are high school graduates and over 14 percent have some university education. Fifty-five percent of the force is 25 years of age or younger. Six percent of the force is over 40 years of age. Nine percent of the force are women.

We believe that each member of the Armed Forces must be well-trained and regularly tested in his or her individual duties. We believe that individual training is only a prelude to team training, the kind of training which gets most of our training effort. We set tasks, conditions and standards for all training whether it be for an Infantry squad exercise or for a large force maneuver involving land sea and air forces. We believe that realistic peacetime training will save lives in wartime, and we also believe it will help preserve the peace by letting our potential enemies know that we are ready to fight.

Training is the key to success in battle. Our armed forces devote a great deal of attention to training and to improving our training techniques. Training is expensive and we want to make certain that we train wisely. We spend a lot of time working on marksmanship, maneuver and command and control in realistic, live-fire exercises and in developing good, well-understood combined arms doctrine. We use computer-driven simulations to train in all sorts of skills from aircraft crews to anti-tank gunners to battalion, brigade and division staffs.

We use instrumented training ranges to help find our mistakes in peacetime. For example, at the Air Force Fighter Weapons Center our pilots train against pilots specially trained to use Soviet tactics in aircraft closely resembling Soviet aircraft in capabilities. Every maneuver, every instrument reading, and every radar command and radio transmission are recorded for evaluation and study. At the Army's National Training Center our tank and mechanized forces maneuver against a force trained and equipped as a Soviet tank regiment and a Soviet motorized rifle regiment. Both forces use lasers closely approximating the range and accuracy of all direct-fire weapons. There are laser detectors on every man and vehicle. The details of the maneuver—all movements, all firing and all radio transmissions—are recorded. All officers and soldiers carefully study the results to find their own mistakes to help improve future training.

Our doctrine stems from our experience that in battle the whole is greater than the sum of the parts. *The fingers of the hand spread apart can be broken, but together they form a fist. Through effective command and control and through a doctrine understood by all, we achieve unity of effort among all arms to concentrate combat power of combined arms forces at the decisive point.* We design our forces and employ them so that this integration is assured in combat—helicopters and close air support aircraft work in close coordination with the ground maneuver and the fire support elements; naval and air units cooperate at sea and near the land. Our exercises and our simulations are designed to train our people to operate automatically in combined arms teams—teams which may involve elements from the Army, the Navy, the Air Force and the Marine Corps.

To help illustrate what I have been trying to say, let me discuss briefly how we would plan to fight the Soviet first echelon tank forces: We will reduce the effectiveness of attacking tank forces by interdicting the defiles and choke points with air and artillery using modern munitions. We will use electronic warfare to disrupt communications. We will slow the attacking force with mines, both planned minefields and mines fired by artillery or laid by helicopter. The main parts of the battle will be fought by the combined arms teams—our own tank, mechanized infantry, and attack helicopter units supported by attack air and artillery.

Here is a picture of our newest Main Battle Tank. (Slide is shown) It is commanded by a staff sergeant, a soldier with six to nine years of service. It has a gunner who probably has three to six years of service, a driver with two to five years of service and a gun loader who has one to three years of service. They drill about five days a week in crew tasks. They fire hundreds of sub-caliber rounds on miniature ranges. They have regular maneuver training as a part of their platoon, company, and battalion in combined arms exercises. About four times each year they will maneuver with Air Force and artillery support. About 35 percent of their training is at night. They fire 134 rounds of main gun tank ammunition each year on difficult, realistic ranges. About half of the firing is at night and all firing is carefully graded.

Here is a picture of our Infantry Fighting Vehicle. (Slide is shown) It carries an Infantry squad commanded by a staff sergeant with six to nine years of service. The vehicle itself has a rapid-fire 25mm gun capable of destroying light armored vehicles and it carries four TOW anti-tank missiles for long-range fire against tanks. The infantrymen can dismount and employ a shorter range, wire-guided anti-tank missile and all the infantrymen can carry hand-held anti-tank rockets. The training and firing tests for the mechanized infantry squad are similar to those of the tank crew.

This next picture is of the Attack Helicopter. (Slide is shown) Its main mission is anti-tank. It carries 16 laser-guided anti-tank missiles and a 30 mm cannon. The missile range is about 6000 meters and it can be guided by the helicopter crew, by another helicopter or by an artillery observer with a tank or infantry company. The crew of the helicopter consists of two warrant officers. One of them has six to fifteen years of service and about 1500 hours of flying time in a helicopter. The other has less than six years of service and about 500 hours of helicopter flying time. They train extensively in computer-driven simulators which reproduce all aspects of their combat mission. They fly about 10 one-and-a-half hour missions each month—almost all of it in what we call "nap of the earth flight" in combined arms training. About 40 percent of the training is at night.

This next picture is an Air Force A-10 attack plane. (Slide is shown) Its main armament is a high-velocity 30mm gun which fires a tank-killing, depleted uranium round. The pilot is an officer, lieutenant or captain, with two to 10 years of service. He had 500 to 1000 hours of flying time. He too trains on flight simulators and he flies about 15 one-and-a-half-hour missions each month. He trains with Army units in combined exercises. If he is stationed in the United States, once a year he will fly his airplane to Europe or to East Asia, or to the Middle East to participate in maneuvers with our own forces and with allied forces.

Our philosophy of command seeks unity and flexibility in execution. We follow the principle that decisions are made at the lowest possible level where tactical flexibility and effective combined arms action is assured. Information flows up and down and laterally. Command guidance, coordinated intelligence, and information flow back up. We try to get new intelligence immediately to all who can use it. We give authority, responsibility, information and resources to those who can use them to best advantage—the combat leaders on the scene. We give our combat leaders *at every level* the necessary information and resources, and then we give them room to exploit the situation or to resolve the problems under a system in which orders are given as broad descriptions of the intended outcome—not as detailed prescriptions of what precisely is to be done.

The defense structure I have outlined is responsive to civilian control. It is a valued principle in our society that the military be subservient to the will of the people as manifested in our civilian leaders. We have four Services in the United States—the Army, the Navy, the Air Force and the Marine Corps. These four Services, each under a civilian leader and a uniformed Chief of Staff, are responsible for the peacetime function of organizing, training, equipping and supporting the forces they provide to the operational commanders. Our operational commanders command forces of all Services and are responsible for all forces in large geographic areas for special missions such as our Air

Defense Command. The operational commanders receive the orders of the President, the civilian Commander-in-Chief, through the Joint Chiefs of Staff, the uniformed Chiefs of the four Services and me as the Chairman. We are the military advisors and the military staff for the elected civilian leaders of the people.

This then is a short overview of our military system. My description is sketchy and incomplete, but I hope it will help you understand us.

Let me conclude by repeating that while our two nations are different, we are also similar in our desire for peace as the best way to advance the well-being of our peoples. Similarly, while our Armed Forces are different, we in uniform have much we can learn from each other. For our part, the U.S. military draws its military traditions from many nations. One of those traditions of military excellence and tactical skill was first found *here, in China.* In the words of Sun Tzu:

> "The general who in advancing does not seek personal fame,
> and in withdrawing is not concerned with avoiding punishment,
> but whose only purpose is to protect the people and promote the
> best interest of his sovereign, is the precious jewel of the state.
> Because such a general regards his men as infants they will march
> with him into the deepest valleys. He treats them as his own
> beloved sons and they will die with him."

This is the concept of selfless service to a cause larger than self which motivates United States soldiers, sailors, airmen and Marines—as I am sure it does your own forces. It reflects the special bond of trust and confidence between the military forces and the society those forces serve and protect.

As one Western philosopher in ancient Greece about the same time as Sun Tzu, Plato said: "Nothing can be more important than the work of the Guardians should be well done .... If shoemakers become inferior and corrupt and claim to be what they are not, the State is not in peril. But if the soldiers, the Guardians of our law and State, only appear to be Guardians and are not, you surely see that they destroy the State utterly." Then, he goes on to say that Guardians or soldiers should be dangerous to their enemies and gentle to their friends, "quick to see, swift to overtake the enemy, and strong." He concludes that bravery is essential but that bravery comes not from physical strength but from spiritual strength.

These ancient principles guide our armed forces. From what I have seen of your people, your country, and your armed forces, I am sure that these same principles motivate you.

**Remarks at the CONGRESSIONAL MEDAL
OF HONOR SOCIETY PRESIDENTIAL
INAUGURAL DAY BRUNCH
Washington, DC
20 January 1985**

I am happy to welcome you to Washington on the eve of the official Fiftieth Inauguration. I bring you the greetings not only of my fellow Joint Chiefs who are here but also the over 3 million soldiers, sailors, airmen, Marines and Coast Guardsmen—active and Reserve. We thank you for your service and for the example that you have set of selfless sacrifice for the security of the Nation.

Yesterday I came back from a week-long visit to the People's Republic of China. That trip home was a stark reminder of the dangers in this troubled world today. In spite of the great sacrifices made and the dangers endured by you and others, the world is still a very troubled place. In fact, there are 23 wars going on in the world today. But, our nation, blessedly, is at peace. My trip home from China—flying over or near the sites of the land, sea and air battle areas of past wars—World War II and Korea—brought to me quite clearly just how fortunate we are today. We are here, a nation at peace, having completed that uniquely American ritual that we perform every four years— electing our President. We are concluding that ritual by peacefully installing him as the leader of the greatest democracy on earth. Many other nations would be witnessing wars or riots or a struggle for power at this very moment. We are not. That is not the way we change leadership in this country. Instead, this morning there was a quiet little ceremony which I just witnessed at the White House and there will be a public ceremony tomorrow that you will participate in.

What about the future? Will we be as secure in 2005 as we are in 1985? There are those in this world who are not all that confident that we will be. In fact, there are some who are downright pessimistic. There is a stunning new book by a French author named Jean-Francois Revel called *How Democracies Perish*. In the opening lines of the book, he described the world as "a democracy-killing machine." And he goes on to say in the book that "Democracy is not basically structured to defend itself against outside enemies seeking its annihilation, especially since the latest and most dangerous of these external enemies, communism, parades as democracy perfected when it is in fact the absolute negation of democracy."

Another French author, Ardant du Picq, in his book *Battle Studies*, said, "There is no military spirit in a democratic society .... A democratic society is antagonistic to the military spirit."

In some ways, both Revel and Ardant du Picq have some good arguments to support their contentions. Although the word "democracy" is liberally sprinkled in the titles of many nations in the world, only a very small fraction of the world's population live in reasonably democratic nations.

191

The pessimism of those two French writers ought to keep us on our toes as we look at the history of the world around us; but their pessimism ought not to frighten us as we look at our own history. The plaque on the corner of the Minneapolis city auditorium which we marched by on the way to the railroad station in 1941 when we were mobilized—I remember reading it—it says: "Participation in the rights of citizenship assumes participation in the duties of citizenship." This is fundamental to democracy; and the duties range all the way from voting to elect our President and legislators to paying the taxes we levy on ourselves. Those duties encompass fighting, yea, even risking death in the battles that "We the People" choose to fight in the defense of this nation and its principles.

You who wear the Medal of Honor are the embodiment of that fundamental principle and are proof of the unbroken history of America's willingness to do what must be done to keep this nation free. You represent a spirit and a virtue which are uniquely American and which refute the predictions of doom for democracy. I want to tell you that the men and women in uniform today embody that spirit as well—a spirit of free men and women not wanting war but ready and willing, if need be, to fight for a just cause.

The men and women in uniform today are worthy descendents of those who served in the past. There are over two million soldiers, sailors, airmen, Marines and Coast Guardsmen on active duty today. There are another million men and women in the National Guard and Reserves. They comprise a force for peace which by its preparedness makes it clear to our potential enemies that they cannot win a war with the United States. We are at peace today because we are strong. If we maintain our strength, we will increase the chances of keeping the peace.

Joachim Von Arnim, the German novelist who lived in the early 1800s, said, "The history of the world begins anew with every man, and ends with him." He meant that one man or one woman *can* make a difference. We have here a roomful of people who made a difference. Aristotle once said, "Virtue was the habit of right choice." Certainly, your bravery was virtuous. What you did was the right choice. Through your sacrifices and the sacrifices of millions of others whose achievements were not so heroic, our nation enjoys peace today.

We have been at peace for over 10 years now. No new Medals of Honor have been awarded except for the tardy but fully deserved award to Sergeant Benavidez. So, there have been fewer occasions to award the Medal of Honor; and the ranks of those of you who wear it are thinning. With the death last week of Charles Kelly, the first enlisted man to receive the award in World War II, there are now only about 250 or so of you in this nation of some 250 million.

But, I know that is just fine with you. I know that in this room there is the hope that there will be no need for bravery such as yours again. And I pray that you are right. War in this modern age, as in every age, is a terrible thing and we need to work very hard to prevent it. The best way for this nation to prevent war is by tending to all the elements of our strength—not just our military strength but our economic strength, our political strength, our social strength, and, most importantly, our moral strength as well.

Our nation seems to learn over and over again that the price of peace and freedom is constant vigilance. The cost of vigilance is high. We will remember that as we debate the defense budget over the next few months. You in this room know that the cost of vigilance in peacetime has never been as high as the price of wars that come from the lack of vigilance. The price of war is not simply paid in dollars for defense budgets; it is paid in the blood of our citizens and in the blood of our allies.

So, if this nation wants to maintain its freedom, it should continue to stand shoulder to shoulder with the other free nations of the world, and continue to accept its responsibilities as a leader of the nation-states of this world. In turn, we the citizens of this country—"We the People"—have to continue to accept our responsibilities as citizens—citizens of a leading nation in this world—and do what we have to do to preserve liberty for ourselves and our posterity in the years ahead.

Once again, on behalf of all the men and women of the Armed Forces of the United States, I want to thank you for what you have done. Thanks for coming to Washington for this Fiftieth inauguration, the great celebration that signifies the freedom that you helped preserve. Thank you very much.

**Closing Remarks to the
SENATE BUDGET COMMITTEE
On the FY 86 DOD AUTHORIZATION
Washington, DC
7 February 1985**

Throughout this hearing I have listened to some assertions from some very respected Senators and I am sorry they are not here now to hear this; but it is my first chance to say it and I think it is very important to say it for the record. It happens to be about things that I think I know more about than anyone else in the room.

The first assertion was, Sir, that we have no clear idea of how we are going to fight effectively. And I want to tell you that that's baloney. We know exactly how we're going to fight. We have a very clear idea of how we're going to fight and we have a very clear idea of how we're going to use the things and the people that the Congress has appointed; and we will do it very well.

The second assertion is that there are no choices being made in what we are going to buy. We have a very elaborate procedure for deciding what we're going to ask the Congress to appropriate for our troops to use on the battlefield. And, we test the equipment and we try it out and we do all sorts of experimenting with it to make sure that it works right.

The third point is that we're not getting value received for what's been put into the defense budget. I just want to tell you that's baloney and anybody who goes out and looks at the Armed Forces of the United States will see that it's baloney. We have the best Armed Forces we've ever had and to say that you don't get value received is just pure bunk.

Remarks at the BIRMINGHAM CITY
COMMAND OF THE SALVATION ARMY
Birmingham, AL
7 February 1985

Thanks for the welcome. It's nice to be back in Birmingham. Mr. Mayor, I've still got the key to the city you gave me in November and I'm happy to know that the lock has not been changed.

This is a great celebration and it is wonderful to be here for this important occasion. Birmingham has always been known as a good Army town and obviously the Salvation Army has known that it's a good Army town, too. I was here last November to help celebrate your 30th anniversary of Veterans Day; and, on behalf of the men and women in the Armed Forces, I thanked the city of Birmingham then for their support for the Armed Forces. I want to do that again. Thank you for your support.

I enjoyed my stay here then, honoring the Veterans. I have a smart, young Marine aide who is with me here tonight. He was there then. He told me afterwards that a kindly lady, about my age, came up to him afterwards and said, "The General gave a nice talk. We thought it was *superfluous*!" This "smart aleck" Marine said, "Well, thanks very much. I thought it was superfluous myself." He said, "I think the General is thinking of publishing it posthumously." So, the lady, God love her, said, "Good! The sooner the better."

I have been in the U.S. Army close to 46 years now and it is nice to be with you in another army, the Salvation Army. I was a little concerned about what I would say. It reminded me of three years ago. I was asked to give the speech at the National Prayer breakfast in Washington. I really did not focus on what to say until the Sunday before the event was to take place. I had from Sunday to Thursday and I hadn't really decided what to say. It suddenly occurred to me that I was going to be speaking to 2300 people in the flesh and then a whole bunch of others over the radio. And I began to get a little nervous.

That morning the Old Testament lesson was from *Jeremiah* and Jeremiah had a problem somewhat similar to mine. He said, "Now the Word of the Lord came to me, saying, 'I appoint you a prophet to the Nations.' And Jeremiah said, 'Ah, Lord God, behold I do not know how to speak for I am only a youth.'"—I knew that part did not apply to me! Jeremiah goes on to say, "The Lord said to me, 'Do not say I am only a youth for to all to whom I send you, you shall go. And whatever I command you, you shall see. Be not afraid of it for I am with you to deliver you,' said the Lord. Then the Lord put forth His hand and touched my mouth and the Lord said to me, 'Behold, I have put words in your mouth.'" I thought about that and I thought I might take some guidance from that passage.

I have only had three speeches in my whole life. One's on tank maintenance; one's on helicopter maintenance; and the third one is on reenlistment. So, I thought I'd just give them the reenlistment speech. And I did.

Now, maybe that's what I'll talk to this group about tonight—reenlistment. The work of the Salvation Army is done quietly and it's an army which fights a special kind of battle. But, it marches under the same banner that the Lord calls us all to march under—and that is, the unifying banner of the Army of the Lord.

I serve in two armies. I am a general in the United States Army, but I'm a private in God's Army. When I was a private in the United States Army—and I was for a long time—the Salvation Army was there. In fact, it was the Salvation Army during World War II which helped create the USO. As many of you know, that service still goes on today. But the Salvation Army wasn't content just to create the USO. It manned service centers throughout the United States and sent volunteers overseas to over 3,000 places where our people were serving in combat. The Salvation Army did the same thing in the Spanish-American War and in World War I. Incidentally, one of those who served in World War I was Chaplain Norman Marshall—remembered for another reason because of his son, who is your National Commander today.

Additionally, some 32 Salvation Army officers served as chaplains in the Armed Forces during World War II and one rose to the rank of Deputy Chief of Chaplains in the United States Army.

That tradition of support to our Armed Forces continues today—that business of caring for the physical and spiritual needs of men and women in uniform who are also serving in defense of this great nation of ours. That is not an easy thing to do. There's a story about a Salvation Army Chaplain in World War II. Just before a big infantry assault, a soldier ran up to him while the cannons were firing away and the soldier said, "Chaplain! Before this attack starts, tell me everything you know about God. Quick!"

Well, that tradition goes on today. That tradition of bringing nourishment for both body and soul continues very actively in the Service. There was a Salvation Army Chaplain who I ran into with the Army out at Fort Ord, California; and there is another one at Lackland Air Force Base. So, it is nice to be here with friends of our Armed Forces, the Salvation Army.

When I look at the Salvation Army today and the U.S. Army, I see that the two armies have many things in common—and one of those is *change*. The Armed Forces of the United States have changed greatly over the years to meet the changing security needs of our nation. Certainly, the Salvation Army has changed since 1880 when the Salvation Army Commissioner George Scott Railton came to this country. America is now different from the America that the Salvation Army served in those days. Commissioner Railton came to the United States in 1880 when we were enjoying the benefits of the Industrial Revolution but also suffering from the problems of a society on the move.

The turmoil of those years is described in Alvin Toffler's book, *The Third Wave*. I'm sure many of you have read it. It describes our history as comprised of three distinct waves: the first wave being the agricultural era of man. That wave began long before Christ and was a gradual change, taking some 2,000 years to spread over the civilized world. The second wave, the Industrial Revolution, was far more rapid and took only about 200 strife-torn years to change the world—bringing with it great physical prosperity but also bringing with it the most destructive of the over 14,500 wars in recorded history—causing great emotional upheaval. And all that led to the Salvation Army.

The third wave—according to Toffler we are in that wave now—is the information wave, and Toffler says it will take about 20 years—only about two more decades—to complete this change in the nature of man's life, and that change will be greater than what we have experienced over the previous 100 generations!

I guess for an illustration you might take ourselves. I don't know about you but I am a representative of my generation. My generation is computer-illiterate. I have a computer terminal in my office and it stares at me and I stare back at it most of the day. We have learned to chat a little bit now but it's not friendly. On the other hand, I am sure you are like me. My children and grandchildren are very comfortable and well-versed in computers and modern communications devices—about like we were with the automobile.

If you look at this rate of change since World War II, we see that Toffler might be right. Man's knowledge has grown so fast that we have learned more in the last 40 years than the accumulation of all human knowledge before World War II back to the beginning of recorded history. We see remarkable things taking place. We see supersonic transportation. We see man in space. We see man going to the moon. We see the world literally grown smaller with nations inextricably intertwined through our economies, our political systems, our common interests, our cultures and through communications and travel. We saw that last night when the President introduced that marvelous, young West Point cadet. It sort of demonstrates the way the world has changed. First, the cadet was a girl, a West Point cadet. Secondly, she came from Vietnam hidden in a boat about 10 years ago—which just tells you how fast the world has changed as well as the present point about what great opportunities there are in this world and in this nation of ours.

All this great change and the knowledge that man has experienced has not brought peace among men or among nations. History has shown us that change in human affairs is not easy and brings challenges as an inevitable consequence; and, if we're not prepared for change, challenges can lead to crisis and conflict. Therefore, we have to look to the future so that we won't be totally surprised. The promise and potential for the years ahead for us is great; but, at the same time, we know that God only gives us a small glimpse of the future and we will only be partially prepared for it. But we as a people and as a nation and you as a city must first weather the challenges that lie ahead. Certainly, we want to pursue our goals as a nation-state at peace. We don't want our future challenged by other nations whose ambitions may be manifested by a tendency to use force. And certainly, I don't have to identify such nations. The President did last night—the Soviet Union.

There are some 20 wars going on in the world today. Every indication that I see tells me that the rest of this century is going to continue to be very much like this one—certainly a lot of change and instability. It is an area which both the Armed Forces of the United States and the Salvation Army have in common—and that's the need to be ready for change.

I want to tell you that I spent the better part of this week explaining to the Congress why I think the Armed Forces of the nation must and can continue to adapt to the changes ahead of us and to protect us from the conflicts that threaten our way of life. A young man from the television station a few minutes ago asked me to explain whether or not I thought we were spending too much for defense and not enough for social programs. I told him, "The two are not connected." I said, "I can tell you we're not spending enough too much for defense. The issue of whether or not we're not spending enough for social programs is another complete issue that the citizens of this country will have to decide. But we must decide to spend enough for defense to defend ourselves and we can afford to do whatever else we need to do."

I explained that same point in Congress this week. I have explained that peace and freedom do not come cheaply. And I have explained to the Congress that the changes in our Defense Establishment that have taken place over the last few years have not been cheap; but they have been important and we are safer for those changes having taken place. I want to report to you sort of parenthetically—not the main theme of this evening—that your Armed Forces today are better than I have seen them in the 46 years that I have been in the Armed Services. By any common-sense measure the nation is safer because of the improvements that have been made. The Soviets must know that and that is why we will be back at the bargaining table next month. The objective of this whole exercise is to reduce the probability of war and maintain the peace.

This is the fortieth anniversary of many of the battles of World War II that took place toward the end of that war. In looking back to the lessons of that war, I recall the words of George Marshall who was Chief of Staff of the Army in 1941, shortly before the United States went into the war. He said in his first Report to Congress that America is embarked on what he called a "great experiment in democracy, a test of the ability of a government such as ours to prepare itself in time of peace against the ruthless and arbitrary action of other governments."

At great cost, we passed such a test in World War II; and I want to tell you that, if we are to continue to enjoy peace and liberty in this great democracy, we have to continue to tend to our military strength. But we also have to continue to tend to all the other elements of our strength—our economic strength, our political strength, our cultural and social strength and, above all, our spiritual strength.

There is a new book by a French author, Jean-Francois Revel, entitled *How Democracies Perish*. In the opening lines of the book, Revel describes the world as "a democracy-killing machine." He goes on to say in that book that "Democracy is not basically structured to defend itself against outside enemies seeking its annihilation, especially since the latest and most dangerous of these external enemies, communism, parades as democracy perfected when it is in fact the absolute negation of democracy."

Now the pessimism of that French writer ought to keep us on our toes. He has a lot of very good points in his book. Certainly, as we look at the world around us, and the history of the immediate past, that pessimism might worry us. But it is my own belief that we need not be overly frightened, though we must be concerned.

When my outfit mobilized almost 45 years ago, we marched past the City Auditorium in Minneapolis, Minnesota. It was about 20 degrees below zero that day. I remember looking at the corner of the Auditorium and there was an engraved marker, a plaque which reads, "Participation in the rights of citizenship assumes participation in the duties of citizenship." That principle is fundamental to the health of our democracy; the duties of citizenship range all the way from voting to elect our Presidents, our Congressmen, legislators and our city governments to paying the taxes that we the people levy on ourselves. Those duties sometimes encompass going off to fight in the defense of this nation and its principles. Those duties also include being responsible citizens who step forward in selfless service to help improve the plight of our fellow human beings.

That concept of selfless service is another thing which the Armed Forces of the nation and the Salvation Army have in common.

The Nation will always need good men and women to serve her. We need good people in our Armed Forces; and, on the other hand, so does the Salvation Army. As Joshua said to his army at the end of a long campaign: "Choose ye whom ye will serve; as for me and my house, we will serve the Lord." It is no accident that William Booth changed the original name of the Salvation Army from the "East London Revival Society" to the "Christian Mission" and finally, in 1878, to the name it has today, the "Salvation Army"— because it is *just that*, an *army* of the Lord. And the key word in any army is "serve" or "service."

The Salvation Army, like the United States Army, has discipline in the concept of service. Members go where they are needed. They follow orders. And that's an important duty for all of us who serve in the Army of the Lord. Christ's first order to Levi was "Follow me." That's the exact same motto for the United States Infantry. Those of you who served in the Armed Forces of our nation know that life in the military is more than just a job. We don't work for the Army, the Navy, the Air Force or the Marine Corps; we serve in it. We don't choose the missions for the Armed Forces—or its wars—but the members are faithful to a higher authority to go out and accomplish the missions. Nor does the service end at the pleasure of the soldier, sailor, airman, or Marine. It ends when the mission is accomplished. It is part of what the British General Sir John Hackett calls the "military's unlimited liability contract." In the case of the Army of the Lord, that contract lasts for Eternity.

When we are called to serve in the Armed Forces, it is not up to us to choose what is important or what is unimportant. There are simply no degrees of importance in the service we perform. Some people in our Armed Forces go on to command great combat units or ships or airplanes or formations in battle; others do obscure staff work in highly anonymous jobs; and some go off to serve in places which their mothers-in-law can't find on the map. But, the key thing is that the service of the generals is no more important than the service of the privates. And that's an important part of military service. All service is important and all service should be well done. The soldier, sailor, airman, or Marine who dies in some obscure skirmish died doing service as important as those soldiers who fought under General Patton in those great battles which brought him to the Rhine River 40 years ago tonight.

St. Paul in *Ephesians* says that we get different gifts but all those gifts are to be used in the service of God. We in the military service are sometimes accused of being impersonal and being concerned with masses of troops and not individuals. I want to tell you that's *wrong*. We know the importance of one soldier in one place can mean the difference between success or failure in battle. The same is true in the Salvation Army. Each individual is important.

You heard Julia Ward Howe's wonderful words being sung by the choir tonight. There is a story about Julia Ward Howe. I think this is one Lawton Chiles told the other day at the National Prayer Breakfast. Julia Ward Howe came to Washington to ask for some help from a senator, to help a fellow who was down on his luck. The Senator told her, "I'm so sorry, Julia. I just can't do it. I'm just too busy to be concerned with individuals." Julia Ward Howe said to him, "That's quite remarkable, Senator. Even God hasn't reached that stage yet."

Joachim Von Arnim, the German Romantic novelist from the early 1800s, said, "The history of the world begins anew with every man, and ends with him." He meant that one man or one woman *can* make a difference. We have here a roomful of people who made a difference. Aristotle once said that virtue was the habit of right choice. Certainly, your choice as members and supporters of the Salvation Army to help others is a virtuous choice. You made the right choice. Through your service and the service of thousands of others like you, volunteers who work for the Salvation Army and other charities, Americans who are down on their luck are put right with God and they are put back on the road to self-respect and improvement.

In the Invocation tonight, we were reminded of Jesus' words when he said, "Whatever you did for the least of these, you did for Me." It is an important thing for us to remember. As I said before, I think it is imperative that this nation tend to all elements of its strength. I want you to know that I and my fellow members of the Joint Chiefs of Staff and Secretary Weinberger and his staff will continue to do all we can to help defend this great nation; and with the help of the Congress and the American people, we will be successful. The health of the Armed Forces today is good, thanks to the investment that "We the People" have made over the last several years. At the same time, as I look out and see so many people here to support the Salvation Army, it's a sign to me that our spiritual health is good as well.

The U.S. Army has a catchy recruiting slogan that says, "Be all you can be—in the Army." I believe that slogan fits the Salvation Army very well; so, I tell you, all you supporters of the Salvation Army, be all you can be—in the Salvation Army. And reenlist today. I have a few words from a couple of great sergeants in God's Army and I'd like to close with those: Sergeant Peter and Sergeant Paul.

I'm going to start with Sergeant Peter. He said some important things. He said, "For this very reason, make every effort to add to your faith, goodness; and to goodness, knowledge; and to knowledge, self-control; and to self-control, perseverance; and to perseverance, Godliness; and to Godliness, brotherly kindness; and to brotherly kindness, love."

And Sergeant Paul had a few words to say about taking care of our equipment and being ready. He said, "Therefore, put on the whole armor of God so that when the day of evil comes, you may be able to stand your ground. And after you have done everything, stand firm with the belt of truth buckled around your waist, and the breastplate of righteousness in place and with your feet fitted with readiness that comes from the gospel of peace. In addition to all this, take up the shield of faith with which you can extinguish all the flaming arrows of the Evil One. Take the helmet of salvation, the sword of the spirit which is the *Word of God*. And pray in the spirit on all occasions with all kinds of prayers and requests. With this in mind, be alert and always keep on praying for all the Saints." And you are all the Saints. Pray also for me. Thank you very much.

**Remarks to the
CHEVY CHASE CLUB
Chevy Chase, MD
28 February 1985**

Thank you, gentlemen. Thanks for the welcome. It is nice to be here tonight. That was an absolutely magnificent meal. It covered most of the places that I have been except Laos and Thailand. Ed, here, knows all about that and I have forgotten what the coleslaw was called which was made from green papaya. But I used to eat that and then when we were flying helicopters, I always thought if I lost a gas-producer in the helicopter, I would just blow into the engine. It was hot. The meal was superb and it made me a little sleepy but I hope I can keep you awake. I eat another meal regularly at this time of the year because it's that time of the year when the trips we make are from the Pentagon to Capitol Hill; and it's called "crow." It is served to us up there quite regularly.

There is a poem that was found in the Ordnance Bureau in 1868. It goes like this—and it sort of describes my life these days:

The Devil came up from Hell one day,
And went straight to Washington City.
He said to a friend he met by the way,
"I shall call on the Armed Services Committee."
He walked into the room with an air quite gay,
And took every one there by surprise,
By bowing and saying, "I'm here for the day—
And I'm the father of lies!"

Then they called in an officer gray and old,
With a character as pure as snow,
And they charged him with lies by contractors told,
And with frauds which he did not know.
Then told him to leave, that he need not reply,
But go forth to the national wrath,
And they sent their report (while the Devil sat by)
To the papers by telegraph.
"Egad!" said the Devil, "I like this well.
You torture a man more here,
Than I in a brimstone lake in Hell.
For there he has no more to fear."

Speaking of crow, I am reminded of a story about a fellow from my home in Crow Wing County, Minnesota. His name was Ole. He went on an errand for his wife, Lena, who sent him to the drug store. On the way home he stopped by the local pub and he spent a good deal of the evening there. Coming home, he tripped over the doorsill and fell flat on his face. Ole looked up to see Lena standing over him and all he could see were her bedroom slippers and then from there on up this towering figure. She looked down at him and he said, "I had a speech all prepared, but I have just decided to take your questions from the floor."

Before I do that, I want to give you a report on the national security as I see it today from the foxhole that I now occupy. Before I get into that I want to read from a Pennsylvania magazine article describing the world situation. And it reads, "War at this time rages over a great part of the known world. Our newspapers are daily filled with fresh accounts of the destruction it everywhere occasions." That statement was written in the same year that your "Bradley House" was built. It was written by Ben Franklin and published in his pamphlet, *Plain Truth*, in 1747. But, certainly, it could just as well have been written today. There are about 20 wars going on in the world today. And the behavior of the Soviet Union with its strong nuclear and conventional forces raises the stakes for us and the rest of the Free World to an unprecedented level.

We can look to our history over the years and we can see that our own peace and well-being and national security have benefited from agreements that we've had with potential adversaries and competitors in the international scene. The Rush-Bagot Treaty of 1818 between Canada and the United States is a good example. We may take for granted the great friendship we have with Canada, our good neighbor and ally to the north; but, in 1818, a few years after the war of 1812, Canada and the United States looked very much like enemies to each other. Yet, the two nations put aside their differences and agreed to a treaty which for all practical purposes demilitarized the Great Lakes and now we have the longest undefended border in the world.

Some people say, "Why can't we do that sort of thing with the Soviet Union today?" Well, certainly there have been great efforts that were tried. But, when one looks at that, you have to be reminded of what Salvador de Madariaga, the great Spanish philosopher and historian who worked for many, many years on the old League of Nations Disarmament Commission, said. He said, "We've got the issue of war and disarmament upside down and backwards. Nations don't distrust each other because they are armed." He said, "They arm because they distrust each other." So, if we're going to work on the business of armaments and what it has to do with keeping the peace in this world, we really have to work on the distrust as much as on the armaments.

This country has a defensive strategy. We have a strategy that is called "deterrence." We say that a sensible balance of forces—nuclear forces and conventional forces for us and our allies—will help us keep the peace and reduce the likelihood of war. We don't seek any superiority over the Soviet Union, but we want to be very sure that the Soviet Union understands that it can't use its military power for coercion to threaten war or to attack us without understanding that they won't succeed. We believe that if we build and maintain forces that are self-evidently capable of frustrating their objectives, then we will keep the peace. And, that is our strategy of deterrence.

I want to give you a little report—I see old soldiers and young soldiers and airmen and sailors and Marines out here and old bosses. I want to tell you that the Armed Forces you have today are as good as any we have had in the 45 years or so that I have been wearing the uniform. And you can be very proud of them. We have extraordinarily good people in the Armed Forces today and they're better equipped, better trained and better supported than they have been in many, many years.

We read a lot about hardware and the arguments about whether we should buy this piece of hardware or that piece of hardware. But I think it is important for us to remember that combat capability is the sum of people, the hardware, the training and the support that they have. And by support I don't just mean the ammunition; I also mean the moral support that they get from the people of this country for the job that they have to do. I can tell you that what you have there now is a well-supported armed force that combines those elements into a very significant combat capability.

You see things like the new tanks we argued over for years and years. Well, I visited units with the new tanks and I saw that the tank gunnery qualification scores for the crews are 46 percent higher than they were a couple of years ago with the old tank—a tank which was a good tank, too. I see that the first-round hits are 83 percent for both night and day. I see the F-16 airplane, the best single-engine airplane in the world. In the bomb competitions, the F-16 pilots today do better with plain, ordinary "dumb" bombs—as the Air Force people call them—than the F-4 pilots did with "smart" bombs three or four years ago. Now, that's a phenomenal increase in capability.

Our alliances also are a very important part of our security and our strategy. This nation is blessed with good allies who share with us common interests and common values and who are willing to join us in the defense of our way of life. NATO is a good example of those alliances. Our East Asian alliances are other good examples. NATO has maintained the peace in Europe for over 35 years. This year we see the 40th anniversary of many of the last battles of World War II. I look around here tonight—how many veterans of World War II are here? The place is loaded with them. That war laid waste to whole nations; yet, at the same time, out of those battles grew a concept of Western security that we have today. Not only did that concept restore the health of the allies, but it also helped bring allies and former foes together as partners in defense of the West and its principles today.

The Soviets too recognize the value of allies. They have worked very hard as a principal part of their strategy, to try and separate us from our allies over the years, as well as to try and limit our arms. They have also worked very hard to try to build their own ties and alliances in the world. They haven't been nearly as successful as we have. As somebody said, "The Soviet Union is the only nation in the world surrounded by hostile communist neighbors."

A good example of the Soviet attempts to separate us from our allies has been over the deployment of the intermediate-range nuclear weapons to Europe. That deployment began in December of 1983; and, from 1979 when NATO made the decision until those weapons began to be deployed in December of 1983, the Soviets did everything they possibly could to separate the United States from its European allies. They were unsuccessful. Those weapons are being deployed in Europe today in spite of what the Russians did. When the weapons began to come in, the Russians walked out of the negotiations—an act for which they were much criticized.

They are now back at the table. The world, I think, has sighed a great sigh of relief, knowing that the two superpowers are now back talking to each other again about the possibilities of reducing both the risks and probability of nuclear war. But we should recognize that these talks will not take away the dangers to peace. The principal Soviet goals will still be pursued. They will continue to try to separate us from our allies and they'll continue to try to limit our arms, by whatever means.

Now, why did the Soviets come back to the table? Well, I conclude by looking at what has happened that it is the synergism of the interrelationship between the steadfastness and unity of the nations of the West, the resolve of the United States to rearm itself and keep itself strong, our willingness to go ahead with our nuclear modernization program and the President's Strategic Defense Initiative.

I believe that the resolve of the West—and the Soviet regard for strength—has convinced the Soviets that it is in their own self-interest to return to the negotiating table. These two elements—good defenses and good allies—if pursued together can continue to provide for peace in the West. But, if we in the West unilaterally limit our arms, whether it is through our own political process or our failure to act when we need to act, then we will hand the Soviets what they are looking for and we won't get anything out of those negotiations.

There is an important vote coming up in the Congress in a couple of weeks, depending on how the politicians manage. It is the vote on whether to continue the production line for the 21 MX or PEACEKEEPER missiles that were authorized last year. I would like to take just a minute and talk about that because we have been before committees of the Congress a number of times in the past weeks testifying about that subject. When I hear the questions from the representatives of the people and when I see a lack of understanding there about what the contribution of that particular weapon is to our security, I wonder about what the rest of the people understand. There are some myths about the intercontinental ballistic missile and its contribution to security. I believe they need to be removed.

One of the first myths is that we are building a first-strike weapon that is destabilizing, and that is going to endanger the world and therefore cause the Russians to build even more weapons or do something drastic. Now, what I want to tell you is that the United States keeps *80 percent* of its strategic nuclear warheads in its bomber force and in its ballistic missile submarine force and only about 20 percent in the intercontinental ballistic missile force. There is no way in the world that the Russian military planners will ever conclude that we are building a first-strike force with 20 percent of our warheads in our ICBM warheads. So, that's a myth.

Then, the second point that comes up often is that the PEACEKEEPER is vulnerable—that we are going to stick it in silos where it will be vulnerable to Soviet attack and it will either invite attack or, because we will have to use it or lose it, we will use it first instead of waiting for them to attack us. I want to tell you that's another myth. If the only thing we had in our strategic nuclear deterrent force was intercontinental ballistic missiles, then the vulnerability of that missile would be of some concern. But when only 20 percent of the warheads are in that force, and when we have a good warning system and a good command and control system, I want to tell you that it is not vulnerable. That's a myth. The Soviets know when we keep our forces in the TRIAD—

bombers, submarine-launched ballistic missiles and intercontinental ballistic missiles—that they can't attack any particular part of the force without having the rest of the force available to retaliate against them.

Now, the idea that we are building a large force that is going to make the Soviets believe we are trying to seek nuclear superiority is another myth that is often heard. During the five-year period from 1977 to 1983, the Soviets added 1,100 modern, intercontinental ballistic missile warheads, with about 5,000 warheads—good, accurate, modern warheads—another 700 submarine-launched ballistic missiles and about 300 bombers. That occurred while we debated whether we should add any or not. They placed their ICBM's in the hardest silos in the world and linked those silos to hardened command centers. And during the same period, we added 135 ICBM's—the last of the last modernization and a few SLBM's and no bombers. In fact, we actually retired more than we added. Now, we rely on that TRIAD—and a good warning system and a good command and control system. We make it very clear to the Soviets that we are not building a first-strike force; that we are, in fact, defensive. But we also want to make it very clear that we have a modern, healthy, nuclear deterrent force so that the Soviets understand they cannot attack us and achieve their war aims.

What I want to tell you about that PEACEKEEPER vote is that *it needs to succeed.* It needs to succeed for a number of reasons. The first is that we need it in the force because it is three times more effective than the missile it is replacing. It puts at risk those things that are of great value to the Soviets and those things they know they need to carry out their war plans. We cannot do that with the weapons that are in the force today.

And the second reason it needs to be passed is because when John Tower and Max Kampelman, our negotiators in Geneva, meet with the Soviets, the Soviets will not see that we are going to limit our own weapons through our own political process.

There is another myth, and I heard that myth was even repeated here: that is, that the Joint Chiefs of Staff don't support the deployment of the PEACEKEEPER and I want to tell you that's a myth. The Joint Chiefs of Staff unanimously continue to support the immediate deployment of that missile system.

We need to get on with that strategic modernization and we need to get on with the strategic modernization not only for our nuclear forces, but we need to keep up the modernization of our conventional forces because the unrelenting buildup of the Soviet forces continues. We can get a little bit complacent because we have had larger defense budgets over the last four or five years than we have had for a long time. We have made some significant improvements in our forces, but the Soviets have not stood still. And we haven't gained much in the overall distance between our forces and the Soviet forces.

Another initiative that is going to come up for a vote soon is the research and development money for the so-called Strategic Defense Initiative. That initiative is a research initiative which says that we should look into our technological genius, which is one of our great strengths, to find out whether or not our sole reliance on offensive retaliation can be mitigated or perhaps even abandoned in the future. Within the bounds of the ABM Treaty, the United States is going to explore the means which might give us the opportunity to combine both offense and defense in the future for our strategic nuclear deterrence. The President has made it clear that this research alters in no way our commitment to deterrence or our commitment to our allies.

Now, the Soviets are intensely interested in this Strategic Defense Initiative. They appear eager to do everything they possibly can to constrain the program. And that is an interesting phenomenon in the Soviets because they are the country with the *only* operational anti-ballistic missile system in the world, and the country that has spent more money on strategic defense than all the rest of the world combined by, I would say, a factor of 10, and the country that is investing huge sums in research in exactly the sort of program that the Strategic Defense Initiative envisions.

Now, responses to the program have been mixed and some are concerned that it will alter the deterrent balance, that it will drive up the levels of armament and that it will make agreement more difficult when we go to Geneva. Certainly, any new technological advance makes arms control negotiations more complicated. We assume that with every other facet of strategic nuclear arms. But I would say to you that we certainly have an argument that the Soviets themselves subscribe to: the concept that a mixture of offensive and defensive systems is compatible with deterrence. The Soviets' own deployments have demonstrated their views of that.

There is another contention that the Soviets may be incited to add more offensive arms in trying to overwhelm the Strategic Defense Initiative with more weapons—or that they won't agree to reductions in offensive weapons because they will need them to overwhelm the defensive systems. I would say to you that as a practical military matter the approach that is being pursued in a layered defense is more likely to provide incentives for the Soviets to reduce or even abandon their ICBM force, perhaps 20 years from now when some of this comes into fruition, rather than have them build more. And, certainly, what the Soviets really fear is the fact that the Strategic Defense Initiative will make their ICBM force ineffective, *not* that they will have to build more.

But, the SDO program is something that will come only in the future. It is a broad research program. We don't have any preconceived notions of the outcome. In the meantime, negotiations can make the contribution to increased stability in the world *if* we can have what the President has asked for: significant, large reductions in strategic nuclear arms.

The accord that was reached in January in Geneva is only a first step. There is a long road ahead. If we are able to persuade the Soviets to make substantial reductions or perhaps even move to a concept that recognizes that both sides can have a defensive organization, it will be a good thing for the world. But, we haven't convinced the Soviets to make such a move in the past; so, the other thing that we need to do is make it very clear to them that we're going to continue to modernize our own forces and keep those forces strong.

We need to go ahead with the modernization of the conventional forces and nuclear forces.

Again quoting from what Ben Franklin said in 1747 in *Plain Truth*: "'tis a wise and true saying that one sword often keeps another in the scabbard. They that are on their guard and appear ready to receive their adversaries are in much less danger of being attacked than those who are negligent."

I would say to you that this is a very important time in the history of this nation and it is a very important time to make sure that the Soviets do understand that we have a sword in our scabbard and not only that but that we will, in fact, use it to defend ourselves. If they understand that, I am confident that we'll keep the peace, not only for ourselves but for our friends and allies in the world. It just simply comes down to making it patently self-evident to the Soviets that we are going to have modern, strong forces so that they cannot succeed with their war plans. I am confident that we will be successful.

Statement before the
SENATE APPROPRIATIONS COMMITTEE
On the Strategic Nuclear Modernization Program
Washington, DC
7 March 1985

Mr. Chairman and members of the Subcommittee.

I am pleased to be here on behalf of the Joint Chiefs of Staff to urge your support for the President's program to modernize our strategic nuclear deterrent forces as our highest military priority.

In particular, the Joint Chiefs urge the immediate and continued deployment of the PEACEKEEPER. Its deployment will strengthen the TRIAD, help ensure deterrence, serve as an incentive for Soviet restraint and provide a sensible climate for more productive negotiations. The PEACEKEEPER is tested and proven; it is ready for deployment; and we need it now.

THE U.S. STRATEGY

Since the end of World War II our goal has been to preserve the peace through strength. This means that we, along with our allies, need to maintain the necessary military strength in addition to the other elements of our national power to make it self-evidently clear to our principal adversaries that they can't achieve their objectives by force or the threat of force. It is a defensive strategy. Our strategy implies several essential components. The first is alliances, such as NATO and our alliances in the Pacific region. We have banded together over the years with other countries who share with us common interests and a desire for peace. The health of those alliances has long depended upon good armed forces, both nuclear and conventional.

Second, we deploy forces in some of the regions where we have alliances. These forward-deployed forces do two things: they deter attack by making it clear to aggressors that their attack will be met by forces which include those of the United States and, second, they lend political strength to the alliances by showing our friends that our commitment is strong. To back up these forward-deployed forces, we maintain a strong central reserve of forces here in the United States, Active, Reserve and National Guard. These forces can go to reinforce our forward-deployed forces or go elsewhere in the world to protect our interests.

To support this concept, we need control of the seas and we have a good Navy to do that. We need the free use of space. We need good intelligence to warn and inform us; we need good mobility to project our power and to sustain it far from our own shores; and we need outstanding command and control to direct our forces.

Overarching all these components are our nuclear deterrent forces and the essential warning and command and control systems. Our strategic nuclear forces are embodied in the TRIAD—a concept which has kept the peace for over twenty years. The TRIAD is designed as a deterrent, not for a first strike. About 80 percent of our strategic weapons are in the bomber and submarine forces. Only 20 to 25 percent of our force is in land-based ICBMs. We maintain the three elements of our TRIAD because each leg of the TRIAD provides special strengths which reinforce the deterrent value of the other legs and help guard against tactical and technical surprise. The TRIAD is the foundation of our deterrent strategy.

THE SOVIET NUCLEAR THREAT

The Soviets continue to modernize their strategic nuclear forces. In contrast to our relatively small force of land-based ICBMs, the Soviet force is over 80 percent land-based, the kind of force most useable for a first strike. In 1982, the Soviets deployed more, highly accurate ICBM warheads than we intend to deploy in our entire PEACEKEEPER program. In 1983, they deployed another 200 ICBM warheads and in 1984 they were nearing completion of the latest phase of the modernization of their current silo-based strategic ICBMs. The Soviet's SS-18 and SS-19 missiles, which could total over 5,000 warheads, are in the world's hardest silos, with a redundant, survivable, command and control network. Moscow is protected by the world's only operational ballistic missile defense system. We expect deployment of newer missiles, the SS-X-24 and SS-X-25.

THE MILITARY RATIONALE FOR PEACEKEEPER

The Soviets continue to spend large sums for offensive nuclear weapons capable of achieving their war aims. In addition, they have extensive programs for active and passive strategic defense. These facts lead to the conclusion that the best deterrent is a US military capability that makes the Soviets' assessment of war outcomes under any circumstance so uncertain and so dangerous as to remove any incentive for them to initiate an attack. This fundamental prescription for deterrence means that the deterrent value of the PEACEKEEPER must be measured in terms of the uncertainty it causes for Soviet war planners in designing an effective ability to achieve their war aims.

The Soviets have taken on difficult tasks for themselves in attempting a war-winning strategic posture. The military requirements for such a capability are extensive, including the need for very sophisticated weapons, large forces and the capacity to execute difficult attack scenarios. These self-imposed Soviet military requirements are the key to an effective U.S. counter-strategy. We believe that the Soviets' war aims are to destroy U.S. nuclear and conventional military capabilities with their land-based missiles while maintaining large reserves for post-war dominance. In order to have high assurance of success, the Soviets need to strike our forces several times and they have the force structure to do that. To counter this Soviet strategy, we need the PEACEKEEPER missile.

The PEACEKEEPER missile is a direct counter to Soviet war aims because it can retaliate promptly with phenomenal accuracy against the Soviet attacking force and other high-value military targets during the conduct of what will necessarily be a prolonged attack. The deterrent value of the PEACEKEEPER comes from this potential to retaliate against Soviet missiles and hardened command posts meant to protect Soviet political and military leaders.

Some have questioned the vulnerability of the PEACEKEEPER system. Vulnerability has to be considered in light of the whole TRIAD of our strategic force. The Soviets cannot attack the land-based leg of our TRIAD in isolation from the other legs of the TRIAD. The Soviets must deal with all legs of the TRIAD and supporting command and control simultaneously. This enormously complicates the achievement of the Soviet war aims. If the PEACEKEEPER was the only element of our strategic nuclear deterrent force, then its vulnerability would be of far greater concern that it is with the ICBM force contributing about 20 percent of our strategic nuclear deterrent force. Within the TRIAD, any potential vulnerability of the land-based leg is compensated by the warning system, the command and control system, and the other legs of the TRIAD.

Deploying the PEACEKEEPER does not mean that the United States is developing a first-strike posture. It is absolutely necessary that we have the retaliatory capabilities to be able to deny Soviet war aims. According to the Soviets' own calculus, the PEACEKEEPER will thoroughly complicate an effective attack. The PEACEKEEPER will add significantly to our deterrent posture and it will be a stabilizing factor in the strategic nuclear U.S.-Soviet equation.

CONCLUSION

The United States delayed its strategic nuclear modernization and we have had to modernize all three legs of the TRIAD at the same time. We are making steady progress with the bomber and submarine force modernization. The TRIDENT submarine program will modernize our aging ballistic missile submarine fleet and the D-5 missile will add new capabilities to the sea-based leg of the TRIAD at the end of this decade. The B-1B program is on schedule; it will be in the operational force next year. It will provide a modern, responsive bomber capable of penetrating Soviet defenses.

The modernization of the ICBM force has had a series of delays well-known to this committee. The delays have not been technological or system delays; the missile is performing superbly. The Joint Chiefs of Staff urge the immediate deployment of the PEACEKEEPER. The PEACEKEEPER is tested and proven, and is ready for deployment. The Joint Chiefs of Staff believe that we must proceed now with the deployment of the PEACEKEEPER in order to maintain the effectiveness of the TRIAD and our deterrent strategy into the next century.

Remarks to the ATLANTA
COMMUNITY LEADERS LUNCHEON
Atlanta, GA
11 April 1985

Thank you. It is nice to be in Atlanta on this beautiful spring day. To be with this group of community leaders is an honor. When I look at the past speakers who have addressed this group, I wonder why Ed Wheeler asked me. I thought perhaps it was a gathering of old handball players. For a fellow who has three speeches—one's on tank maintenance, one's on helicopter maintenance and the third's on reenlistment—it is an honor also to be here the year of the 150th anniversary of Oglethorpe University and, I guess, the 200th anniversary of the death of James Oglethorpe.

Coming into the Atlanta airport is always a thrill. We have a little Bible class at our church. One of the older ladies, a member of the class, asked the pastor, "How do you get to Heaven? What's the route to Heaven?" Well, for the Lutheran folks, you get a good dose of Grace by faith and so forth but the pastor said, "There are probably a number of routes. I don't know exactly which route you take; but, whichever way you go, I know you have to change planes in Atlanta."

I have a bit of a cold and if I sound like I'm talking through my nose, it is because I just returned from a trip to Eastern Europe and I have a "communist" cold. Like all things communist, it seems to hang on longer than it is welcome. We live in what was characterized in the Invocation as a "troubled world." I think one need only to read what is in the headlines of the newspaper on any given day to be reminded of the fact.

There are some 20 wars going on in the world today. There have been millions of people killed in wars since World War II. And it looks like a dark and dreary world. *Harpers Magazine* at one time had an article that said, "It is a gloomy moment in the history of our country. The domestic situation is in chaos; prices are so high as to be utterly impossible. The political cauldron seethes and bubbles with uncertainty, Russia hangs like a cloud dark and silent upon the horizon. Of our troubles, no man can see the end." That was *Harpers* in 1848. The world in 1985, like in 1848, is a dangerous place.

There are a number of contributions to the instability of the world. Certainly, I'm not expert enough to tell you what they all are. But I look at the Soviet Union and the massive military buildup that has taken place over the past 25 years and I can only conclude that it is one of the major factors in the instability of the world today.

Some years ago an author said, "Look eastward to that prison house of peoples, Russia. There is only one way of dealing with Russia and that is the way of courage." The author was Karl Marx. Many years later another author wrote, "The Soviets view their relationships with the West as played not in the spirit of cooperation, but with a competitive zeal designed to further Soviet interests at the expense of the opposition .... Recognizing that the Soviet Union approaches issues from a different orientation ... the United States should ... bolster its will and rise to the challenges with a degree of resolve ... in terms comprehensible to the Soviet Union. It should avoid any unilateral restraint and accommodations because this type of behavior is interpreted by the Soviet Union not as an invitation to cooperation but as an opportunity which must be exploited."

That is from the Master's thesis of Major Arthur P. Nicholson, when he finished the Naval Post Graduate School in 1980. As you know, Major Nicholson was killed by a Soviet soldier the week before last.

We live in an interdependent world—interdependent in terms of politics, in terms of social structure and, more than anything else, in terms of economics. When I first put on the uniform, the United States was a net exporter of oil, not much by today's standards—but 20,000 barrels a day was not insignificant in 1939. Today, we import 3.3 million barrels a day and that is down to almost half what it was 10 years ago. The same can be said of a number of things. Last year we had a trade imbalance of $100 billion, a trade deficit. Now, I don't cite that fact to pass judgment on trade deficits, I simply cite it to give some idea of the magnitude of our economic ties with the rest of the world. That $100 billon is more than the Gross National Product of many nations in South America or in Africa. So, our ties with the rest of the world are very great, particularly in the economic sense.

This is the time of the year for us when we go to the Congress to testify in support of the President's defense budget. We've gone through that series of hearings for the most part, and I sense that there are three "burning questions" in the minds of the members of the Congress this year. Because the Congress represents "We the People," I would say that those three "burning questions" also are on the minds of "We the People." So, I would like to talk about those three questions. The first is "How much is enough for defense?" The second is, "Are we spending the money that we are spending for defense sensibly?" And, the third question is, "What do we do about nuclear weapons?" I am sure there are other "burning" issues but I would like to address those for a few minutes and then save some time for questions.

The first question is, "How much is enough?" Well, there are a number of ways that one might measure how much is enough. People say, "Since we're at peace, it must be enough." Or you can use a regression analysis and look back at years in the past when we had what was considered to be a stable world situation and say that that might give us some guidance. You might look at the peacetime years between the Korean War and the Vietnam War. If we did, we would see a number of facts. The first is that that was the time we had unquestioned nuclear superiority. Secondly, we as a nation were willing to spend about 8 percent of our Gross National Product for defense over a period of about 10 years' time. We maintained an Army which was about 200,000 stronger than the Army we have today. We had a 900-ship Navy in contrast to the 450-ship Navy we have today. We had 26,000 airplanes in the Air Force in contrast to the 13,000 airplanes we have today. We had a National Guard and Reserve that were much stronger than what we have today. We had an Individual Ready Reserve that had one and a quarter million people in it in contrast to the 300,000 or so that are in today.

We could look back at 1979, five or six years ago, when we were willing to spend only 4.9 percent of our Gross National Product for defense and we would see an Army that was 16,000 under its authorized strength which was then 250,000 below that strength I mentioned earlier. We would see a Navy that was short 22,000 Petty Officers. We would see Armed Forces that were short about 5,000 pilots. We would see that we were recruiting about 50 percent high school graduates and about 40 percent of those that were enlisted in the Armed Forces were in the lowest mental category acceptable to the Armed Forces. And, you would also see a world in which U.S. power had fallen to a low point.

There are a number of ways to determine how much is enough. I would suggest to you that neither of those regression analyses is necessarily the way to do it. One ought to look at the world and determine how to proceed for the years ahead. You should look at your strategy and decide how best to meet that strategy at the lowest cost to the taxpayers.

Now, as we go through this, you might see some other answers to that question but the only thing that I will tell you further on that particular question is that we should be guided by the words of Winston Churchill in a talk to Britain in the 1930s. He said, "We can afford what we need for defense. What we cannot afford is to say, "We only need what is convenient to provide."'

I want to tell you today that our Armed Forces are reasonably healthy, and I'd like to go on to that next question, which is, "Are we spending sensibly what we spend for defense?" We have spent a trillion dollars for defense in the last five years, so what have we produced? That is a good question, and one that deserves an answer. So, I'd like to talk a bit about what the money has produced. What I would like to tell you in the first place is if we had stayed at the 1980 level, we would have spent very close to a trillion dollars anyway. What has happened? An additional $300 billion was spent for defense over the last five years over and above the 1980 level. Where did it go? About $80 billion went for people; that is, improvements in people's pay, additional inducements to get good people in, and keep good people. About $110 billion went for equipment, new equipment. Thirty-seven billion dollars went for improved support; that is; building up the war reserve stocks.

What did it produce? Well, I want to tell you now that over the last few years 93 percent of the people enlisting in the Armed Forces are high school graduates. Only about 7 percent of those enlisting are in the lowest mental category acceptable for the Armed Forces. The reenlistment rates have gone from about 25 percent for first-term enlistees to about 52 percent. For career soldiers, sailors, airmen and Marines, the percentage has gone from 63 percent to 83 percent. What I want to tell you is that is the heart of the improvement of your Armed Forces. People are the heart of good armed forces. The United States has learned and relearned that lesson throughout its history and I tell you that as citizens we don't need to relearn it again. Let's remember that.

The pilot shortage has been about cured. The Navy Petty Officer shortage has been cured. The Army's non-commissioned officer shortage has been cured. So, the people situation is in pretty good shape. And it's in far better shape than those numbers show you. Because the turbulence has been reduced, and because the training attrition is down, we need to bring in fewer people, and stability in the force is there to do the job better because they have been on the job longer.

But, what did we get for equipment? Many times I read about criticisms of the equipment that we have purchased. I want to tell you that the fundamental axiom of American defense—and this is not a new one—is that we will make up for shortages in manpower by providing our people the best possible equipment that we can get for them. We think it is better to expend hardware and energy than it is to expend life and blood.

Today we have some of the best airplanes in the world. We have added 2400 of the new M-1 tanks and another 2200 of the new M-2 Fighting Vehicles. The Navy has gone from 493 to 523 ships while it retired 50 World War II vintage ships. But it is the combination of people and equipment that has made the difference. And what glues that together is the training, that extra $37 billion that was added to improve training. We have done tremendous amounts of research and development trying to find and improve ways to keep our military equipment in the field in operation. And that has paid off in good training.

I would just like to say a few things. The F-16 airplane in the Air Force today in today's bombing competitions does far better than the F-4s, the airplane it replaced. The F-16 does it with "dumb" bombs. That is, with just plain, ordinary bombs with no guidance it does better than the F-4 did with guided missiles a few years ago. And with a one-man crew instead of a two-man crew and with improved operational ready rates the airplane has far exceeded anything that we ever had with the F-4. The maintenance man-hours and flight hours are far better than was ever expected.

Then, there is the tank force, for example: The M-1 tank was greatly criticized and almost lost in Congress because of the criticism that was raised over that tank. That tank has now been fielded in large numbers. I visited a tank force in Europe last year; and, with the combination of better tanks and better people and better training, that tank force in Europe has an operational ready rate of about 94 percent. That is in contrast to about 70 percent for the old tank force. More importantly, the tank can fight at night and in the daytime and the tank crew qualification scores are 46 percent higher than they were four years ago. The first-round hits in tank gunnery qualifications are up to 83 percent in contrast to around 50 percent a few years ago.

Now, if you just do a little mathematics in your head: with 2,000 tanks in the field and a 70 percent operational ready rate, it means that 1400 tanks are ready to go out and meet the enemy. If you have a 94 percent operational ready rate, it means that over 1800 tanks are ready to meet the enemy and that means you have another armored division's worth of tanks *ready*. Now, if your first-round hits are 83 percent instead of 53 percent, and the tank is able to fight 24 hours a day instead of 12 hours a day, you see that you have an almost exponential increase in combat capability. The same is true across the board. Go to the naval forces and you see that, with the addition of the AEGIS cruisers to the carrier battle groups, we have increased the air protection for our carriers about nine times what it was before that AEGIS cruiser was available.

I could go on and on but what I want to tell you is that the taxpayer is getting value received from the money put into defense. Do we always do it right? No. The answer is categorically "No." I can cite the $700 toilet seat, or the $435 hammer or whatever it happens to be. The people say, "Well, what do you do with tax money given for defense purposes?" Well, we work very hard to try to avoid such excesses. I want to tell you that we have two million people wearing the uniform full-time. We have another million wearing it part-time in the Reserves. We have a million civilian employees out there. That is about 4 million people. Most of them are working very, very hard to do their jobs well; but I have been around long enough to know that no matter how dumb it is, somebody is out there doing it wrong. It is just the way human nature is.

I got a letter from a fellow just recently. He said, "Dear General Vessey, Congressman So and So has been airing a political TV commercial in which he claims the Pentagon pays $435 for a hammer. In the Review and Outlook column of the *Wall Street Journal*, the editorial entitled "The Ponderous Pentagon" states the Pentagon pays $100 for a hammer. My question is which is right? How much does the Pentagon pay for hammers? Does the Pentagon buy second-hand hammers? Maybe you could get them cheaper that way. I have an extra one in my garage that I will let the Pentagon have for free. I am proud to be an American and if I can save America $435 (or even $100) by giving up a hammer, I would be proud to do so! Let me know if I can help!"

So I wrote him a letter. I said, "Thanks for your letter about hammers. You are absolutely right in implying that either $435 or $100 is too much to pay for a hammer. I inquired into the matter to try to get answers to your questions. First, how much does the Pentagon pay for hammers?" The General Services Administration tells me that the Defense Department bought 83,000 hammers from the General Services Administration this past year. The prices varied from $6.40 to $8.70. Most of them were of the $6.40 variety. In a routine audit this past year, Navy auditors discovered that as a part of a weapons system support contract, a contractor had prorated support overhead charges on some common tools, among them a hammer. Under that contract, the hammer cost $430. Needless to say, the Navy corrected the contract and recovered the excess charges for the hammer and the other common tools. So, the answer to your question is that the Pentagon pays somewhere between $6.40 and $8.70 depending on the type of hammer."

"I, like you, would be happy to give up one of my hammers if I thought it would save the taxpayers from spending $100 or $435. Fortunately, I think both of us can keep our hammers in good conscience."

The next question that I would like to talk about briefly is, "What to do about nuclear weapons?" Now, the first thing I'd like to say about that is that nuclear weapons are here. They are here in this world and we can't change that. Some people think that God let man invent golf for the entertainment of the rich. Those of us who had to dive for golf balls in water hazards know that that's not the case. We know God let man invent golf to teach him something about life. And the most important thing that it teaches man is the ball is where it lies. So, you have to play it from there. And we are where we are in this world. God may forgive our sins but He won't give us any "mulligans." Nuclear weapons are out there and we have to deal with the world the way it is.

We have returned to the negotiating table with the Soviet Union in Geneva with a policy that says that we want to have drastic reductions in the level of nuclear weapons. Now, I looked up the last speech that Mr. Chernenko gave in which he said that he agreed we need to have reductions in nuclear weapons, perhaps to move to a world that has no nuclear weapons. I looked at President Reagan's speech just before we returned to Geneva and he seemed to be saying the same thing. So, maybe our negotiators can sit down there and find some reasonable way to reduce the number of nuclear weapons.

In the meantime, it is important for us to recognize that the first element of our strategy is our strategic nuclear deterrent force. We have not built a force to attack somebody else. We have built a force to try to make it clear to our potential enemies that they cannot attack us and succeed. I would like to point out a few facts about our strategic nuclear force. We keep about 25 percent of the warheads in our strategic nuclear force in ballistic missile warheads. That is the most dangerous type of warhead, the type which, in large numbers, could be used for a first strike. The Soviet Union keeps about 70 percent of its strategic nuclear warheads in ballistic missile warheads. So, we have to make it clear that we have no intentions of shooting first, of striking anybody else. But we also want to make it clear that the Soviets can't strike us and achieve their war objectives.

We keep the rest of our nuclear force in bomber weapons or ballistic missile submarines. There are a number of issues before the Congress this year and have been for a number of years to modernize that force. We believe it is important for that force to be a modern force. We believe it is important for that force to be a modern force for a whole bunch of reasons. First, for safety. Second, for effectiveness, so that potential enemies will know that we have an effective force. And thirdly, if we get to a markedly reduced level of nuclear weapons through negotiations, we want a force that continues to be an effective deterrent force because that is our strategy. We don't want a war. We don't want any kind of a war. But we don't want to be paralyzed by the fear of war as we go about our business in this world of nation-states in which we live.

The President appointed a commission a couple of years ago that is commonly called the "Scowcroft Commission" to examine this issue. That commission came up with some very sensible recommendations. They are in the public domain. If you are at all unsure about the nuclear weapons issue, I would suggest that you read that report because it brings right up to the forefront the importance of modernizing our force. A few weeks ago the Congress voted to go ahead with the so-called MX, the PEACEKEEPER Intercontinental Ballistic Missile, and to modernize that force, at least partly. Now, another set of votes will come up later this year and I would suggest that they are important votes. They are important votes for "We the citizens" and it is important for our elected representatives.

I would say one last thing about the issue of nuclear weapons negotiations and that is that the level of weapons will not necessarily reduce the danger of war. Salvador de Madariaga, the Spanish philosopher and historian who worked for many, many years on the old League of Nations Disarmament Commission, wrote in his memoirs that mankind has the issue of war and disarmament upside down and backwards. He said that, "Nations don't distrust each other because they are armed; they arm because they distrust each other." And if we really want to reduce the danger of war in this world, we have to work on the mistrust. If we settle the mistrust issues, the level of armaments will then automatically go away.

I would say to you that in this issue of defense of the Nation, "We the People" have an obligation to ourselves but there is also another obligation and that obligation is laid out in the Preamble of the Constitution where it says "Preserve the blessings of liberty for ourselves and our posterity." When Congress votes for the defense budget in May, they will not be voting for defending ourselves today. Those budgets have already been taken care of. What they are voting for is defending our posterity in the years ahead.

It is reminiscent a little bit of the TV ad—I've forgotten the announcer's name. The man comes on the TV with a burning house in the background and he says, "When is the worst time to find out that you don't have the right insurance on your house?" Well, the answer is self-evident in the ad with the burning house in the background. And I would say to you that the same thing applies to national defense. When is the worst time to find out that you don't have the right national defense? That's during a time of trouble for the Nation because you don't pay then in dollars. You pay in the blood of our citizens and that is what we do not want to do. And I am absolutely convinced that by maintaining the right levels of defense for this nation we can keep the peace. We don't have to go to war and we can keep the peace not only for ourselves but for our posterity.

Letter of Resignation to
Honorable Ronald Reagan
President of the United States
The White House
Washington, DC
12 April 1985

Dear Mr. President,

I respectfully request that I be retired from active duty on 30 September 1985. I realize that the date is eight months ahead of the date on which my second term as Chairman, Joint Chiefs of Staff, would terminate under the law, but I believe it is a good time for me to leave. Thanks to your leadership, that of Secretary Weinberger, and the support of the Congress and the American people, our Armed Forces have made extraordinary improvements in the last few years. As for replacing me, there are at least five very well-qualified officers from which you can choose, and any of those five will do the job very well.

You do not need another report on the improvements in the armed forces; I would simply call your attention to your last meeting with the Joint Chiefs of Staff and tell you that the Armed Forces are in the best condition I've seen them in my 45 years of service. On the other hand, we must remember that the readiness of the Armed Forces and the state of our defenses must be tended continually. Like the freshness of bread on the shelves of a bakery, readiness of the Armed Forces must be tended daily. We must prepare for tomorrow as we deal with today's problems. I realize that the nation must deal with many problems beyond those of defense, but, frankly, I am worried about the direction to which the Congress is turning in dealing with the defense budget this year. I urge your continued support for the necessary improvements in our defenses needed to secure the peace in the years ahead.

The Joint Chiefs of Staff are functioning quite well. They have good relationships with you and with Secretary Weinberger. They have had their own operations and procedures under continual review over the past three years and set in motion some substantial improvements in defense planning and the formulation of military advice. Needless to say, we are not inhibited by lack of room for more improvement, but I believe you have the right set of Chiefs and the right Secretary of Defense to make the needed improvements.

Lastly, it has been a great honor and privilege to serve the country under your leadership and to work with the dedicated people who help you "provide for the common defense." Cap Weinberger's model of selflessness, competence, and diligence has been great for the Defense Department. I ask to leave in September only because my wonderful wife has saluted and obeyed for the past 40 years; she cheerfully endured numerous family separations, countless short-notice moves, life in strange places, and difficult living conditions. I promised to have her in our home in Minnesota before the first snow of the 85-86 winter. I must keep my promise.

Very respectfully,

Extract from
COMMENCEMENT EXERCISES AT
NORWICH UNIVERSITY GRADUATION
Northfield, VT
18 May 1985

This is a happy, wonderful spring day in the Vermont countryside. It is a great day for families and faculty and for you graduates. I am pleased to be here, particularly in this the bicentennial year of the birthday of Captain Alden Partridge. He not only founded America's first private military school but he also provided the foundation for today's ROTC program which has been the bulwark of providing officers for the Armed Forces of the United States—and not only for the active forces but also for that legacy of our great Militia heritage, our Reserve and National Guard.

One of the briefest commencement addresses ever given goes like this:

"You have finished your education in a time of uncertainty, unrest and unprecedented change .... Don't conclude prematurely that the individual is unimportant and that you can abdicate your responsibility for making the tough, hard decisions that you may wrestle with for most of your lives. You live in a country that is healthy while much of the world is either lean or hungry. There will be all kinds of alarums and excursions (but you cannot) say, 'Let someone else make these hard decisions as to what our policy and our purpose should be.'"

That commencement address was given about 150 years ago by the great German philosopher, Goethe; and, I say to you that it is as applicable today as then. Ten days ago, we marked the 40th anniversary of the end of World War II in Europe. In spite of the sacrifices made and the dangers endured by millions of freedom-loving people—including 1600 Norwich graduates who fought in that war—the world is still a very troubled place. In fact, there are about 20 wars being fought as you graduate today, if you define a war as a conflict in which uniformed forces are engaged and people are being killed.

Blessedly, our nation is free and at peace today. What about the future? Will we be as secure in 2025 as we are in 1985? There are those who are not confident that we will be. In fact, there are some who are downright pessimistic. There's a new book by the French author, Jean-Francois Revel, called *How Democracies Perish*. In the opening lines of the book, he describes the world as "a democracy-killing machine." He goes on to say, "Democracy is not basically structured to defend itself against outside enemies seeking its annihilation, especially since the latest and most dangerous of these external enemies, communism, parades as democracy perfected when it is in fact the absolute negation of democracy."

In some ways, Revel has some good arguments to support his contentions. Although the word "democracy" is liberally sprinkled in the titles of many nations in the world, the United States is only one in a very small minority of reasonably democratic nations.

That observation should keep us on our toes as we look at the world around us; but it should not frighten us as we look at our own history. Von Arnim, the 19th century German novelist and a colleague of Goethe, said, "The history of the world begins anew with every man, and ends with him." What he meant, I believe, is that one man and one woman can make a difference. That is the essence of our democracy. I remember reading a plaque on the Minneapolis City Auditorium as my outfit marched off to war as we were mobilized during World War II, 45 years ago. It says: "Participation in the rights of citizenship assumes participation in the duties of citizenship." The full participation by each citizen is fundamental to democracy; and the duties range all the way from voting to elect our President and legislators to paying the taxes we levy on ourselves. Sometimes, those duties encompass fighting, even risking death, in the battles that "We the People" choose to fight in the defense of this republic of ours.

Much has been said throughout your years here about the great responsibilities the graduates of Norwich have as citizens and as soldiers. Alden Partridge said that Norwich would provide not only an education but also a military background which would "qualify graduates for the correct and efficient discharge of their duties when their country may require their services." Last night, many of you swore an oath which you reaffirmed this morning as officers in the Armed Forces of the Nation to defend the Constitution of the United States against all enemies. As you accept those responsibilities, all of us here today and all Americans will be placing in you our highest trust.

But there is a second reason we have placed our highest trust in you, a reason that people sometimes forget—each of you, *in or out of the military,* are also the embodiment of our nation's values. In some ways that second responsibility outweighs the first, because without those values, our freedom would be an empty exercise in self-indulgence.

To protect our nation's values, the decisions you make must be based on principle rather than expediency. It can mean that you choose the harder right instead of the easier wrong.; and that may mean that you sometimes must stand alone, supported only by your convictions. Perhaps these words are alien to your experiences at Norwich because, for the past four years, you have lived in a community whose code is one of integrity. You have been supported by faculty, by fellow students and by parents who try to live by the principles of this institution. Whatever temptations you may have had over these four years to let your standards slip, you have prevailed. But, today, you are leaving this community and you are entering a world which is neither so guided nor always so supportive.

But, I am not concerned because the greatest thing about Norwich is not its faculty, good as it is; nor its impressive tradition of training the citizen and the citizen-soldier; nor the physical beauty of the campus in this part of Vermont. The greatest thing about Norwich is you—the young men and women who will perpetuate the values of this institution and of this nation which you will serve.

You have the talents and the values and perseverance that it takes to be the real heroes and heroines of your generation—the embodiment of "We the People," the "We" who have kept the Nation free and who will pass on the blessings of liberty to our posterity, just as you will one day pass those blessings on to your posterity.

I want to close with a prayer for you. This prayer comes from the Order of Matins in the *Lutheran Book of Worship*. It is a good prayer for military people and a good prayer for you graduates on Commencement Day. It goes like this:

> "Lord God, You have called Your servants to ventures of which we cannot see the ending, by paths as yet untrodden, through perils unknown. Give us faith to go out with good courage, not knowing where we go, but only that Your hand is leading us and Your love is supporting us. Amen."

That is my prayer for you and I give you my congratulations. Best wishes to all of you.

**Address at the COMMENCEMENT
CEREMONIES FOR 1984-1985 COMMAND
AND GENERAL STAFF COLLEGE
Fort Leavenworth, KS
7 June 1985**

You finish the Staff College at an exciting time; and if you look out at the world, you will see that it is also a troubled time. You see war in Afghanistan, war in Kampuchea, war in the Persian Gulf, and war here in Central America in this Hemisphere. Certainly, our look at the world today might lead us to believe that the world is headed for a major conflict; but our job is to do our part to see that it doesn't happen.

For you in the Armed Forces of the United States, you leave at a particularly interesting time as far as your profession is concerned. There is more going on in the development of tactical concepts, in equipment modernization and in cooperation among the Armed Services of our country and with our allies than ever before in history. Those of us who are in the business of trying to set the course for the future have tried to leave you three tools for the future: good people, extraordinarily good equipment, and good training concepts. Looking at the past and what we had in the past and looking at what we have today, I can tell you that we've done that. Perhaps, the best of that is the people. You also have extraordinarily good equipment. It is not perfect equipment. It was designed by fallible human beings and built by other fallible human beings and operated by a third set of fallible human beings. Yet, it is good equipment, extraordinarily good equipment. What is more important is that the Army, Navy, Air Force, and Marine Corps have all invested tremendous amounts of money for research and development in training for the future. We have today the best training concepts that we have ever had.

The most exciting part for you is that we are absolutely uninhibited by lack of room for improvement. There is a tremendous amount of good and important work for you to do out there—such as the development of tactical concepts to take advantage of those tools that I mentioned to you. So, as you confidently move into the future to do your work, I encourage you to preserve what is useful from the past but march into a future which is a changing future.

Look back at your roots, and I want to talk to you a little about your roots—about your roots as officers and about the roots of the institution you serve, the Armed Forces of the United States. I realize that I am talking to officers from other nations and to some civilian graduates of the college; but I think you will see that the concepts that I will lay out apply to your nation and to you civilians as well.

You have chosen to serve the Nation through service in the Armed Forces. The key word is "service." You don't work for the Army, Navy, Air Force, or Marine Corps; you serve in them. And that is a completely different concept than working for them. Britain's Sir John Hackett called it the military's "unlimited liability contract." That's a good name for it. You don't choose the wars you fight; you don't choose the places you serve; but, sometimes your duty will take you to places where you will risk life and limb. The reason for your service is because "We the People" agreed to provide for our common defense. You have chosen to serve the Nation; but there is an important corollary: the Nation has chosen you to serve. That is a unique relationship. The people of this nation want peace, but they want a confident peace. They don't want to be paralyzed by the fear of war as they march on in the days ahead. The people of the Nation need to have confidence that you don't advocate war, but war is, in fact, your business and they need to know that you are ready for it. By being ready for it, you help ensure the peace.

There is a marvelous dialogue in the "Second Book" of Plato's *Republic* where Plato has Glaucon and Socrates talking about the attributes of the armed forces of that day. Plato has Socrates saying, "Nothing can be more important than that the work of the Guardians should be well done." He said, "If shoemakers become inferior and claim to be what they are not, the state is not in peril; but if the Guardians of our city only appear to be Guardians and are not Guardians, you surely see that they utterly destroy the city."

Socrates and Glaucon then go on to describe the attributes for the Guardians. Guardians should be "quick to see, swift to overtake the enemy, and strong." Socrates adds they should be brave, but their strength must be spiritual as well as physical. Then, between them they decide that one man cannot practice many arts, that war is an art and must be studied and practiced, and that the higher the duties of the Guardians, the more time and skill and application will be required. They conclude that the Guardians ought to be dangerous to their enemies but gentle to their friends; and, by their friends he meant the citizens of the Republic. Then they wonder about whether or not these conflicting attributes can be found in a single person.

Through the years, most civilized nations have wrestled with those issues about their armed forces: how to have warriors with the necessary skill and ferocity in times of war and not have them be a menace to the society in times of peace.

Our Forefathers of this great nation were concerned about these issues and they were notably skeptical about military power. In fact, in 1784, the Continental Congress declared that standing armies in peace were inconsistent with the principles of the Republic. The Congress reduced the Continental Army to about a hundred officers and men and then stationed them as far away from civilization as they possibly could. And I suspect that some of your orders today may indicate that we still do the same thing.

That skepticism was later developed in the *Federalist Papers,* and it all relates to why our military, which springs from the society it serves and is sworn to defend, embodies the principles that govern the society. We the people in the military are a part of "We the People." That is why our military forces have never produced the so-called "Man on Horseback," and why we

222

have not strayed from the duty of defending the Constitution as was originally intended—that is, protecting the society but not policing the society.

You, the men and women of the Armed Forces today, are our nation's Guardians; you are the warrior class of today. You have chosen to give up some of the benefits of liberty so that the society as a whole can exercise those benefits and liberties in full. As with Socrates' Guardians, your duties will require more time and skill and art and application. That is why you have come to the Command and General Staff College. As with the Guardians of Plato's Republic, nothing is more important than that your work be well done. Your skill, your concept of service, your values, and your loyalty will carry you through whatever duties you have to perform in the years ahead. The skills you learned here are important. It is essential that you hone them as you go to your next assignment; but it is also essential that you hone that concept of service.

A message I would like to leave with you is that there are no degrees of importance in the services you perform. Some of you will command aviation units or tank units or infantry units. Others will work in logistics supplying weapons and equipment or doing research and development. Some will be buried in the anonymity of staff work. Some of you will go to faraway places that your mother-in-law won't be able to find on the map. Wherever you go, the duty is important and each set of duties is as important as the next.

A year ago on Memorial Day, my present squad, the Joint Chiefs of Staff, participated in the burial of the Unknown Soldier from the Vietnam Conflict. We were offered a limousine ride from the Capitol to Arlington Cemetery; but I said, "No, we'll march." We fell in and we marched; and despite all this business about bickering among the Joint Chiefs of Staff, I want you to know that we marched *in step* three miles from the Capitol to the Tomb of the Unknown Soldier. We did that for one reason, and that was to demonstrate our belief in the code that there are no unimportant duties, that whoever has fallen serving his country, even if he is unknown, has performed very, very important duties.

Twenty or 25 years from now, one of you by the Grace of God and through the confidence in you or your fellow members in the warrior class, may be serving as Chairman of the Joint Chiefs of Staff or as Chief of Staff of the Army and standing up here on the podium harassing the graduating class. For whomever that is, I want to tell you one thing: it is important for you to recognize today and then that your duties are no more important and no less important than the duties of your classmates who did not rise to those high ranks. The officer is a servant of the Nation; he is a servant of his superiors; and he is a servant of those who are subordinate to him. And it is important that, whatever rank you hold in the authority of whatever office you have, you recognize that you serve the Nation by serving your fellow soldiers by your professional competence and by your dogged and unceasing care and concern for the men and women entrusted to you.

Inseparable from the concept of service is the concept of integrity. The citizens of this nation place great trust in you as Guardians of the Republic.

They will continue to judge all of us by rules stricter than they apply to themselves. If you buy a $435 hammer, you're going to get hammered for it even though you bought 83,000 hammers for $6.40; and that is the way it should be. The people of this nation *should* do that because, ultimately, their security rests with you and with us. The people of the Nation have entrusted the Armed Forces with the most awesome weapons ever known to man. And they have entrusted them with hundreds of billions of dollars of their hard-earned treasure. But, more importantly, they have entrusted the leaders of the Armed Forces with the lives of their sons and daughters who serve in the Armed Forces and with their own lives and their security for today and for the years ahead.

Don't confuse integrity with infallibility. There is a great tendency to do that. As Gary Cooper said in *High Noon*, "You should aim to high-regarded." But you should remember that you are human and fallible, and that those who serve with you and those you will lead are also human and fallible. The code of the Guardian has plenty of room for fallibility. And certainly, the higher up the flagpole you go, the more of your fallible backside will show. There is room for that. But there is no room for lack of integrity or for those who place themselves above duty, above their comrades, or above their country. Careerism is *the one great sin* in the Armed Forces and it has no place among you in the warrior class.

Now, you may sit there and say, "Well, that's alright for you to say when you're on your lofty perch as Chairman of the Joint Chiefs of Staff, because you've made it; but we want to get ahead." I know you want to get ahead and I applaud that, but, if you get there over the bodies or careers of your comrades, you have served the Nation poorly.

There's a marvelous passage in the last pages of Field Marshal Bernard Montgomery's book. He said, "There are times in war when men must do hazardous jobs, and when success and the Nation's fate depend on the courage, determination and tenacity of officers and men. When those who set duty before self give of themselves to see the task committed to them through to its completion, they win the day and the highest honor that mortal man can give."

To the international students here today, let me say, "Thanks for attending." I hope that your attendance has been as valuable for you as it has been for us. I am sure that the faculty and the students here have enjoyed your company and profited from your presence as members of the class. It is my firm belief that nurturing contacts among the military forces of the nations of the world will help reduce the risk of war. I know that my own friendships with my classmates of the 43 nations represented in my class of the Command and General Staff College have served the security of the Free World. In the past year alone, in the line of duty, I have met classmates from five of those nations.

I also want to say a word to the families. Your husbands or wives, as the case may be, have reached an important point in their careers. It is important to them and it is important to the Nation. It is important to you. They needed your support as they went through the school and they need your support now as they go on to new and more demanding duties. I realize that this lecture is not necessary for you families because if you had not supported them, they would probably not be here in the first place. Nevertheless, I would like to read from a speech that tells a little about military families. It was a speech given by Karen Nicholson when a memorial was dedicated in honor of her husband, Major Arthur Nicholson, who was killed recently by a Soviet sentry. She said in her speech:

> "To belong to the military is to belong to a very special family. Perhaps because we are so often away from our loved ones, a bond develops that you can find nowhere else. And that love and concern has opened many doors and has stood by us in the past weeks. Nick was the most patriotic person I have ever known. And that's why he made the military his life. He felt that each and every day he did something for his country, for his family and for everyone he knew. He devoted his life to understanding other people, especially the Soviets, in the hope that through friendship and knowledge of each other he could contribute to world peace. He didn't want to die and we didn't want to lose him, but he would gladly lay down his life again for America."

Now, I read that in recognition that the family serves as surely as do the people in the family who wear the uniform. I acknowledge your great importance to the military community; and, as you leave here, I want you to know that you go with my thanks and the thanks of the other members of the Joint Chiefs of Staff for the sacrifices that you make. You go with our best wishes for you and your families for the exciting days ahead. In the Liturgy for Morning Prayer in the new *Lutheran Book of Worship*, there is a prayer which is a good prayer for Service men and women and their families. It goes like this:

> "Lord God, You have called Your servants to ventures of which we cannot see the ending, by paths as yet untrodden, through perils unknown. Give us faith to go out with good courage, not knowing where we go, but only that Your hand is leading us and Your love is supporting us."

I want you to know that that's my prayer for you and I give you my congratulations. It has been a pleasure to be here. Best wishes to you all.

Honorable Bill Nichols
Chairman, Investigations Subcommittee
Committee on Armed Services
House of Representatives
Washington, DC
21 June 1985

Dear Mr. Chairman,

In accordance with your May 23, 1985, letter to the Secretary of Defense, enclosed are my responses to questions on the organization of the Joint Chiefs of Staff.

In addition to answering these questions, you asked that the Secretary and I provide separate statements of our views on matters specified in your letter to the Secretary of April 24, 1985, specifically, "Three legislative proposals: a bill (HR 2265)...that includes many of the provisions of the House-passed 98th Congress JCS bill that were not enacted in the fiscal year 1985 Defense Authorization Act; a bill introduced by Representative Ike Skelton; 1983 Department of Defense JCS recommendations that were not enacted in the 98th Congress, ... the JCS-related portions of recently published studies by the Georgetown Center for Strategic and International Studies and the Heritage Foundation."

This letter will address itself to those matters specified above. However, before I do so, I want to review some background which may not be known by all members of the Committee.

On 14 June 1983, I along with all members of the Joint Chiefs of Staff testified before your Subcommittee. The topic was improving the effectiveness of the Joint Chiefs of Staff. That testimony relates directly to the scope of the hearings you are to hold, and since all members of the JCS at that time had an opportunity to express their views, I would respectfully refer this committee to the transcript of that hearing.

When I became Chairman in June 1982, I agreed with my colleagues on the JCS that we would undertake a review of our organization and our way of carrying out our responsibilities. As a basis for that review we recognized that the effectiveness of the JCS is a direct function of the relationships the JCS maintain with the Secretary of Defense and the President, with the Commanders in Chief of the Unified and Specified Commands (the "CINCs"), and with each other as members of the JCS. Accordingly, we decided to address the issue personally rather than involve our staffs. We also agreed that we would specifically address the recommendations for change made by my predecessor, General Jones, and those made by General Meyer, then a member of the JCS.

We agreed on four criteria we would apply to all proposals for change:

—Would the change improve our ability to wage war if we're ever forced into one? The ultimate test is the ability to move from peace to war and to fight the war to a successful conclusion, should deterrence fail.

—Would it provide the President and the Secretary of Defense better and more timely advice?

—Would it better ensure that the requirements of the commanders in the field, the Commanders in Chief of the Unified and Specified Commands, are met? These Commanders in Chief are the ones who will execute the war plans and fight the battles; and their needs were a key part of our review.

—Would it improve the ability to allocate national security resources more wisely and efficiently—helping the President and the Secretary of Defense to meet their difficult responsibility of getting the most security from a fixed budget?

The Secretary of Defense asked us to add a fifth criterion, which we added:

—Would the suggested changes maintain our national legacy of civilian control of the military?

As the starting point for our examination, we used the duties of the JCS prescribed in Section 141, Title 10, US Code. Our examination of those duties specified in the law confirmed for us that those are the correct duties and responsibilities for the JCS. Our examination also confirmed that the challenge for any "reorganizer" is how to enhance the effectiveness of the Secretary of Defense, because he is the key man in the Defense Department, a man whose duties go considerably beyond those of most Cabinet officers.

We concluded that reform must focus on how he uses the JCS, his military advisors, as a part of the entire DOD organization. His effectiveness depends on how well the JCS carry out the duties prescribed for them in the law and on the three interdependent relationships I mentioned earlier. Further, we concluded that the existing law already gives us most of the latitude we need to improve the effectiveness of our own operation. In cooperation with Secretary Weinberger, the JCS are working to do that now. Many improvements have already been made; and others are underway. The JCS believe that with the continued support of the Secretary we have the opportunity within existing authority to continue to improve our effectiveness.

Nevertheless, we also concluded that some of the changes needed would require changes in the law. The JCS made recommendations to that effect to the Secretary. These changes were incorporated in the DOD bill submitted to both Houses of Congress on 18 April 1983. The JCS recommendations which were incorporated fully in that bill had two parts:

First, we recommended that statutory restrictions on the size of the Joint Staff and tenure of its officers be changed to augment and strengthen their support to the Chiefs. The changes were necessary so that the size of the Joint Staff can be adjusted when necessary to ensure it has the number of experienced officers needed to assist the JCS and the Secretary of Defense in carrying out their assigned responsibilities. The Congress adopted many of these proposals in 1984, but the 400 officer cap on the size of the Joint Staff remains and should be removed.

Second, we recommended that Title 10, U.S. Code, 124, be amended to place the Chairman in the formal chain of command. The Chairman presides over the Joint Chiefs of Staff; and he communicates, at the direction of the President or the Secretary of Defense, orders to the Commanders of the Unified and Specified Commands. The proposed legislation would make explicit the Chairman's functions as a link between the Secretary of Defense and the Unified and Specified Commands, an arrangement which already works well in practice. This legislation was not enacted and I continue to believe that it needs to be.

In our examination of other proposals for change, we concluded it was not necessary to specify that the Chairman is the principal military advisor. The Chairman has ample opportunity to provide advice under existing law. We concluded that the Chairman should not have a full-time, four-star Deputy or Vice Chairman. Similarly, the JCS gave careful consideration to the concept of a national council of senior military advisors apart from the Chiefs of the Services and concluded that such a council was not required. We also concluded that it was not necessary or appropriate to revise the law to subordinate the Joint Staff specifically to the Chairman. The Chairman is already responsible for the management of the Joint Staff and its Director on behalf of the Joint Chiefs of Staff.

Mr. Chairman, with this as a background, I will comment on other proposals for change as you requested I do in your letter. Elements of those proposals which have not already been discussed or which are not specifically included in the questions provided are discussed below:

The provision that "subject to the authority, direction, and control of the Secretary, the Chairman supervises the commanders of the combatant commands and acts as their spokesman on operational requirements" is consistent with the JCS proposal that the Chairman be placed in the chain of command. As you are aware, the Authorization Bill of 1984 has already codified the Chairman's role as spokesman for the CINCs, a procedure which works well in practice.

The JCS do not agree with the provision which would authorize the CINCs or the members of the JCS to comment formally on reports and recommendations of the Joint Staff before the JCS review them. This provision could lead to inflexible rules which would hamper timeliness and quality through bureaucratic layering in the staff process. The views of the CINCs are always sought as a matter of course when time permits and when appropriate.

In summary, Mr. Chairman, the JCS duties detailed in Section 141 of Title 10 US Code, are the correct duties. Carrying out those duties requires three healthy relationships: (1) the relationship between the JCS and the President and the Secretary of Defense; (2) the relationship between the JCS and the Commanders of the Unified and Specified Commands; and (3) the relationship among the JCS themselves. All of the people involved, the President, the Secretary of Defense, the members of the JCS, and the CINCs of the combatant commands must work to keep the relationships healthy if our present system or any mutation I can foresee is to work effectively. The Administration proposed two law changes which I believe would improve the present organization. Otherwise, the law as now written with the changes to the law enacted in the Fiscal Year 1985 Authorization Act give ample authority to the JCS to perform their duties if those relationships I pointed out are healthy.

Questions and Responses

Question One. What should be the JCS Chairman's role as a military advisor to the President and Secretary of Defense?

General Vessey. I believe the Chairman's role as a military advisor should be as it is currently established in the law. He is a member of the Joint Chiefs of Staff and the members of that body serve as the principal military advisors to the Secretary of Defense and the President, and the National Security Council. He represents the Chiefs in many fora and he has the responsibility of conveying the views of all the Chiefs. It is not necessary that he be given authority to give advice in his own right. That is already covered in existing practice.

Question Two. How much control over the Joint Staff should the Chairman have?

General Vessey. The law already gives me all the control over the Joint Staff I need. Even before the changes passed by the Congress and approved by the President last year in the Authorization Act, Title 10, Section 143 in subparagraph C provided for the Joint Staff to perform such duties as the JCS and the Chairman prescribe. The Joint Staff is the corporate staff of the JCS and should be available to all the Chiefs. The Chairman of the Joint Chiefs of Staff manages the Joint Staff and its Director on behalf of the JCS. The law clearly gives the Chairman the authority to task the Joint Staff either independently or on behalf of the JCS. Last year, the changes in the law explicitly gave the Chairman the authority to select the officers to serve on the Joint Staff. As the law reads, it seems implicit that the Chairman owes an accounting to the JCS for his management of the Joint Staff on their behalf. As can be seen from the words in the law and from actual practice during my tenure as Chairman and in my observations of past Chairmen, the Chairman has extraordinary authority over the Joint Staff in directing its use to serve the JCS.

Question Three. Please explain how assignments to the Joint Staff are made now that the law governing selection of Joint Staff officers has been changed. How many names are you requiring to be included on the nomination lists cited in the law? What procedures have been established to ensure that nominated officers are selected from among the most outstanding Service officers?

General Vessey. The recent changes to the law were helpful and give me more flexibility in the management of the Staff. Those that give the Chairman tenure authority and selection and retention authority over personnel assigned to the Joint Staff are especially helpful. I have discussed this matter with the Chiefs and they are committed to ensuring that the Joint Staff is staffed with the most outstanding officers. Let me state at this point, however, that the men and women we have on the Staff now are top-notch, and they are working hard to give the Joint Chiefs the support they need.

A new Department of Defense Directive, "Duty with the Organization of the Joint Chiefs of Staff (OJCS)", currently being staffed, implements Title 10, United States Code, Section 646, and issues policies and procedures concerning the assignment, promotion and retention of officers assigned to the OJCS. In short, this new DOD directive, applying to the OJCS and the Military Departments, solidifies the personnel processes for nominating and selecting only the most outstanding officers for assignment to the OJCS. It further supports career enhancement and professional development initiatives commensurate with being selected for and serving a successful OJCS assignment. The expanded authority of the Chairman, Joint Chiefs of Staff, to request multiple nominations to facilitate selection decisions to staff the OJCS enhances the Chairman's prerogative for personnel management of the OJCS. All assignments to the OJCS are nominative. The option to decline nominations that do not meet stipulated selection criteria is actively exercised as is the management option to by-name request the assignment of specific personnel. Requests for multiple nominees to consider for fill of selected billets is exercised as appropriate.

Question Four Should the JCS Chairman be a member of the National Security Council (NSC)?

General Vessey. The JCS are the principal military advisors to the President, the Secretary of Defense and the NSC. That arrangements is probably satisfactory; however, making the Chairman a statutory member would serve as a reminder of the need for military advice. The key issue here is that the Nation's senior civilian leadership should receive military advice from the Nation's senior military leaders. Under this Administration, Joint Chiefs of Staff advice is heard at all NSC deliberations. The present arrangement is probably satisfactory.

Question Five Should the JCS Chairman have a deputy?

General Vessey. The JCS were unanimous on this issue. The Joint Chiefs of Staff do not support creating a four-star Deputy or Vice Chairman. There are some very good arguments for having a Deputy Chairman, but the difficulty lies in the relationships between a Vice or Deputy Chairman and the other Chiefs. The Joint Chiefs of Staff could not agree on a charter for a Deputy Chairman which satisfactorily defined those relationships and, consequently, unanimously opposed establishing a Deputy Chairman position. We prefer our current system of a quarterly Acting Chairman in my absence. The Chairman has a three-star assistant and the Joint Chiefs of Staff fully support this position and the role of this individual. Our system of a quarterly Acting Chairman is working well. It has the significant benefit of exposing the Chiefs to my duties and enhances their ability to perform as members of the Joint Chiefs of Staff.

Question Six. Would strengthening the JCS Chairman's hand help to ensure a stronger voice for field commanders?

General Vessey. It is difficult to answer this question because it is not clear what is meant by "strengthening the JCS Chairman's hand." Nevertheless, the issue of how we ensure that the CINCs' views are heard is an important one.

The CINCs are charged with carrying out our war plans. Their needs are central to the PPBS process. As such, steps have been taken for the CINCs to fulfill the role established for them by the National Security Act. Through their active participation in Defense Resources Board summer program review and Defense Guidance development, the CINCs have a significant influence in PPBS both in their own right and through me, their spokesman for operational requirements. The Unified and Specified Commanders' views are often solicited and they have direct access to me and I to them. I also encourage them to air their views at our periodic CINCs' conferences and we in the JCS actively seek their views and evaluate their requirements as we advise the Secretary on the budget.

The CINCs have adequate authority to lay out their requirements to the Services through their component commanders as well as lay out those requirements directly to the Secretary of Defense and the JCS. Programs and budgets and resource allocation at the national level produce the forces and support given to the CINCs through the component commands. Consequently, the issue of giving the CINCs a stronger voice is more a question of the resources that have been allocated or which are available to be allocated to each CINC rather than a question of his voice in Washington. In the Unified Command Plan, there are some CINCs with unusual Service component structures, usually for reasons of economy. In those cases, the JCS have to pay particular attention to ensuring that the CINC's connection with the Services and the JCS themselves is clear and unobstructed. The second part of the issue concerns how the CINC influences how the forces under his command are equipped, supplied, and trained for the likely missions. Here again the CINC has the same channels open to him that he has on budget matters; that is, to the Services through his component commanders, as well as directly to the Service Chiefs on Service-unique matters and to the JCS on joint operations matters. The CINC himself has a great deal to do with the training of his forces, particularly with joint training. He works with the JCS to establish the Joint Exercise Program for his command. The JCS have also involved the CINCs deeply in the development of joint doctrine tactics, techniques and procedures. It is an effort to ensure that the voices of the CINCs are heard in force development.

Question Seven. Should the unified and specified commands have liaison officers in Washington?

General Vessey. This has both advantages and disadvantages. We have some CINCs who have liaison officers in Washington now but their functions vary and are highly specialized to support the unique needs of those CINCs. We have all the flexibility we need to establish or to disestablish such liaison offices should circumstances warrant; but we do not want them to become mandatory or too large.

Question Eight. Please explain the structure and functions of the Organization of the Joint Chiefs of Staff and the Joint Staff. What is the relationship of these bodies to each other? Include an explanation of the numbers of personnel assigned to each of the elements of both organization and their duties.

General Vessey. The structure of the Organization of the Joint Chiefs of Staff and Joint Staff has been evolving ever since the Joint Chiefs of Staff were formally established by the National Security Act of 1947. This act provided for a Joint Staff not exceeding 100 officers operating under a Director appointed by and responsible to the Joint Chiefs of Staff. In its initial form, the Joint Staff had three main components, headed by Deputy Directors for Strategic Plans, Intelligence and Logistic Plans. The Joint Secretariat and certain other elements of the JCS organizations were not counted as part of the Joint Staff. This distinction between the Joint Staff and other supporting elements still exists today. Amendments in 1949 to the National Security Act of 1947 raised the permissible number of Joint Staff officers to 210. Between 1949 and 1958, increasing workloads of the JCS and the broader JCS duties enacted in 1958 required expansion of the Joint Staff to the 400 limit which still exists today.

During the decade of 1960s, a number of additional agencies were established to deal with areas of concern that assumed increased importance, such as arms control negotiations, counterinsurgency activities, and the need to produce a wider range of studies and analyses. During the same period, the manning necessary to discharge the responsibilities of the numbered J-Directorates increased, accounting for virtually all the spaces under the Joint Staff's statutory limit of 400 officers. With the approval of the Secretary of Defense, the new agencies were usually established in a status outside the Joint Staff but subject to the supervision of its Director. The title used was often that of "Special Assistant to the Joint Chiefs of Staff" for a particular function. As a consequence, the term "Organization of the Joint Chiefs of Staff (OJCS)" came into use to include all the directorates and agencies under the Joint Chiefs of Staff, both within and outside of the Joint Staff. The Joint Staff is considered a part of the OJCS with the only distinction being the legislative ceiling imposed on the size of the Joint Staff—no such ceiling exists on the size of the OJCS. This differentiation has existed for some ten years and has been regularly reported to Congress through OSD via the annual Defense Manpower

Requirements Report (DMRR) which shows the total authorized end-strength for the Organization of the Joint Chiefs of Staff.

The current report reflects 1562 positions, of which there are 850 officers, 369 enlisted, and 343 civilians. Included in this overall total are the 376 officer positions currently authorized in the Joint Staff. The Joint Staff consists of the Office of the Director, Joint Staff, the Directorate for Manpower and Personnel (J-1), portions of the Directorate for Operations (J-3), the Directorate for Logistics (J-4), the majority of the Plans and Policy Directorate (J-5), and the majority of the Directorate for Command, Control and Communications (C3S). The remaining activities within the OJCS are primarily associated with the Office of the Chairman; the National Military Command Center (NMCC), the National Emergency Airborne Command Post (NEACP) and the Alternate National Military Command Center; JCS representatives to various international activities and negotiations; the Strategic Plans and Resource Analysis Agency (SPRAA); the Joint Analysis Directorate (JAD); the Joint Planning Staff for Space (JPSS); and associated automation and resource management functions in support of the entire OJCS.

Question Nine. How can we be sure that civilians in the Pentagon are not making decisions that more properly should be made by the military?
General Vessey. The Joint Chiefs make few decisions, per se. Our function is to advise the President, the Secretary of Defense and the NSC and to carry out the policies of the Secretary and the President.

My view is the civilian leadership should establish broad policy guidance, establish objectives, set fiscal guidance and supervise—leaving to the Joint Chiefs of Staff the military functions of advising on military matters, developing military strategy and war plans, maintaining readiness and conducting military operations. I believe that the heart of maximizing the DOD decision making process is improving the effectiveness of the Secretary of Defense by improving the support rendered by the Secretary's military staff, the Joint Chiefs of Staff. Through our proposals and through the Joint Chiefs of Staff fulfilling their responsibilities under the law, the Secretary of Defense would receive better, more timely military advice on matters pertaining to military policy, strategy, planning, and programming. The Secretary and his civilian staff would then be able to focus more attention on matters of policy and management.

Question Ten. Do civilians in the Office of the Secretary of Defense become involved improperly in the business of the Joint Chiefs of Staff?
General Vessey. No, not really, but there is a problem in that the military personnel in OSD tend to provide military advice which should be coming from the Secretary's military staff, the JCS.

Question Eleven. Can't something be done to simplify the massive, complex organization of the Office of the Secretary of Defense which encompasses, in effect, a number of large defense agencies as well as the Secretary's immediate office?

General Vessey. This is really the Secretary's business but I do have a few thoughts. First, the Defense Department indeed is big, but it should be big because its responsibilities are large. The Secretary of Defense has responsibilities which are unique and go considerably beyond those of any other Cabinet officer. He is a Cabinet officer to the President. He is also manager of the biggest agency in the Free World. Its budget exceeds twice that of the AT&T before the breakup, General Motors, General Electric and US Steel combined. Third, he is a member of the National Command Authorities and as such is directly responsible for the defense of the Nation.

In view of the weight of his responsibilities and many demands made on him, he needs a large staff and Congress should not indiscriminately limit his authority or flexibility to adjust his staff and his organization to meet his needs. At the same time, the Secretary of Defense needs to police his organization continually to insure clarity in lines of responsibility and to insure that unnecessary overlap and duplication does not stifle the advice and assistance he needs.

Statement before the
SENATE APPROPRIATIONS COMMITTEE
Subcommittee on Defense
On the FY 86 DOD Appropriations
25 June 1985

Mr. Chairman and members of the Subcommittee.

I report to you that the military posture of our armed forces is sound. The forces are manned with good, capable people; their armament is being improved with good, modern equipment; their training has been improved; and they have better support behind them. By every commonsense measure, our forces are more ready than at any time in the recent past. These improvements are due to the support of the American people and the Congress; and, on behalf of the men and women in our armed forces, the Joint Chiefs of Staff and I thank you for your support. We ask for your continued assistance in the FY 1986 budget.

The Nation should neither be complacent nor accept the notion that these past three years can somehow erase the decline in real growth over the 1970s or eliminate the gap caused by the continued growth of Soviet power. The Joint Chiefs of Staff have looked at the threats to this nation's security and at our strategy. We believe this year's original budget request was sensible. It was neither massive nor excessive. It was a reasonable response to threats to the national security and to the requirements of the military strategy of the United States. Reductions in the President's requested budget will slow the momentum of improvements to our deterrent posture and they will affect readiness and retard responsiveness in a crisis.

The Joint Chiefs of Staff do not advocate these cuts. However, we participate fully with the Secretary of Defense in the development of the amended budget before you now. We participated understanding the reductions had to be developed. The threats to our interests have not slackened; but, if the defense budget needs to be cut for reasons other than defense, then the way the Secretary has laid out these cuts has the support of the Joint Chiefs of Staff.

Good people are the heart of our forces, and I am pleased that the favorable trends reported last year generally continue. Recruitment and retention are good. About 50 percent of the force are careerists. We have a fine corps of non-commissioned officers. By every standard, we have well-disciplined, dedicated, capable Service men and women who are proudly serving their country. We need to continue to support the programs which will ensure our Armed Forces are manned by intelligent, trained, well-disciplined soldiers, sailors, airmen, and Marines.

Our forces are better equipped. New, good equipment from long-delayed modernization has made its way into the hands of our forces—Active, reserve and National Guard. In FY 84 alone, the equipment added to the force included the following important items:

— 769 M-1 Tanks
— 598 BRADLEY Fighting Vehicles
— 120 BLACKHAWK Helicopters
— 209 PATRIOT Missiles
— 72 Multiple Launch Rocket Launchers
— 11 APACHE Attack Helicopters
— 187 New F-15, F-16 and A-10 Fighters
— 46 Ships (including 16 warships) and 282 Aircraft for the Navy
— Plus thousands of trucks, small arms and communications items.

We have added not just quantity to our force but, more importantly, greatly increased capability. A few examples:

— M-1 ABRAMS Tank—Average tank gunnery qualification scores 46 percent higher than those of M-60A3 crews. Last year, a U.S. tank company in M-1's scored the highest in the prestigious Canadian Army Trophy competition against the best tank crews and tanks in the Free World.
— M-2 BRADLEY Fighting Vehicle—High-speed battlefield companion to the M-1. More armor protection for the crew; TOW missile and cannon firepower; and greatly increased mobility in comparison to the M-113 Armored Personnel Carrier (APC).
— F-16 Fighter—The best single-engine fighter in the world. Maneuverable, agile, maintainable (needs only half maintenance-man

hours of the fighter it replaced). Phenomenal bombing accuracies; does as well with conventional bombs as F-4 did with guided bombs.
— M-16A2 Rifle—Lightweight, dependable, versatile, improved accuracy, improved sustained firing capability for the Infantryman.
— AEGIS on the TICONDEROGA Class Cruiser—Provides up to nine-fold increase in air defense firepower for the protection of the Fleet.
— SL-7 Roll-on/Roll-off (RO/RO) Fast Sealift—USNA ALGOL during September 1984 REFORGER exercise moved 271 tracked vehicles, 652 wheels, 230 military containers—loaded in only 36 hours, and capable of traveling from Beaumont, TX to Antwerp, Belgium, in six days instead of 13.

Our forces are well-trained and they know how to fight together in ways which capitalize on the advantages the new equipment can offer. We are emphasizing joint and combined training. The training is realistic and innovative. The forces are trained and measured against high standards. Support and sustainability programs are on-hand as new equipment is fielded to ensure that the new equipment is integrated effectively. In the past three years the funding for ammunition and spare parts has grown by over 25 percent. Within those areas we have doubled funding for war reserve spares, and in Europe alone, Army ammunition on the ground is up about 16 percent.

All these factors—good people, good equipment, good training and support—add to our strength. The Joint Chiefs of Staff believe that this improved military posture helps deter war and can help provide a climate for sensible negotiations with the Soviets. A strong national defense helps ensure the peace and safeguard our security.

Your support is important for the continued security of the Nation and that of our allies. Regrettably, our security and that of the West are not assured. Even under the best of circumstances, the second half of the decade of the 1980s will continue as a period of challenges to our security and as a period of widespread instability. The Soviet Union has been unrelenting in its buildup of military power and in its willingness to use or to threaten to use that power either directly or through the use of its surrogates.

As the Congress considers the defense budget, I urge the members to remember the need for day-to-day readiness. Crises too often give little warning of their approach. The lessons learned since World War II show us that no matter how good the preparations, orderly mobilization is very difficult and very costly once growing tensions indicate immediate danger. Under modern conditions, hastily building new, battle-ready forces is not practical even if the national treasure is spent without restraint. An Army, Navy, Air Force and Marine Corps, in-being and maintained in readiness, are the best military guarantors of our security. They add weight to our diplomacy and support the other elements of our national power.

Every indication the Joint Chiefs of Staff see tells us the Soviets will most likely continue on the path they have been on, fielding stronger nuclear and conventional forces on the land, on and under the sea, in the air, and in space.

The United States has no plans to match the Soviet buildup weapon for weapon. Certainly, the Joint Chiefs do not believe this should be done or need to be done. However, this nation and its allies simply must do what is needed to counter the Soviets with a military posture which makes clear that the Soviets cannot achieve their aims by starting a war or threatening war.

The Joint Chiefs believe that our strategy provides this nation with a sensible approach to preserve the peace and to provide for our national security. It is not a new strategy. It is the strategy of deterrence which we have pursued for nearly forty years. The success of that strategy rests on ready, modern Active and Reserve Component forces, both conventional and nuclear, and on the maintenance of strong alliances.

THREAT

While being pleased with the improvements in our own forces, we must remember that the Soviets have not been standing still. The momentum of the Soviet military buildup, unequalled by any peacetime nation in history, will carry Soviet force expansion and modernization programs well into the 1990s. With this pace of modernization over the last ten years, the Soviets have produced about three times as many aircraft and about four times as many tanks and other tracked vehicles as the Untied States. They have deployed a large and powerful navy. The Soviets have the world's only operational anti-satellite weapon.

Soviet forces have always enjoyed significant quantitative advantages. To counter this, the United States has traditionally relied on the qualitative advantages afforded by its technology. The Soviets, however, are continuing to field new equipment, much of it comparable to that produced in the West; and our qualitative edge is narrowing. The Soviets have achieved military advantages through a willingness to devote large resources to research and development, through adaptation and outright piracy of Western technology, and through their willingness to accept inefficiency in order to field new equipment rapidly. They devote twice the resources to research and development as the United States and they produce five times as many scientists and engineers—over 400,000 annually. In the past ten years, the Soviets have produced some 40 major aircraft developments, 60 major shipbuilding developments, 60 ballistic missile and space system developments, and 45 in ground forces. They develop new jet engines and several new rockets every year and they are presently testing two new attack helicopters.

With the momentum of investments in their military forces over the past decade and with sustained levels of effort in research and development, net Soviet combat power in every theater has increased. In the ground forces in the European Theater, for example, the Soviet Union along with the other countries in the Warsaw Pact has continued to increase its strength in armor, anti-armor and heavy fire support. The Soviet air forces are now flying third generation attack and fighter aircraft throughout the Warsaw Pact. They have deployed the MiG-29 FULCRUM with look-down/shoot-down weapons systems and are expected to deploy the SU-27 FLANKER with similar capabilities. The Soviet Navy has by far the world's largest submarine fleet with 376 ships. There are 250 BACKFIRE bombers, over 120 of which are dedicated to naval aviation and global anti-ship missions, and the BLACKJACK—comparable to the B-1B—will be operational by 1988. Their surface combatants are among the most modern in the world, and they are now building a nuclear-powered aircraft carrier we believe will be large enough to operate conventional take-off and landing, high-performance jet aircraft.

Most ominously, the Soviets continue to modernize their strategic nuclear forces. In 1982, the Soviets deployed more highly accurate Intercontinental Ballistic Missile (ICBM) warheads than we intend to deploy in our entire PEACEKEEPER program. In 1983, they deployed another 200 ICBM warheads and in 1984 they were nearing completion of the latest phase of the modernization of their current silo-based strategic ICBMs. The Soviets' SS-18 and SS-19 missiles, which would total over 5,000 warheads, are in the world's hardest silos, with a redundant, survivable command and control network. Their Moscow complex is protected by the world's only operational ballistic missile defense system. We expect deployment of newer missiles, the SS-X-24 and SS-X-25. We have yet to deploy a single PEACEKEEPER missile.

Soviet power is a reality that cannot be assumed away. With a population exceeding ours by only 17 percent, they have active armed forces two and a half times larger and ready reserves exceeding ours by about a factor of ten. We must continue to face up to the realities of Soviet military power this year and in the coming years with a sustained program that demonstrates the steadiness of our resolve to defend our interests.

WHAT THIS BUDGET PROVIDES

The Joint Chiefs believe that the revised budget for FY 86 supports the Nation's strategy, though at a lesser degree of confidence than we would have liked. We participated in the formulation of this budget, and we are satisfied that the proper balance has been struck at the reduced resource levels which have been set. There is sensible balance in the resources provided for nuclear and conventional forces. Today's readiness needs are balanced with the need for modern forces in the future. The budget provides growth in research and development activities to help maintain a qualitative advantage for U.S. forces in the years ahead.

STRATEGIC NUCLEAR FORCES

The JCS support the full deployment of 100 PEACEKEEPER missiles. The Congress needs to understand that every JCS analysis of the military requirement for the modernized ICBM confirms the need for 100 MX missiles. I recognize that the Congress in adjusting the FY 86 military budget may not be able to find a way to authorize the full number of missiles in the President's original budget. Whatever decision is made, I strongly urge that the Congress set in motion the necessary provisions for completing the program for 100 missiles.

All the original justification for deploying the MX remains in effect. The only things that have changed since the Bipartisan Scowcroft Commission confirmed the need for 100 MX missiles are the steady and unrelenting additions to Soviet strategic forces. One hundred MX missiles make a critical contribution to deterrence because the MX threatens what the Soviets value most, their hardened ICBM's and leadership.

Our TRIAD of strategic nuclear forces is the umbrella under which all our deterrent forces operate. The TRIAD is designed as a deterrent, not for a first strike. About 75 percent of our strategic weapons are in the bomber and submarine forces and 25 percent in ICBM's. We maintain the three elements of our TRIAD because we believe each leg of the TRIAD provides special strengths which reinforce the deterrent value of the other legs and which help guard against tactical and technical surprise. The TRIAD has been the basis of our deterrent posture for over two decades.

The United States delayed its strategic nuclear modernization, and we have had to modernize all three legs of the TRIAD at the same time. We are making steady progress with the bomber and submarine force modernization. The TRIDENT submarine program will modernize our aging ballistic missile submarine fleet and the D-5 missile will add new capabilities to the force at the end of this decade. The B-1B program is on schedule; it will be in the operational force next year. It will provide a modern, responsive bomber capable of penetrating Soviet defenses.

The modernization of the intercontinental ballistic missile force has encountered a series of delays well known to this subcommittee. The delays have not been technological or system delays; the missile is performing superbly. The Joint Chiefs of Staff urge the immediate deployment of the PEACEKEEPER. Its deployment will strengthen the TRIAD, help ensure deterrence, and strengthen the position of our nuclear arms negotiators. The PEACEKEEPER is tested and proven, and it is ready for deployment. We must proceed now with the deployment of the PEACEKEEPER in order to maintain the effectiveness of the TRIAD and our deterrent strategy into the next century.

Research and development on the small ICBM is proceeding. It will add the new dimension to the ICBM forces in the mid-1990s.

STRATEGIC DEFENSE INITIATIVE

The Joint Chiefs support the President's Strategic Defense Initiative (SDI) to have this nation employ its technological talent to determine whether an alternative to sole reliance on offensive retaliation is feasible. Within the bounds of the ABM Treaty, the Unites States is exploring means by which we might end the dominance of offensive ballistic missile weaponry. The cuts being considered in this important program will severely restrict our ability to continue research and will cause us to lag behind the Soviet Union—the only nation in the world with an operational ABM defense system.

CHEMICAL

The Soviets have extensive offensive and defensive chemical warfare capabilities. Our lack of a modern chemical retaliatory capability detracts from our overall deterrent posture. Should deterrence fail, our forces would be fighting at a great disadvantage in spite of the strides we have made in improving defenses against chemical weapons. Unless we modernize our chemical munitions and continue to provide for a sensible research and development program to prevent technical surprise, we provide little incentive to the Soviets for negotiating a verifiable arms control agreement prohibiting chemical weapons. This budget provides for long lead-time items and facilities in order to begin production of binary chemical weapons, weapons which are safer to store and to employ and which help reduce the likelihood of Soviet use of chemical weapons.

NEGOTIATIONS

The Joint Chiefs fully support efforts to obtain genuine, equitable and verifiable reductions in armaments. Arms control and other related negotiations are being pursued with the idea that equitable and verifiable agreements can contribute to security and stability. Negotiations are not a substitute for force modernization; rather, negotiations and our modernization programs are mutually reinforcing. We must modernize our own systems even while we seek genuine reductions in force levels through negotiations.

PEOPLE

No matter how good the strategy or excellent the equipment, good soldiers, sailors, airmen and Marines remain the heart of our defense forces. This nation has very good people in its armed forces today because of the Nation's renewed pride and faith in those people and the willingness to pay the price for adequate security. The men and women in uniform need to know we will give them the best possible equipment, training and support for their difficult tasks; and they need to know this nation will provide reasonable pay and compensation for them and adequate support for their families. As we continue into a period of economic recovery and as we face a declining manpower pool, we must guard against the erosion of pay, retirement, and other benefits. We surely do not want to return the forces to the unstable personnel picture of the mid-1970s. The budget provides the right amount of support.

CONCLUSION

In conclusion, I want to repeat what I said before this Committee a year ago: this nation and its allies must remain strong and steady. Last year I reported to you that we were making progress in reversing the decline of the 1970s in our general purpose forces and that we were in the early stages of modernizing our strategic nuclear deterrent forces. That progress must continue in order to maintain the effectiveness of our deterrent strategy.

When the Joint Chiefs look at the Soviets' forces, we see forces that are very large and capable of offensive operations on a global scale. We see their willingness to use their forces and those of their surrogates in Asia, Europe, Africa, and in this hemisphere to achieve their aims. Our forces are designed for deterrence. That has been our strategy since World War II, and it's been a sensible strategy.

The Joint Chiefs have examined the strategy and the threat, and we believe that this budget, though now reduced below a level we requested, will allow more modest improvement in our forces by providing good people, good equipment, good training, and good support. As I said at the beginning, we need not match the Soviets weapon for weapon or man for man; but, this nation absolutely must continue to deal with the unrelenting growth of Soviet power and with the realities of an increasingly interdependent and dangerous world. I urge your support for the President's defense budget.

**From a Letter to an
American Citizen in California
7 August 1985**

Thank you for sending me a copy of your letter to the President about the issue of keeping the peace in this nuclear age. As a Christian, a citizen, a professional soldier, and a father of three children, I join you in your quest for a stable and peaceful world. I understand your concerns and share with you an abhorrence of war, particularly the thought of nuclear war. But, as we go about our business in this world of nation-states, the United States cannot be paralyzed by the fear of war in the pursuit of our political, economic, social and cultural objectives. We cannot allow ourselves or our allies to be coerced by Soviet power.

Our purpose is to "wage the peace." However, nuclear freezes or even the reduction of nuclear warheads by themselves do not necessarily reduce the risk of war. We should not be afraid to negotiate with the Soviets, but such efforts must be within the context of preserving our security. Failure to recognize this point may well lead to an increase in the probability of nuclear war. This is why I support *both* the President's strategic modernization programs and the negotiations in Geneva.

As much as you and I would like to, we cannot wish away nuclear weapons. But we can act responsibly; and, I firmly believe that, as George Washington said, "... if we desire to secure peace, it must be known that we are at all times ready for war." Being ready for war is a campaign against war; it is expensive and does involve risk, but it is far cheaper in both dollars and blood than actual conflict.

Again, thanks for your letter and I want you to know we are on the same team.

Remarks at the
ACTIVATION OF U.S. SPACE COMMAND
PETERSON AIR FORCE BASE
Colorado Springs, CO
23 September 1985

It is a beautiful, brisk morning here in Colorado, and I am pleased to be here on this fine day to preside over this important ceremony.

By law, with the advice and assistance of the Joint Chiefs of Staff, the President, through the Secretary of Defense, has the authority to establish unified and specified commands in strategic areas.

The President has approved formation of the United States Space Command as a unified command and General Bob Herres as its first commander. Forces assigned are represented here today. U.S. Space Command now joins the other United States unified and specified commands worldwide helping the United States and its allies in maintaining the peace.

The United States Space Command is created in response to a recommendation of the Joint Chiefs and the Secretary of Defense to consolidate our military activities in space. USSPACECOM is composed of the Air Force and Naval Space Commands—and a new Army element. The Command will support our unified and specified commanders worldwide. The Command will serve the national security interests and the needs of the United States and its allies by providing an organizational structure that will centralize responsibilities for more effective use of space systems.

The United States Armed Forces use space systems to preserve national security by performing such functions as communications, weather forecasting, navigation, and warning. This new command will improve the use of current systems and will enhance planning for future use of these systems in these areas. *The U.S. military use of space is just as is our use of the land, sea and air: non-aggressive. It threatens no one.* These activities, which began over 25 years ago, are consistent with our commitment to the peaceful uses of outer space and with all U.S. treaty obligations.

It is important for the world to remember the United States' strategy. Our strategy is one of deterrence. We maintain forces in readiness both here in the United States and deployed in regions of the world where we have alliance commitments and vital interests. It is an alliance strategy, and we are fortunate to have good allies such as Canada and our partners in NATO and elsewhere who share with us common interests and a willingness to join in the defense of the freedom we cherish.

USSPACECOM will be an important part of that strategy. It was formed as a unified command with men and women of all four of our Services. It was formed after close consultation with Canada. And it will complement the mission of the North American Aerospace Defense Command, NORAD.

Its mission is defense. Our nation has no intent to attack anyone. By the maintenance of strong, ready deterrent forces, we want to prevent war.

There are several things the Command will *not* become. It is not a force built to escalate the arms race. It is not a force built to achieve dominance for the United States. The Command will make its contribution to that fundamental element of United States strategy, the prevention of war, and do it in the same way that the other unified and specified commands do. The Command will be ready to carry out its directed wartime missions as circumstances should require.

Forming the Command is a signal to everyone concerned, friends and possible foes, that the United States has a great interest in maintaining the peace and that we stand ready to defend those interests and to help promote peace and stability in cooperation with our friends. The Command will be a force for peace by being ready for war.

I have known and worked with General Herres for several years. He is an officer with great talent as a planner and strategist. You who have known him as Commander in Chief of the Aerospace Defense Command understand that reputation. I tell you soldiers, sailors, airmen and Marines who come under his command today that you have a top-notch commander in whom the President, the Secretary of Defense and the JCS have great confidence. I charge you to continue to give your best and to help keep this nation secure by keeping us strong and ready.

Finally, I bring you special greetings from Secretary Weinberger. And, on behalf of the Secretary and all members of the Joint Chiefs of Staff, I wish you Godspeed as you take on your important duties.

Remarks at the
RETIREMENT CEREMONY FOR
GENERAL JOHN W. VESSEY, JR.
Andrews Air Force Base, MD
30 September 1985

Mr. President, you and the Vice President do a great honor to the Armed Forces of the United States by participating in this ceremony today.

It is a great time to be in the Armed Forces of the United States. It is a great day to be a soldier. I hope we have the Recruiting NCOs all around the building here and are signing up new recruits after this wonderful ceremony. I want to say thanks to the troops that put it on. It's the first military operation that has taken place in the last three years and four months that I've not been cut in on.

Concerning the ceremony itself, I have often said that I plan to build an anthology of retirement and change of command speeches after I left the Service and publish it as "Service Humor." I don't really want to contribute to anybody else's anthology; but as I went out this morning and took my jog from Quarters Six down along the edge of Arlington Cemetery, I looked out over the city and I could see that the city was shrouded with a pre-dawn haze. I couldn't help but think of the contrast of that view of Washington last night when the Washington Monument, the Lincoln and Jefferson Memorials, and the Capitol were sparkling in the Harvest Moon.

And I thought as I looked at that morning haze that those symbols of the foundation of our liberty and freedom—the principles upon which this nation is built, the principles in our Constitution—sometimes get a little bit out of focus as they were this morning in that haze. And we need to reflect on how we let them get out of focus and to reflect on the importance of protecting them.

So, I thought, well, maybe I ought to risk being in somebody's anthology and to say something here at this ceremony. There is a natural proclivity for the old guys leaving to give one last lecture, and I thought of that. And I thought maybe I should give a lecture to the American people, thanking them for their support for the Armed Forces and for a strong defense—and tell them that their support is needed in the days and years ahead—that their support for a strong defense should not be a one-shot operation.

I thought I might tell them what Winston Churchill said to the British people before World War II, "We can afford what we need for defense. What we can't afford is to say that we can afford only what is convenient to provide." I thought I might remind them that they won't wish away nuclear weapons, that they won't wish away the Soviet threat and that as you go to negotiations with the Soviets, Mr. President, you need a firm defense of the United States as a building block for those negotiations. But I've said all that before. The American people don't need that message, so that shouldn't be the lecture.

Then I thought of talking to those patriots who represent "We the People" in the Congress and thanking them for their support for a strong defense. But

I also wanted to tell them that I've listened to a number of *their* lectures over the past few years when I went over to testify. I thought I might tell them that they deserve to get maybe a 60-second lecture from me today. And I thought I'd tell them that they dabble too deeply into the defense budget. They get too far down into the details and they get lost; so, sometimes they don't get the Appropriations Bills out on time. The combination of those two probably wastes more of the taxpayers' money than they are trying to find in savings by dabbling into the depths of the defense budget.

I thought about telling them, respectfully, of course, that, while they are diddling around with the notion of reorganizing the JCS, their own organization for dealing with defense sadly needs reform. And I thought I might tell them in the language of the modern-day soldier to "get their act together"—to get on with two-year authorization bills and multi-year procurements, to clean up the committees and stop dabbling in the details of the Defense budget, and to judge us by broad objectives and whether we meet those objectives and whether we do it with reasonable Defense budgets. But, I've said all that before; so it didn't seem that that lecture would be appropriate.

I thought of lecturing my fellow members in the Armed Forces about the great responsibilities the people of this nation have laid on them and how important their diligence, their alertness, their teamwork, their loyalty and their perseverance are to the security of this nation today and in the years ahead. I thought of reminding them of the importance of being alert, being ready, and being well-trained. And the importance of doing all those things with the knowledge of the taxpayers' dollars—and to take care of the equipment and supplies that have been provided to them. But I've said all that before; so, there is no need for that lecture.

And I thought of all sorts of other lectures .... To my Russian counterpart about the foolishness of attempting to start a war with the Western allies. Or to our allies about the importance of providing adequate contributions to the common defense. Or to my fellow members of the JCS about keeping up the good work. Or lectures to defense contractors and to American workers about the importance of quality work in the defense materials upon which the lives of these people here depend. But I've given all those lectures so there is no need to repeat them.

Then I thought of all the people I should thank .... Maybe to thank the Lord for His help. But we do that every day. Or to thank everybody in the military chain of command for the help they've given me—from you, Mr. President, on down to the lowest private, even to the ones just recruited or re-enlisted today. Or thanking my old comrades like General Bolte, my World War II commander. Or Lux Holbein, the Chief of Police in Hanau, Germany, who came all the way from Europe for this ceremony and who helped me get five of my stalwarts out of jail 30 years ago.

And I could thank all the security people and the workers in the Pentagon who have made life easier; but, there are far too many people to name and I hope you all know that I'm grateful.

I thought of thanking Avis for successfully packing the household goods for the 29th time and getting them shipped off without any help from me. Or thanking the children for not mutinying for a dozen or so moves during the middle of the school year; but, they are all grown up and they know I'm grateful.

By the time I thought of all those things to say, my run was about over and I was back at the Chairman's house; and the first glimpse of the morning sun silhouetted through the haze the Capitol and all those monuments down there. It occurred to me that the principles upon which this nation rests are firm—that when you look out there at the Capitol you can't help but be reminded of the Preamble to the Constitution—"We the People." And as I thought about Arlington Cemetery in which all those gravestones are there for all the other "indispensable" people who preceded me, I was reminded that defending the country over the past 209 years has been steady business—steady work—and will continue to be in the years ahead. I have a very good man replacing me. So, I put the flag out in front of Quarters Six and, as I put it in the bracket, I thought that, in addition to all the JCS problems and all the undone work I was leaving Bill Crowe, I leave him that very good, 20-buck bronze eagle that I bought for the end of that flag pole.

It occurred to me that probably the best thing to do here this morning was to give to my fellow citizens the same charge that Saint Paul gave to the Hebrew Christians when he said, "Let us run with perseverance the race that has been set before us." And then just simply say, "Thanks. Thanks, troops."